BIRDS ✦ PEACE ✦ WEALTH

BIRDS ✦ PEACE ✦ WEALTH

ARISTOPHANES'
CRITIQUE OF THE GODS

Three Plays Translated by
WAYNE AMBLER
and **THOMAS L. PANGLE**

PAUL DRY BOOKS
Philadelphia 2013

First Paul Dry Books Edition, 2013

Paul Dry Books, Inc.
Philadelphia, Pennsylvania
www.pauldrybooks.com

Printed in the United States of America

Library of Congress Cataloging-in-Publication Data
Aristophanes.
 [Works. Selections. English]
 Birds, peace, wealth : Aristophanes' critique of the gods / three plays translated
by Wayne Ambler and Thomas L. Pangle. — First Paul Dry Books edition.
     pages. cm.
 ISBN 978-1-58988-078-8 (alk. paper)
 I. Ambler, Wayne. II. Pangle, Thomas L. III. Aristophanes. Birds. English. 2013.
IV. Aristophanes. Peace. English. 2013. V. Aristophanes. Plutus. English. 2013.
VI. Title.
 PA3877.A3A47 2013
 882'.01—dc23

                                                          2012045543

CONTENTS

DIVINE COMEDY
Aristophanes' Critique of Zeus

ARISTOPHANES HAS ALWAYS been understood to have set the standard for what great comedy can be. His genius was established most obviously by his creation of wonderfully engaging, madcap plots, by his deployment of wildly hilarious, original metaphors, by his witty coinages of bizarre new words, and by his wickedly apt nicknames for famous people. No doubt, Aristophanes also shows little inhibition against using humor of the raunchiest variety. Scholars rightly stress that his plays are also highly political, taking up such serious issues for the Athenian democracy as the ongoing Peloponnesian War, the dubious power of demagogic leaders such as Cleon, and the harmful effects of new and radical intellectual forces such as Socrates, the sophists, and Euripides. Animating the present volume, however, is a concern with a deeper dimension than all these: we are convinced that the comedies of Aristophanes were written also as explorations of fundamental and enduring questions of civic and human existence. We take as genuine the poet's repeated proclamation that he is the educator of his audience, and thereby the educator of the city or society, in the most important matters—justice and piety—and that, as such, he is superior by far in wisdom to Socrates and all that the latter stands for and embodies as philosopher and natural scientist and educator of only a tiny elite.

Although our approach will distinguish this volume from those which focus on Aristophanes' humor, literary gifts, or analyses of Athenian political problems, we are not blazing an entirely new trail. Philosophers of the stature of Hegel and Nietzsche expressed deep admiration for Aristophanes' wisdom, even if his most obvious talent was his capacity for producing laughter. Hegel observes that "it certainly goes against our German seriousness" to admire a vulgar jokester; but Hegel then uses this observation to turn against the kind of seriousness exhibited by his fellow countrymen. As he goes on to say, "this poet . . . was thus no ordinary joker and shallow wag who mocked what is highest and best, and sacrificed all to wit with a view to making the Athenians laugh. For everything has to him a much deeper basis, and in all his jokes there lies a depth of seriousness."[1]

But in what does Aristophanes' "depth" consist? Where is the "seriousness" to be detected in such a mocker? It is instructive to start from Hegel's focus on the *Clouds* for its forceful presentation of the dangers represented by Socrates' aggressive effort to settle all questions by his dialectic. While "Reason" may seem to be a benign or even noble principle, to be encouraged in all college classes and promoted almost as a discipline unto itself under the heading "Critical Thinking," it can show also a darker side, and the arch-reasoner Hegel finds this illuminated by Aristophanes' presentation of Socratic dialectic:

> The exaggeration which may be ascribed to Aristophanes is that he drove this dialectic to its bitter end; but it cannot be said that injustice is done to Socrates by this representation. Indeed, we must admire the depth of Aristophanes in having recognized the dialectic side in Socrates as being a negative; and—though after his own way—in having presented it so forcibly.[2]

Hegel sees in Aristophanes' *Clouds* the disclosure that Socratic reasoning teaches "the nullity of the laws" and that "the payment of debts can be disregarded." More generally, "the power of judging in Socrates' method is always placed in the subject," so "where this is bad, the story of Strepsiades must repeat itself." Aristophanes' riotous comedy provokes Hegel to reflect on the dangerous consequences of promoting Socratic dialectic as a way of testing authorities and hence as an untested authority itself. Hegel here identifies a profound issue which strikes at the heart of biases still strong today. As he does so, he also pays tribute to the power of comedy to reveal through exaggeration, and thus to teach.

---

1. *Lectures on the History of Philosophy*, trans. E. S. Haldane, 3 vols. (Lincoln: University of Nebraska Press, 1995), 1.426–30. [*Vorlesungen über die Geschichte der Philosophie*, ed. Michelet, in *Werke*, ed. Marheinete et al. (Berlin: 1833), 14.85–89.]

2. Ibid.

Nietzsche differs radically from Hegel in his final assessment of Socrates, but he too treats Aristophanes as an admired guide to the fundamental issues.[3] Nietzsche sees Aristophanes as sharing and elucidating Nietzsche's own view that "the syllogistic whip" of Socratic dialectic represented a mortal threat to the noble culture of the Greeks: "The unerring instinct of Aristophanes was surely right when it included Socrates himself, the tragedy of Euripides, and the music of the New Dithyrambic Poets in the same feeling of hatred, recognizing in all three phenomena the signs of a degenerate culture."[4] Nietzsche not only honors Aristophanes for having anticipated elements of his own critique of Socrates, he also ranks Aristophanes as a great creator, along with Caesar, Homer, Leonardo, and Goethe (*The Will to Power*, 380). To be sure, Nietzsche's critique of Socrates does not rely solely or even mainly on Aristophanes. It is Plato's much more flattering or beautiful portrait of Socrates that Nietzsche makes the basis of an argument close to the one made by Hegel on the basis of Aristophanes: Nietzsche contends that even in the Platonic portrait of Socrates, Socratic dialectic reveals itself as corrosive, not only of the authority of law, but also of life-giving musical art, and especially tragedy: "Optimistic dialectic drives *music* out of tragedy with the scourge of its syllogisms; that is, it destroys the essence of tragedy" (*The Birth of Tragedy*, section 14, p. 92). And in a passage that could easily be based on the experience of Aristophanes' Strepsiades and his son in the *Clouds*, Nietzsche submits that this "optimistic dialectic" is based on a hope that is ultimately disappointed:

> Anyone who has ever experienced the pleasure of Socratic insight and felt how, spreading in ever-widening circles, it seeks to embrace the whole world of appearances, will never again find any stimulus toward existence more violent than the craving to complete this conquest and to weave the net impenetrably tight. . . . But now science, spurred by its powerful illusion, speeds irresistibly toward its limits where its optimism, concealed in the essence of logic, suffers shipwreck. (Ibid., section 15, p. 97)

---

3. Leo Strauss introduces his classic interpretative study of Aristophanes (*Socrates and Aristophanes* [Chicago: University of Chicago Press, 1966]) by stressing how Aristophanes' presentation of "the problem of Socrates" foreshadows Nietzsche's; Strauss notes that Nietzsche "uses Aristophanes' critique of the young Socrates as if it had been meant as a critique of the Platonic Socrates" (6–8).

4. *The Birth of Tragedy*, section 17, trans. Walter Kaufmann (New York: Vintage, 1967), 107. And consider also that Nietzsche commends Aristophanes' "profound instinct" in presenting Socrates as "the first and supreme *Sophist*, as the mirror and epitome of all sophistical tendencies" (section 13, pp. 86–7).

In Nietzsche's eyes, then, Socrates is a boaster: he promotes his dialectic optimistically, as if it were able to resolve fundamental questions conclusively, but his dialectic proves much more able to corrode the existing tradition than to erect a new one of comparable nobility.

What Hegel and Nietzsche say about the Aristophanean critique of Socratic critical thinking provides major clues to what Aristophanes holds to be the distinctive virtues of comedy as a vehicle for promoting and conveying wisdom. Aristophanes does not tire of asserting his vocation as a teacher of his audience, and a teacher in the most important matters—justice, war and peace, piety or religion, love, the nature of wisdom. His attack on Socrates as a teacher has as its reverse side Aristophanes' claim to be, himself—in and through his comedies—the truest teacher of the Athenians. What is the basis of this claim? His comedy, Aristophanes contends, teaches above all insofar as it provokes thought, and thoughtful questioning, and critical and self-critical reflection. What makes comedy such an excellent promoter of *critical* thinking? Comedy characteristically debunks or deflates, and its targets can include what is authoritative or powerful and therefore usually dangerous to criticize—even impermissible to criticize. Comedy can provoke and enable the audience to think critically about what are otherwise uncriticizable institutions, leaders, customs, and beliefs. Comedy can get away with this because comedy is by definition not "serious," but only playful; comedy and its critique is thus much more easily brushed off or excused than is explicitly "serious" critique.

The comic poet is permitted to be outrageous in public because it is presumed he does what he does only or largely for the sake of laughter. Nothing is serious for him, so—somewhat like the Fool in *Lear*—he wins the right to speak more freely than others. He need not portray the Athenian wartime leaders as knowing what they are doing; he can even present the almighty Athenian people themselves as if they are a bit dim-witted and susceptible to flattery (as he does in the *Knights*). Similarly, he can suggest that Zeus is not worthy of the beautiful temples and solemn ceremonies men devote to him. He can even represent on stage the possibility that the gods have abandoned men to their destruction (as occurs in the *Peace*). The comic poet can put such thoughts on center stage even at a religious festival. Wise comedy can provoke "safe" critical thinking—criticism of authorities that leaves the authorities intact even while, often by wildly exaggerated caricature, it reveals underlying absurdities and limitations of conventional wisdom. This applies especially to the theme central to the plays included here: the relationship between gods and men. Because Aristophanes as comedian need not defer to the "official" or conventional views of his audience, he is able to provoke thought about the gods' possible responsibility for the deep imperfections of human life, about the ability of adroit human beings to defeat or destroy the gods, and about the relationship between piety and important social conventions.

No doubt tragedy can also challenge conventions. Indeed, Aristophanes criticizes Euripides for doing so too boldly. When characters representing radical ideas appear on the tragic stage, however, they fail. Threats to justice, the established laws, and the gods pervade tragedy; but these threats are more often than not defeated, through dramas that allow or force their protagonists to finally recognize their "tragic flaws." In the three comedies included here, however, it is the most radical and unconventional characters who triumph: rather than seeing tragic flaws punished, we see comic virtue rewarded, even though this virtue entails radical impiety.[5] Because it appears to be a mere joke, however, the outcome gives no offense.

Not the least of the spurs to taking Aristophanes as a profound thinker and teacher is found in Plato. Aristophanes is assigned an impressive role in Plato's *Symposium*, and this notwithstanding such responsibility as Plato may assign to Aristophanes' *Clouds* for the trial and execution of his teacher (*Apology of Socrates* 18c8–d2, 18b4–c1). The *Symposium* is devoted to speeches that at once praise and analyze love, understood both as a human phenomenon and as a god. Why do we love what we love? Do we really love what is good? Or, is it what we regard as belonging to or akin to us that we most truly love? Is our loving likely to lead us to happiness? These are fundamental questions we continue to ask and that exact a toll if we answer them poorly. Plato has Aristophanes invent a myth as a way of presenting his answer to such questions; and although this myth is riotously funny, it is also so memorably evocative that it has never ceased to be the object of fascinated study. The myth is, in short, entirely worthy of being included in Plato's philosophic treatment of love. By having Socrates single out Aristophanes' myth in his ensuing speech, Plato makes it even clearer that Aristophanes' hilarious con-

---

5. Consider the case of Euripides' lost play *Bellerophon*, which Aristophanes parodies in his *Peace*. Like Trygaeus, Bellerophon has a bone to pick with the gods and attempts to confront them by riding the winged steed Pegasus to heaven. He is cast back down to earth, however, as a cautionary tale to other mortals.

tribution embodies in comic dress a profound effort to understand love and related issues.[6]

Plato further honors Aristophanes by making him one of the two intrepid companions who spend the wee hours of that night drinking and talking with Socrates—although by the morning it turns out to be only Socrates who never passed out and who appears sober, hangover-free, and ready for the challenging conversations of the next day (223c2–d12). We think it is fair to say that apart from Socrates himself, only a very few characters in the thirty-plus Platonic dialogues are treated with such respect as Aristophanes. It would seem that in Plato's view, at least, there is no reason to assume that an author of comedy cannot also be a profound thinker, a point which may be suggested also by Socrates' concluding thesis of the *Symposium*—that it belongs to the same author to know how to compose both comedy and tragedy (223d2–5).

A tradition has it that Plato also wrote, "Seeking to acquire a temple which would never fall, the Graces found the soul of Aristophanes." Whether true or not, this accords with the presentation of Aristophanes in the *Symposium*, a presentation that recommends that we approach this comic poet as someone worthy of Socrates' company and of Plato's respect. Two other legends have been passed down which express the sense that Plato held Aristophanes in great esteem. One reports that Plato sent the plays of Aristophanes to Dion of Syracuse as the best way of coming to understand the character of the Athenians; another has it that on Plato's death, a copy of Aristophanes was found under his pillow.[7]

Plato is not only our guide as to how we would study Aristophanes, he also helps to introduce the unifying theme that has led us to bring these three particular plays together into a single volume. That theme is the critique of Zeus and the Olympian gods. To explain the origin and cause of love, Plato's Aristophanes invents the myth that human beings were once spheroids with four arms and four legs but who mostly rolled their way to and fro; to humble this then-uppity species, Zeus

---

6. In his reported dialogue with Diotima, Socrates presents her as having considered the view animating Aristophanes' speech, that love is directed toward what is "one's own," what belongs to oneself (*Symposium* 205d10–206a5; cf. 212c4–6). It is true and important that Diotima does not accept this view and opposes to it the view that love or *erōs* is of what is good, whether it belongs to oneself or not. We do not claim that Socrates or Plato agrees with Aristophanes—to the contrary!—only that they take him seriously as a thinker and hence encourage us to do the same.

7. On the latter, see Nietzsche, *Beyond Good and Evil* 28, where he takes this as sufficiently apt as to be a fact.

cut them right down the middle, as one might do by applying a taut wire to a hard-boiled egg (*Symposium* 189d–190e). Each half then longed to be reunited with its other half, and this longing is what we know as love. Funny as it is in such minor respects as in the image of these rolling spheroids with their eight appendages, the myth is also partly tragic, for it shows the splitting to be permanent and (at best) only intermittently and imperfectly subject to love's remedy. Our never-to-be-fully-satisfied longing for restored wholeness exists in large measure because of a cruel, clumsy, and utterly un-philanthropic action by the king of the gods, who with an amusing but brutal lack of imagination threatened to halve the halves if they did not conform their actions to his wishes. Based on Plato's presentation of Aristophanes' understanding of love, at least, the comic poet is critical of Zeus, and hence begins to indicate why "Aristophanes' Critique of the Gods" is the subtitle for this volume.

Zeus and the Gods in Aristophanes' Plays: An Overview

A survey of Aristophanes' eleven surviving comedies shows that while the gods are regularly invoked in pious oaths and prayers, it is nevertheless the case that the gods' characters and powers are not infrequently called into question by the mortals on stage.[8] This is not to say that the existence of the gods is denied—except by Socrates and his ilk. Indeed, in as many as six of the comedies, one divine being or another actually appears onstage.[9] In four of these, the *Frogs* and the three plays included here, the gods featured onstage are central to the plot. Each of our three plays is distinguished by featuring a mortal hero who directly challenges the legitimacy of the rule of Zeus, and does so on plausible and coherent grounds. Aristophanes does not leave it at having his protagonists utter despairing laments about the defects of the prevailing divine dispensation; his heroes act vigorously to correct the misrule of the king of the gods, by substituting the worship of divinities whose superiority is powerfully manifest in terms all human beings can understand. The Aristophanean heroes certainly do not think that Zeus deserves obedience by the

---

8. An especially amusing example is Nicias's proof that the gods must exist since they so clearly hate him (*Knights* 31–34).

9. Hermes makes a brief but important appearance at the end of the *Clouds*, as does a certain Amphitheus in the *Acharnians*. Although the chorus of Clouds admits that the Athenians do not yet recognize them as goddesses (578), they lay claim to being divine, and what is more, they seek to join, and thereby to transform, the pantheon of gods lawfully worshipped by the Athenians.

mere fact that he is the divine king; they do not live in patient forbearance of the ills of the world; and, in contrast to Dostoevsky's Ivan, for example, they do not threaten, in despair or anger, to "return their ticket" to live in such a misbegotten world. Rather, when they find Zeus to be guilty of misrule, they go on the attack, with radical religious innovation. Amazingly, each revolution is spectacularly successful, and Zeus's rule is either overturned or severely curtailed by a determined mortal's root-and-branch religious reform.

Through these comedies Aristophanes provokes, in the minds of at least the strongest in his audience, the thought that determined, shrewd or wise mortals might be able to transform the prevailing religion, to reshape the rule believed to be exercised over mankind by divinity. And as one recognizes and reflects on the fact that Aristophanes indicates a deep spiritual kinship (though not an identity) between himself and these heroes of his, one begins to discern that the comic projects of Aristophanes' heroes are wildly exaggerated, but thereby deeply revealing, reflections of the poet's own much more subtle educational project for the citizenry. The success of this educational project—varying widely in its impact on various portions of the audience, but going even beyond the accomplishment of Euripides[10]—provides the compelling empirical evidence for the correctness of the comic poet's answer to the question, "What is a god?" This success vindicates the comic poet's claim to unrivalled wisdom in regard to the most important of all matters.

Thus the three comic heroes in the plays included here raise the questions of whether there are gods, who they might be, how powerful they are, and how they might be changed or eliminated. Although the precise form of such questions changes from age to age, these are questions that are inseparable from political life; and they certainly are powerfully present in our own day. We have already mentioned Nietzsche in this regard, but let us add that the great theorists and architects of the modern liberal state designed its contours partly with an eye on the goal of diminishing the role of religion in the public square. Not unlike our three comic heroes, they wanted to reduce dependence on "Zeus" and his priests. In his place, and like our three heroes, they sought peace, wealth, and human rulers liberated from exaggerated piety. And nowadays the so-called New Atheists are pressing the case that it is high time for a final defeat and elimination of the powers of darkness that, in their view, have cost us so much blood and treasure. As

---

10. See the *Thesmophoriazusae*.

their most eloquent exponent puts it over and over again, "Religion poisons every-thing."[11] Aristophanes was not a modern liberal; still less would he agree with the New Atheists' advocacy of universal public atheism. He does, however, put dissat-isfaction with the gods at the center of the three plays included here, does bestow victories on the human critics of those gods, and does invite us to think with him about the justice of their causes, the tactics behind their victories, and the limits of their successes. We can best begin doing so if we contrast our heroes' successes with Socrates' failure.

Aristophanes vs. Socrates on Zeus and the Gods

Once we see that our three plays are united in that each represents a successful assault on supreme divinity, it becomes evident that they stand together also as an instructive contrast to the disastrously unsuccessful impiety of Aristophanes' Socrates—whose hubris is defeated and punished at the end of the *Clouds*. Why, we are prompted to wonder, is Socrates punished for his kind of impiety, whereas our three protagonists become triumphant heroes for theirs? The clues are evi-dently to be found in the differences between the two kinds of impiety, and be-tween the two kinds of impious protagonists. Socrates' attack on Zeus consists in bluntly affirming, and teaching, the nonexistence of Zeus, and of all traditional di-vinities—rather than seeking to replace Zeus's and the other traditional divini-ties' rule over and within society with a rule of better providential deities. And the threat to Socrates from his boldly open denial of the existence of caring, providen-tial gods becomes manifest as the dramatic contest between father and son reaches its climax (*Clouds* 1464–77). The suicidal danger incurred by the arrant impiety of Socrates and his circle is underscored by what are almost the last words of the play: "Chase them! Strike them! Stone them! Do this for many reasons, but espe-cially because they were knowingly unjust to the gods." The god Hermes even ap-pears onstage to support the violent actions taken against the godless Socrates and his students. When we consider, in contrast, the three plays included in this vol-ume, we are led to see that in the poet's eyes Socrates' mistake is in the *way* he rebels against Zeus, *not* in his disposition to do so. A closer synoptic and compar-ative look at these four plays will lend strength to this interpretation and thereby

---

11. Christopher Hitchens, *God is Not Great: How Religion Poisons Everything* (New York: Hach-ette, 2007).

shed light on Aristophanes' understanding of the gods and how to defeat or even "destroy" them (*Birds* 186, 1514).

In contrast to the heroes of our three plays, the Socrates of the *Clouds* is presented as dwelling in Athens without serious complaints about his own or the city's condition. He is content with his little school or "thinkery"; and although he suffers various comic setbacks, he endures them with equanimity while remaining enjoyably absorbed by his scientific investigations and teaching. We learn that while Socrates happily ponders and instructs, Athens is at war: it is the extreme hardship of this war that drives Trygaeus, at the outset of the *Peace*, to wonder whether Zeus is aware of the high human toll the war is taking; but in contrast to Trygaeus, Socrates is unmoved by the war-induced sufferings of his fellow Greeks.[12] We also learn that Socrates is dirt poor—but again, whereas the hardship of living in poverty, and sympathy for his fellow impoverished farmers, drives Chremylos, the hero of the *Wealth*, first to Delphi and then to attempt to restore sight to the god Wealth, poverty as a personal or social ill does not trouble Socrates. Last but not least, Socrates lives in the midst of a citizenry notorious for pursuing endless lawsuits and constantly levying fines: it is such incessant litigiousness that drives Peisthetairos, the hero of the *Birds*, to abandon Athens and fuels or justifies his attack on Zeus; but Socrates, although he is a master at teaching tricky courtroom rhetoric, pursues his private life without litigious passions. Seeming to need little or nothing from either the Athenians or the Olympian gods, Socrates is not impelled to plot escape from or revolution against the powers that be.

Accordingly, the action of the *Clouds* is initiated not by Socrates, who has no great troubles or needs, but by Strepsiades—who, like the three heroes of our plays, and the Greeks in general—is driven to desperation by lawsuits, poverty, and war. Most acutely, Strepsiades is drowning in debts arising from the equestrian enthusiasms of a son whose expensive tastes outstrip his family's resources, rendered precarious by the consequences of war. At his wits' end, Strepsiades turns in desperation to Socrates' little thinkery, where he hopes to learn how to win any case in court, be it just or unjust, and thus to escape financial ruin by defrauding his creditors. Socrates, the man least in need of victories in court, appears most able and willing to teach others how to achieve such victories and thus exploit their fellow

---

12. Unless noted otherwise, "Socrates" will always mean the Socrates presented by Aristophanes, not necessarily the Socrates of whom we read in Plato and Xenophon. With regard to the limited or nonexistent effect of the war on Socrates, however, see also Xenophon, *Apology of Socrates* 18.

citizens. In his encounter with Strepsiades, Socrates in no way discourages the old father from his unlawful enterprise; rather, he assures him of complete success, if only he will learn what Socrates has to teach.[13]

Immediately on meeting Strepsiades, Socrates takes the theological offensive: he belittles the old man's religious belief and offers to teach him the truth about the gods (*Clouds* 247–54). The teaching begins with assertions and proofs that Zeus does not even exist, and that his purported functions as maker of rain, thunder, and lightning are carried out by the Clouds (364–94), while his function of punishing perjurers is simply not performed at all (395–411). The would-be pupil initially resists these strange new teachings (366–411), but is soon won over, and proclaims in his own name that Zeus does not exist (822–28). Perhaps surprisingly, Socrates suffers no immediate ill consequences for having directed such openly impious teachings to a rather ridiculous old visitor to his school. That Socrates is not promptly hauled into the courts of a city where not believing in the gods of the city could be punished by death may be explained in part by Strepsiades' failure to understand fully his teacher's meaning: when Strepsiades hears Socrates insisting that instead of Zeus, Necessity or Vortex is supreme, Strepsiades understands Socrates' words in light of Greek myths about the dethroning of one god by another (of Ouranos by Chronos, and of Chronos by Zeus—374–81). By supposing that there is now a new divine king, Strepsiades is protected against the true Socratic teaching that there never has been any divine king whatsoever, and never will be, thus leaving all things under the sway of mere necessity (395–407). In other words, Strepsiades learns to parrot Socrates' scientific views, without grasping their full theological radicalism.

After Socrates has judged Strepsiades to be too old and stupid to learn his lessons, the father's hopes turn to persuading his son Pheidippides to take his place as a student of Socrates. Even though the youth has nothing but contempt for Socrates and his associates, and appears to be unconcerned with the toll his expensive habits are taking on his father, Strepsiades manages to persuade him to go to Socrates' thinkery; perhaps Strepsiades learned something from Socrates about persuasion after all. As the first stage in the education of the youth, Socrates stages a debate between the personified cases for living justly and living unjustly—a debate in

---

13. Socrates shows a similar indifference to the unlawful consequences of his education even after he succeeds in teaching Strepsiades' more competent son (1148–53).

which the case for injustice wins decisively. The drama of this event makes it seem an especially imprudent exercise for Socrates to carry out in a city in which one may be executed for corrupting the youth; yet because Pheidippides remains unimpressed, even this crushing defeat of the Just Argument entails no immediate threat to Socrates.

The decisive turn toward Socrates' downfall occurs during his offstage education of Pheidippides. Although the poet prudently and responsibly keeps this education offstage, its powerful effects are made evident by the way it transforms Pheidippides—to his father's horror. Prior to his private encounter with Socrates, Pheidippides was absorbed by the excitement of horse racing and eager to spend his days among like-minded enthusiasts, and he actively resisted going to Socrates' school (102–04, 119–20). When he returns home from Socrates' thinkery, he is a changed man—and completely enthusiastic about his new self. As he puts it:

> How sweet it is to spend my time on novel and clever matters,
> And to be able to look down with contempt on the established laws.
> For back when I used to apply my mind only to horsemanship,
> I couldn't even say three phrases before I made a mistake.
> But now, since he himself has made me stop all this,
> And I associate with subtle opinions and arguments and thoughts,
> I think that I will teach that it is just to beat my father. (1399–1405)

Other evidence of Pheidippides' decisive transformation at Socrates' hands includes his confidence that Zeus does not exist (1469–71), his new preference for the morally shocking Euripides over the more traditional poets Aeschylus and Simonides (1354–75), his trust in his teacher Socrates as the decisive authority on questions he cannot answer (1430–32, cf. 1467), and his view that it is perfectly just for a son to beat not only his father but his mother as well (1440–46, 1321ff.).

It is no surprise that when Strepsiades gets a close look at the effect on his son of Socrates' "liberating" education, the enthusiasm the father once had for that education turns to revulsion: Strepsiades wanted his son to learn how to pull off only a little injustice, enough to escape a few debts; what he gets is the overthrow of everything he holds dear. Zeus, the king of the gods, proves to be tied to concerns of far deeper importance to Strepsiades than his debts: not least, his son's filial respect or affection for mother as well as father. After his son shows just how far he has traveled down the path blazed by Socrates, Strepsiades finally sees that Socratic science leads to the renunciation of even the most fundamental laws undergirding the family. No wonder the father races back to his former religious beliefs and seeks to punish those he holds responsible for having corrupted his son. Since the old man can see that it is highly unlikely that he could out-argue Socrates, the clever teacher of courtroom rhetoric, and get the philosopher punished by a court proceeding, Strepsiades has no recourse except to attack Socrates with violence. But first, of course, Strepsiades reaffirms the existence of the king of the gods (1470–85).

Strepsiades never considers that Zeus himself will punish Socrates for his impiety, perhaps in part because Strepsiades has come to hold himself responsible for what has gone wrong (1452–64); but neither did Strepsiades expect earlier that he himself would be punished by Zeus for seeking to learn how to get away with perjury in the courts. Strepsiades, we may say, manages to believe in Zeus as a defender of the moral order while yet believing that Zeus is in need of human assistance to do his job. Strepsiades becomes Zeus's required ally and vindicator, and burns Socrates' school to the ground as the curtain falls.

Whereas Plato's Socrates goes willingly to his death while leaving behind the beautiful and powerful message that the unexamined life is not worth living, the Socrates of Aristophanes' *Clouds* is chased off stage as his thinkery is burned down, leaving behind the much less beautiful but still powerful message that the examined life comes with no guarantees of a salutary outcome, and even, or perhaps especially, under Socrates' tutelage, may prove corrosive of our dearest attachments.

Zeus and the Gods in Birds, Peace, *and* Wealth

Having examined Socrates' failure, let us now consider the success of the three heroes of the plays in this volume—and first of all, the triumph of the hero of the *Birds*, the most radical of our three heroes. Peisthetairos does not deny the existence of Zeus, but instead wins over the birds as his allies and then leads them in a successful revolt against Zeus and the other Olympians.[14] In the course of consolidating his grip on his allies, Peisthetairos does not shrink from grilling some of them for dinner, while simultaneously outwitting three divine plenipotentiaries so as to secure for himself Zeus's beautiful companion, Basileia. She comes

---

14. For an extended discussion of Peisthetairos's rise to power over the birds, see Wayne Ambler, "On Tyranny in Aristophanes' *Birds*," *Review of Politics* 74:2 (2012) 185–206.

complete with the full supply of Zeus's powers, including his feared thunderbolt, and Peisthetairos cruises to victory with only a brief and ineffective moment of divine resistance to his daring revolution (1189–1261). Those in the audience who are sympathizers with the traditional gods, and who must have rejoiced at Socrates' downfall, wait in vain to see Peisthetairos struck down as Socrates was. Aristophanes could easily have made fun of Peisthetairos as he did of Socrates, thus sending a message to any others who might have been tempted to take lightly the power of the gods. But instead of depicting Peisthetairos's impious revolution as a failure, Aristophanes ends his play with the triumph of this shocking character: the very last line of the play even celebrates the apotheosis of Peisthetairos as "the highest of the divinities."[15] The same author who ended the *Clouds* by burning down the school of a teacher whose radical thoughts on Zeus and justice caused distress in but a single Athenian family now allows the hero of the *Birds* not only to criticize Zeus but to defy and even replace him. What does Aristophanes teach by depicting such successful impiety on so grand a scale?

While the *Birds* is the most radical of the three plays in which Zeus is successfully defied, it does not diverge in spirit from the *Peace* and *Wealth*. In the *Peace*, the protagonist is deeply vexed that the war with Sparta has gone on so very long. Trygaeus evidently assumes that Zeus wants to be good to the Greeks, for he first concludes that Zeus must simply be unaware of the harm being done down on Earth (63). Trygaeus thus decides to ascend to heaven to inform Zeus of the dire situation down among the Greeks and to try to get the supreme deity to bring the war to an end. On just his second attempt Trygaeus enjoys an unlikely success, flying aloft on a giant beetle that feeds on and is voraciously attracted to dung. The creature, which has the power to conduct humans on an ascension to heaven and to the gods, does not imply a very flattering notion of the destination. Our hero calls attention to his own courage, for this is after all an especially dangerous way of going to heaven: if even a single outhouse door is left ajar, the beetle will veer sharply back to earth, throwing his rider to his likely death. On the other hand, Trygaeus

---

15. The *Birds* was originally performed soon after a convulsive incident in which religious statues all over Athens were mutilated and sacred mystery rites were reportedly mocked in secret blasphemous ceremonies. Prominent Athenians, including Alcibiades, were accused of being responsible and many were severely punished in a hysterical witch-hunt. See Thucydides 6.27–28, 6.53, and Andocides, *On the Mysteries*. Aristophanes' play shows no sign whatsoever of endorsing the religious reaction: all to the contrary—Peisthetairos is, in Strauss's words, "that super-Alcibiades" (*Socrates and Aristophanes* 305).

is certain that he has no need of carrying food to sustain the dung-beetle once he gets to heaven. When Trygaeus and his mount arrive at the residence of the gods in heaven, Trygaeus learns that the Olympians became annoyed at having to watch and listen to the Greeks suffering in the war below, so they moved further away to escape the racket, and abandoned human beings to the rule of a single god, War, who has buried alive the goddess Peace and is preparing new tortures for men. Trygaeus learns, then, that Zeus's failure to help human beings is not merely the result of ignorance; Zeus is knowingly unleashing new woes upon the Greeks—even if he does so indirectly, through the agency of the fearsome god War.

Trygaeus is now faced with the choice of either submitting to this divinely-ordained outcome or turning against the king of the gods. Trygaeus is evidently convinced that Peace is deeply beneficial to humans, and on no good grounds forbidden to them. He unhesitatingly rebels and decides to try to excavate the goddess, even though this requires him to defy both War and Zeus, the latter of whom has threatened to execute anyone who makes such an attempt (371–72). Trygaeus digs up Peace with the help especially of peace-loving farmers; he then brings her back to earth in triumph, with her two attendants. While Zeus and the Olympian gods are not directly overthrown, they are utterly defied; and human beings now direct their worship and their prayers to Peace herself, who is called "the greatest of all the goddesses" and "the most benevolent of the gods," while War, Zeus, and most other Olympians fade into insignificance (308, 584–602). Sacrifice is now offered to Peace, not to other gods, and the very nature of the sacrifice is altered: no fatted ox or big fat pig is offered up to Peace in lurid, gory ceremonies, but instead a peaceful animal, a little lamb, is sacrificed in modest fashion and out of view. Prayers are also offered to the Graces, the Seasons, Aphrodite, Yearning, and Hermes. Ares, the god of war, is explicitly excluded as a target for prayer (456), and the other Olympians are simply overlooked. Aristophanes teaches that when human beings are gripped by the importance of peace, gods of a more militant disposition may be driven from the scene, and if human beings can secure Peace (or peace) by their own efforts, the felt need for Zeus and kindred divinities may dwindle or even evaporate. The gods thrive only when human beings think they need them, and the pantheon can be radically transformed so as to suit newly perceived needs.

At the same time, however, none of the characters in the *Peace* shares Socrates' view that Zeus simply does not exist. Zeus is confronted, not denied; and he is replaced, not merely overthrown or thrust aside. How Peace will fare as a substitute for Zeus over the long haul is a matter for serious questioning; for even in the moment of greatest enthusiasm, the Greeks are not all equally zealous in unearthing her or in honoring her (464–507). Still, Peace is surely a great source of hope to the war-weary; their defiance of Zeus in the name of Peace will be rewarded much more richly than by, say, the ascetic life of Socratic investigation. The Greeks have a clear and present reason to overthrow Zeus and to elevate a more beneficent deity; and they look forward to the joys that doing so will bring.

As Trygaeus triumphs over War and Zeus in order to bring much-longed-for Peace to the Greeks, so in the *Wealth* the lead character, Chremylos, triumphs over Poverty and Zeus in order to bring much-longed-for Wealth to the Athenians. The actions of Chremylos have their origin in a comic version of Glaucon's wonderful question to Socrates at the beginning of Book II of Plato's *Republic*. Chremylos asks whether he should perhaps be teaching his only son to be unjust rather than just. After all, he wants his son to be happy, but he has noticed that the just and god-fearing people like himself are poor, while the unjust have prospered; so should he not be teaching his son to change his ways and become an unjust rogue? Unlike Glaucon, Chremylos turns for guidance not to the philosopher Socrates but to the oracle at Delphi. As a consequence, he learns that the reason bad people are often wealthier than good ones is that Zeus long ago blinded the god Wealth, who is for that reason unable to recognize the deserving and distribute to them a larger share of his blessings. And why did Zeus do this? Out of envy for good men (87–92): what a charmer is Zeus! On learning this, Chremylos becomes determined to remedy this unjust situation by restoring the vision of the god Wealth; and he is not at all deterred by the knowledge that his plan is directly opposed to the will of Zeus— just as Trygaeus, the hero of the *Peace*, was undeterred by Zeus's threats. Amusingly, the god Wealth himself is completely intimidated by Zeus, so he is hesitant to seek to undo his divinely ordained blindness. The mortal Chremylos, however, is strengthened in his commitment to his project by the conviction that his conspiracy is a just and even a pious one. Just and pious people live miserable lives, so on their behalf he is in the right to defy Zeus, the source of their misery. Chremylos insists on this especially in a fierce debate with the hideous goddess Poverty, who tries both to threaten him and to explain how wonderfully good it is for human beings to be so poor (415–609).

Chremylos succeeds in restoring sight to the blind god Wealth and, consequently, in spreading wealth to all decent Athenians. This joyous result also has the amazing effect of putting to an end all prayer and sacrifice to the Olympian gods, for the

Athenians who have a sure route to wealth within their own power no longer turn to the Olympians for what has come to seem to all Athenians uncertain and unneeded assistance. Wealth seems able either to supplant or to provide for all other goods. Lest this dramatic decline of the gods be missed, Aristophanes has it reported by a discouraged and hungry priest of Zeus the Savior that the decline of devotion to the gods is so extreme that no one worships anymore in the temples—which are now used only as public latrines (1182–84).

Taken together, the *Peace* and the *Wealth* suggest that piety can be transformed if and when the prevailing gods can no longer be defended as good or just in ways intelligible and important to ordinary people. Put differently, our two rebellious human heroes possess—and what is more, evoke in the audience—what is at best a contingent devotion to supreme deity: their piety is derivative, not primary or fundamental; it is based on the premise that divinity must be beneficent in helping humans to secure such basic goods as peace and wealth. When Aristophanes' heroes put the existing gods to the test of this premise, and find the gods fail the test, the mortal heroes, as strong-souled men of action, are ready to lead the way in replacing the existing gods so as to achieve what is good, under better gods of human institution.

The *Birds* is not devoted to a single major perceived good for human beings, like peace or wealth, but is far broader in scope, and its planned solution is even more radical. Its protagonist leads a revolution directly against the Olympian gods, and his goal appears to be power—power which he promises to the birds but in fact achieves for himself (163). Peisthetairos defends his revolutionary efforts by showing what poor excuses for ruling gods the Olympians really are. They are ineffectual: Apollo is supposed to heal the sick, and Demeter is supposed to feed the hungry, but Peisthetairos mocks the thought that these divinities really perform these services (577–85). Truly great gods, worthy of human devotion, would gobble up the pests that damage the fruit we grow in our gardens; but so useful a service appears to be beyond the power of the Olympians! Yet their inaction does not keep the gods from expecting to be treated well by humans. They demand that mortals labor to build in the gods' honor, at great expense, beautiful temples with golden doors, where abundant sacrifices are offered to the gods. How much better would be birds as our gods! Birds eat caterpillars, and you can make the birds happy with a few handfuls of birdseed: you don't need a hecatomb of well-fatted oxen to sate the hunger of birds! As for a dwelling place, a little bush will please birds even more than an elaborate temple with a carved pediment and massive marble columns (610–626); and of course one need not fear that birds are going to behave like Zeus and rape one's wives and daughters (554–60)! As the birds catch the spirit of Peisthetairos's impiety, they add, for their part, that Zeus seats himself solemnly in the clouds but deems himself to be too august even to lift a finger for those on earth who have pressing needs (726–28).

Although the heroes of the *Peace* and the *Wealth* successfully ignore Zeus's threats and reverse key policies, they do not attack him directly. Peisthetairos, however, takes the war directly to Zeus and the rest of the Olympians. His comic battle plan depends on, and vividly reveals, the weakness of the Olympians: he will have his avian allies wall off the air, which divides heaven and earth, thus keeping the savory sacrificial aromas from reaching and nourishing the gods. Thus cut off from the vapors below, the Olympian gods will be starved into submission or even destroyed (183–86). The poet grants him success; Zeus is destroyed (1514). Zeus not only fails to do anything good for human beings, he also is utterly incapable of defending himself once he is attacked by a resolute mortal. His response to Peisthetairos's assault is pathetic. He first sends Iris to investigate and soon thereafter sends three confused gods to negotiate. These gods quarrel among themselves and appear to bring only a very weak hand to the negotiating table; there is talk of Zeus wielding a thunderbolt, but we never get a glimpse of one. The divine plenipotentiaries do little but capitulate. In a different incident, soon after the birds sing an ode calling attention to their keen vision, Prometheus is able to escape Zeus's detection simply by opening a parasol (1506–09): Zeus lacks an eagle's eye. And in response to Peisthetairos's offer to help the gods punish humans who renege on their oaths to the gods, Poseidon is eager to secure this help—thus admitting that the gods are not effective enforcers of their own decrees.

The flimsiness of Zeus's purported strength is equally displayed in the *Wealth* and the *Peace*. In the former, even though Poverty makes a spirited defense of herself and threatens the rebels with destruction, Zeus never appears or otherwise supports his would-be defender. Indeed, Zeus is eventually starved into joining the man who defied him (1188–90). In the *Peace*, Zeus even appears to be unaware that Trygaeus has arrived in heaven and is violating his explicit orders that no one may excavate Peace. Trygaeus accomplishes this excavation with a mass of Greeks who are making a huge racket, but neither War nor Zeus has the slightest idea that this rebellious operation is taking place. Nor does the successful excavation of Peace elicit a response. Zeus's most decisive action in the entire play is to move further away from human beings, abandoning them to War.

All three of our plays present the gods as needy beings. Zeus may adopt the posture of august self-sufficiency, but he and his fellow-Olympians are very much dependent on human beings. This is comically represented by showing the gods to be in need of the nourishing vapors from the sacrifices offered up by men below. Hence, in the *Birds*, the gods are subject to being starved into submission by walls built in the sky to cut these vapors off. The Olympians are also in need of the sexual opportunities offered by mortal women, and hence are doubly frustrated by the walls. But behind this wildly absurd tactic of building a wall in the air to weaken the gods is an entirely serious suggestion: the Olympians may be destroyed if men stop believing in them and sacrificing to them. In fact, this is what happens to them in the *Birds*—the comic and unbelievable tactic of building a wall in the air to starve the gods is replaced by an absolutely believable and realistic tactic of persuading people to stop sacrificing to them (1515–20, 1236–37). The Olympians are truly destroyed not by anything physical, like walls, but because the Athenians cease to worship them (cf. 518–38). If the power of the Olympians comes only from men's belief in the Olympians, then ending these human beliefs results in the end of the gods' power. What lives by opinion dies by opinion.

Crucial to the success of our comic heroes' projects, and a point that must be stressed as revelatory of a major part of Aristophanes' understanding of human nature in its piety, is that the goods which men seek from the gods are mundane. The most striking evidence in this connection is that the gods Wealth and Peace are represented as largely satisfying mortals' needs for the gods, while in the *Birds*, Peisthetairos explains that what mankind wants in order to be satisfied is simply a longer, healthier, and more prosperous life (586–609). Not one of Aristophanes' characters looks to Zeus for the sake of eternal life or moral perfection. According to Aristophanes, what men look to gods to help them acquire are peace, wealth, health, long life, the cheerful countenance of kindly tranquility, well-watered plough-lands, baskets of eels, sweet dried figs, the joy of love, and the delights of the arts and festivity.[16] Aristophanes does not use the gods, or anything else, to devalue the concerns or the pleasures of daily life. Aristophanes does not portray humans

---

16. *Peace* 999–1009, 1141–58, 1316–29; *Birds* 584–610, 704–36; *Wealth* 134, 500–16. The Graces, the Seasons, Aphrodite, Yearning, and Hermes, who assisted in the excavation of Peace, will presumably continue to have a place in the revised pantheon of the *Peace* (456), though it is striking that the Olympian Hermes does not appear after line 725, when Trygaios leaves heaven; nor is he even mentioned after this point, save in a single oath (963).

as in need of something beyond themselves to which they may express devotion and for which they may make genuine sacrifices. Thus Chremylos, for example, defends himself as just, but only as moderately, and thus sensibly, just. He seeks to be just so long as being just allows enjoyment of the blessings of prosperity; he is at least strongly inclined to abandon justice if it is not rewarded or accompanied by such blessings. The solution that Chremylos and the other Aristophanean protagonists seek is not Glaucon's—a heroic and transcendent kind of Justice whose value is so great as to be worth choosing even if it leads to the just man's being tortured on the rack and crucified. Aristophanes' characters turn to the gods for ordinary satisfactions and pleasures, and the gods who displace Zeus do so by appearing more likely to fulfill these needs and to help satisfy these pleasures. The new ruling gods do not demand that humans overcome their earthly and earthy needs and pleasures, and do not offer great rewards for such overcoming.

Yet it would be incomplete to say that for Aristophanes and his characters the gods represent nothing more than longed-for helpers and supporters of mankind's quest for basic satisfactions. Not all traditional divine beings fare as badly at Aristophanes' hands as Zeus does in the three plays in this volume. Even the same god may be viewed differently depending on circumstances and his different responsibilities. When imagined as a music-maker among the gods, for example, Apollo is celebrated in the *Birds*, not debunked; it is when he is considered as a healing god for human beings that he is treated scornfully for his failures (*Birds* 209–22, 772, 584). Along with Apollo in his association with music, the Muses and the Graces are elevated, not ridiculed (although unworthy poets are of course teased, even if they profess a connection with the Muses).[17] If we look beyond Zeus and beyond the *Clouds* and the three plays translated here, Dionysius is the orthodox god who most draws our attention.[18] The patron deity of the theater, his importance is confirmed—not without comedy, to be sure—in the *Frogs* by his service to both tragedy and to the city. Aristophanes' presentation of Dionysius, as well as the Graces and the Muses, returns us to this thought: the comic poet's consideration of the gods

---

17. For a few characteristic passages on the Muses or Graces, see *Birds* 659, 781–82, 1100, 1320; *Peace* 41, 456, 775, 816. For the teasing of a poet who relies too heavily on a claimed connection with the Muses, see *Birds* 905, 908, 913, 924, 937. In keeping with the comprehensive claims made on behalf of wealth (143–46, 160–64, 181–83), there are no references to the Muses or Graces in the *Wealth*—which is accordingly, as Strauss puts it, Aristophanes' "most humdrum" play.

18. Dionysius does not appear in the *Clouds*, but when Aristophanes is onstage as the lead Cloud, he refers to Dionysius as "the one who raised me" (519).

is not limited to what they do or do not do for us; it extends to how our thoughts about them affect and express what we do and how we live. While the most pressing question is the one raised in the *Clouds*—namely, whether piety is not a necessary source of supporting sanctions for duties and restraints essential to the family and the city—Aristophanes does not lose sight of the influence of imaginative thoughts about deities that inspire the human creation of beautiful music, poetry, temples, and statues (*Birds* 612–16, 1109–10; *Peace* 615–18). Aristophanes' plays do not constitute a blanket rejection or debunking of all personal deities; we must never forget that Aristophanes presents himself as one of the Clouds. Reflection on this and the kindred but contrasting apotheosis of the Titanic Peisthetairos may point to the implicit Aristophanean suggestion that human piety also expresses, in and by its more admirable and beautiful or charming gods, humanity's natural aspirations to the most spiritually rich enjoyments.

The Limits of Aristophanes' Critique of the Gods

If Aristophanes' criticism of Zeus and his rule or dispensation is far-reaching, it is not without limits. To repeat the most crucial point, not one of Aristophanes' heroic rebels goes so far as Socrates—simply denying the existence of Zeus or other gods.[19] In each of our plays, minor or novel deities displace Zeus and the main Olympians; and these new, or newly promoted, divinities are heralded in the very titles of the plays in which they become supreme. The heroes of these plays call for a new and improved pantheon, not a mechanistic or godless universe. Aristophanes implies that the case against Zeus must be made in the name of new gods; even a boastful tyrant like Zeus would be hard to dislodge if the alternative were nothing. (And from a human point of view, Socrates' impersonal "god" vortex is no god at all.) In contrast to vortex, the birds, for example, are new and improved per-

---

19. Not only does Socrates deny the existence of Zeus, but he seems to deny all personal deities. His professed devotion to the Clouds gives way quickly to the claim that it is "vortex" (*dinos*) that "compels" the motions of the clouds, motions that Strepsiades had attributed to Zeus (367–80). Socrates' oaths to "breath, chaos [or 'yawning void'], and air" do not make him a theist, nor even does an occasional oath to the god he explicitly denies (694) or to the Graces (773). Socrates' last reference to the Clouds in the play occurs less than one-third of the way in (423–24), and his student Pheidippides attacks Zeus in the name of vortex, not the Clouds (1470–71). It is not surprising that the Clouds, who invoke eight conventional deities in the parabasis and act to defend them, are ready to see Socrates punished by the end of the play (1458–61).

sonal divinities. They promise to do better than Zeus did in helping human beings find their way to abundant food, longer lives, amorous conquests, and a measure of wealth. The god Wealth promises to reward the just and make it unnecessary to choose between virtue and prosperity. And the goddess Peace promises to enable men to tend to their vines and enjoy the fruits of simple lives in the country. Great but solid hopes attend them all and sustain the forces arrayed against Zeus. Aristophanes' heroes are not anti-theistic; they seek new gods who come closer to living up to standards implicit in the human conception of and natural directedness to divinity.

Another, related—and crucial—limit on Aristophanes' critique of the gods comes to sight when we observe that the overthrow of the traditional gods is by no means accompanied by a revolution in or against traditional morality. To be sure, in the *Birds* at least, the birds promise precisely such a revolution. They announce to human beings that living as birds will eliminate the need to sacrifice pleasures in pursuit of noble action. Indeed, they say that all the shameful actions repressed by law will not merely be allowed but will even be noble, so there will be a complete transvaluation of values. Just as Socrates' ace student Pheidippides had outrageously defended the beating of fathers, so too do the birds (753–59). But contrary to the promise of these lines, and unlike Socrates, Peisthetairos is on the scene to act against this moral breakdown. He directly forbids what the birds had promised: in the new order, there will be no father-beating, and justice and moderation are imperative.[20] Peisthetairos leads a wildly radical revolution against the Olympians, yet he is careful to find a way to protect the moral and theological core on which his new city (and his own rule)—like any city and any civilized rule—will depend. Cities inescapably need citizens formed to defend the laws, not to find pleasure in looking down upon the laws with contempt.

The *Peace* suggests similar limits in what theological revolution will durably achieve. Even at the moment when he is enjoying his great successes in heaven, Trygaeus learns that Zeus is not in fact wholly responsible for the war. Trygaeus is persuaded by Hermes after only a few reminders of the historical record that, con-

---

20. Peisthetairos excludes eight people from the new city; he welcomes no one (1343–71, 992–1020). While justifying his exclusions, he defends the law and what is moderate and just (1045, 1345–57, 1433–35, 1448–50). In particular he redirects a father-beater to the Thracian front (cf. *Clouds* 1405–39); he excludes an astronomer who reminds of Socrates; and he attempts to persuade the sycophant to find a decent way to make a living.

trary to the view that Zeus thrust the war upon them, the Greeks themselves bear much of the blame. It is true that the Olympians did not work earnestly or effectively to establish peace, and true as well that Zeus finally decided to give Greece over completely to War—and, in most ungodly fashion, did so just in order that he not have to listen any longer to the Greeks' cries for help! But the Greeks themselves turned down chances to make treaties, and the Athenians are represented as having started the war for shameful reasons (605ff.). The very action of the play supports the main features of Hermes' report: not all Greeks favor the excavation of Peace, and Trygaeus himself is less troubled by war in Megara or Sparta, for example, than by war near his own farm in Athens (246–54). War in the abstract is thus not the problem, as Aristophanes' humans see it; it is one's own sufferings in war that are to be avoided. And although Trygaeus successfully absconds from heaven with the goddess Peace, it is not clear that this virtually lifeless, passive, statue-like being will do much to ensure the blessings the Athenian farmers associate with her. Although her heart was reported to be in the right place, she achieved nothing before her entombment by War. When the Greeks began to fight, she simply disappeared (614). She is credited with no independent powers to stop the fighting. She does boast that she came to Athens on her own initiative (665–68), but she came only after the events at Pylos gave peace a chance. Even then, she could do nothing to get the Athenians to ratify a treaty. If she is weak as compared to mortals, she was also no match for War once he was unleashed by Zeus. War, after all, can shout, move under his own power, give terrifying orders, and bury her. The latter part of the play shows divisions among the Athenians, both by trade and by inclination, and one may expect the divisions will again prove too lively for the goddess to pacify.

Speaking more generally, Aristophanes teaches that overthrowing Zeus by overthrowing opinions about Zeus does not eliminate the course of nature and the power of chance. But nature and chance forever frustrate or impede the satisfaction of natural human needs and longings. This is the deepest reason why nothing can do away with the human need for gods. It is an odd thing to say about a play in which men grow wings, but the *Birds* does not depict a fundamental conquest of nature. One may also say that the meaning of "the gods" is equivocal. On the one hand, the intermediate causes of what is most important in our lives may be traced back to the gods. When we think like this, we may hold the gods to be responsible, for example, for our poverty, for our apparent good and bad luck, and perhaps even for the moral demands or dilemmas we face. The gods are the fundamental causes of everything.

At the other extreme, which we take to be closer to Aristophanes' own view, one might try to sort out various causes that underlie these and other aspects of our lives, without tracing those causes back to the gods. We might trace some to chance, others to nature, and still others to law, for example, and to the opinions that human beings hold about the gods. While these opinions will have powerful effects, a change in them does not change nature, chance, or the need for law. In this second view, the discovery of these other causes limits the importance of the gods; this weakening makes their overcoming possible, but also limits its consequences. In Aristophanes' plays, the gods are responsible only for those things for which the opinions of men about the gods are responsible. It appears possible, based on Aristophanes' plays, to overthrow the Olympian gods, and it also appears they deserve it, but the scope and consequences of such an exciting triumph are more limited than might first be thought. Changes to the pantheon may be wished for and encouraged, but the charms of peace, wealth, and natural pleasures will wax and wane with circumstances, even when their influence is increased by associating them with supporting deities. It is worth noting in this connection once again that Aristophanes appears on stage as a Cloud—and the Clouds invoke eight deities, one of whom is Zeus (563–606). Aristophanes along with his Clouds seems more favorable to Zeus than are Socrates and his other rebellious characters. Zeus is shot through with faults, as Aristophanes abundantly shows, but gods will always be needed and—vulnerable though they are—they may not always be so easily replaced. Aristophanes is able to laugh at the Olympians, and at some more than others, without lapsing into a bitter polemic or advancing ardently a program of reform promising once and for all to make things right between men and their gods: that would be to make Aristophanes himself a subject for comedy, for—as he seems to see it—there is no solution to the divine comedy that can resolve once and for all the problems that plague the human situation (and it is by the human situation that gods are judged). Zeus and other gods can be overthrown, and they deserve it. The *Birds*, *Peace*, and *Wealth* encourage kinder and gentler lives for their worshippers. But will Trygaeus and Peace be sufficient to keep the Greeks deeply and durably devoted to peace? Will Chremylos and Wealth be able to solve forever the problem that is forecast by Poverty? Will Peisthetairos and his natural deities live up to the attractive promises that helped to show Zeus's pronounced defects? Some gods are better than others, but all gods, both new and old, have their work cut out for them.

A NOTE ON
THE TRANSLATION

LANGUAGES ARE SO DIFFERENT that translation cannot be done mechanically; it always requires difficult judgments. Moreover, translators often have different goals. Aristophanes is obscene and offensive, for example, so some may incline to tone his vulgar humor down, as most did a century ago. And he is very funny, so translators naturally try to ensure that their translations are also funny, even if a certain witticism may lead one to stray from the most precise rendering of the Greek text. Because Aristophanes' diction was generally easy for an ancient Athenian to understand, it also may seem reasonable to strive for comparable familiarity in English. "Zeus" may therefore become "God," for example; "just" may become "right" or "fair" or "deserved"; and "soul" may go untranslated altogether. And of course we all enjoy liveliness and variety of expression, so we would like these qualities to be prominent in our English renderings.

The problem is that such tempting adjustments may keep readers from seeing and considering important interpretations of the play. For example, in the parabasis of the *Clouds*, Aristophanes says he wishes to be believed to be *sophos* (520), a word we always render "wise." The close cognates of this word are used at least eighteen times in the *Clouds*, and they certainly appear to be tied to the most important questions raised in the play: Is Socrates as wise as he thinks he is (94, 489, 841)? Is the comic poet Aristophanes in some or even all respects wiser than the philosopher Socrates? Did Aristophanes write his plays for wise spectators in particular (525–26)? Is the Unjust Speech wiser or more foolish than the Just Speech (895, 899, 1057)? Is the radical Euripides wiser than more traditional poets (1370, 1378)? As noted above, however, translators of Aristophanes are tempted to use multiple renderings of the same or related words for the sake of variety, humor, and vigorous diction. Thus, in these eighteen passages linked by *sophos*, the leading recent translation uses eleven different words, including "sage," "sophisticated," "brainy," "ingenious," "smart," "sagacious," et cetera.[1] This is a pleasant variety of words, but they cost the reader the accumulated weight that comes from repeating the same word, which helps one see that wisdom is indeed a central theme of the play. Lost at the same time is the opportunity to compare different claims arising in passages sharing a strong linguistic link. To put this more sharply, we think the comic poet means it when he presents himself as superior in wisdom to the philosopher Socrates; we think he is serious as well about a related question, one raised in Socrates' "thinkery" and put on stage for Pheidippides: is it wise to follow the traditional laws even if doing so requires one to abstain from leading the most pleasant or best life possible? In the hope of enabling our readers to recognize and to study issues like these, which we consider to be of massive and enduring importance, we are cautious in our pursuit of other charms.

The distinctive feature of our translations is that they strive to be as faithful as possible to Aristophanes' Greek and to be as consistent as possible in the way they render it into English. We have established these priorities in the belief that Aristophanes is worthy of study not only as a comic poet but also as a thinker; these two categories are not in his case at war with one another. Our introduction defends this case; although difficult of access, the provocative studies of Leo Strauss demonstrate in far greater detail how rewarding a careful study of Aristophanes' thought can be.[2] If Aristophanes has a claim to a kind of wisdom as well as to hilarious wit and linguistic brilliance, it becomes that much more important to be painstakingly accurate in moving his plays from an ancient language into a modern one that is very different.

Because there are multiple and conflicting manuscripts of Aristophanes' plays, translators must first determine what text to translate. Fortunately, new and better editions of his Greek texts have recently been published, and we have taken advantage of them. Although we have been cautious about accepting proposed emendations or corrections of the manuscripts, we have certainly considered them.

We are indebted to the texts, annotations, and translation suggestions in the following: Victor Coulon, ed., and Hilaire Van Daele, trans., *Aristophane Comédies*,

---

1. Jeffrey Henderson, ed. *Aristophanes: Clouds, Wasp, Peace* (Cambridge: Harvard U. Press, Loeb Library, 1998).

2. See in particular *Socrates and Aristophanes* (Chicago: University of Chicago Press, 1966) and *The Rebirth of Classical Rationalism* (Chicago: University of Chicago Press, 1989), essays selected and introduced by Thomas L. Pangle, esp. 103–34, 171–73. There are of course other scholars who show great respect for Aristophanes as a thinker, but they are far from representing a majority view.

2nd ed., vols. 2, 3, 5 (Paris: Les Belles Lettres, Budé, 2002 and 2009); F. W. Hall and W. M. Geldart, eds., *Aristophanes Comoediae*, vol. 1 (Oxford: Clarendon Press, 1906); Jeffrey Henderson, *Aristophanes*, vols. 2, 3, 4 (Cambridge: Harvard University Press, Loeb Library, 1998, 2000, 2002) and *The Maculate Muse*, 2nd ed. (Oxford: Oxford University Press, 1991); S. Douglas Olson, ed., *Aristophanes Peace* (Oxford: Oxford University Press, 1998); and Leo Strauss, *Socrates and Aristophanes* (Chicago: University of Chicago Press, 1966).

In addition to disagreements over what Aristophanes actually wrote, uncertainties accompany the assignment of lines to a particular speaker. While there are traditions that assign lines, these traditions are not easily traceable to Aristophanes; the text itself may be our best guide to what speaker spoke particular lines.[3] Only in cases of special importance do we note disputes over the text or over the assignment of lines to a particular speaker.

For more complete statements on the challenge of translating ancient Greek and the principles we follow, see Thomas L. Pangle, *The Laws of Plato* (New York: Basic Books, 1980), pp. ix–xiv and Xenophon, *The Education of Cyrus* (Ithaca: Cornell University Press, 2001), trans. Wayne Ambler, pp. viii–x.

---

3. J.C.B. Lowe, "The Manuscript Evidence for Changes of Speaker in Aristophanes," *Bulletin of the Institute of Classical Studies* 9:1 (1962) 35–39.

BIRDS

DRAMATIS PERSONAE[1]

EUELPIDES [= "Of Good Hope"]
PEISTHETAIROS [= "Persuasive Comrade" or "Persuaded by Comrades"]
BIRD-SERVANT OF TEREUS
TEREUS, having become a Hoopoe Bird
CHORUS OF BIRDS [and its **LEADER**]
PRIEST
POET
ORACLE-COLLECTOR
METON, a geometer
INSPECTOR [of new colonies, for Athens]
SELLER OF DECREES
MESSENGERS
IRIS [the messenger goddess]
HERALDS
A FATHER BEATER
KINESIAS, a dithyrambic poet
IMPOVERISHED "SYCOPHANT" [a false accuser, who harassed the rich with
    lawsuits in order to get money by settlements]
PROMETHEUS
POSEIDON
TRIBALLIAN [a barbarian god]
HERACLES

[Mute Characters:
XANTHIAS and **MANODORUS**—also called **MANES**: baggage-carrying slaves who
    accompany Euelpides and Peisthetairos
PROCNE
BASILEIA or **QUEEN**]

---

1. Bracketed material lacks manuscript authority; it is intended only to facilitate a first reading of
the play. Line numbers are borrowed from the Greek texts of the plays; they will not always be sequential in English.

[Enter **Euelpides** and **Peisthetairos**, the former with a jackdaw, the latter with a crow, and two servants carrying luggage.]

Euelpides [to his jackdaw]: Right on? Is *that* what you are bidding—
toward where the tree appears?

Peisthetairos [to his crow]: Split yourself!
[To Euelpides]: This one croaks to go *back*!

Euelpides [to his jackdaw]: Why is it, you rogue, that we are wandering up
And down?! We'll perish with this route of weaving about!

Peisthetairos: Woe is me—persuaded by a crow,
To go a roundabout route, more than a thousand stades[2] long!

Euelpides: Ill-fated am I, persuaded by a jackdaw,
To wear off the nails of my toes!

Peisthetairos: But where on earth we are, I no longer know!

Euelpides: But from here you could presumably find your way to the
fatherland?

Peisthetairos: By Zeus, not even Execestides[3] could do it from here!

Euelpides: Groan!

Peisthetairos: Pal, you go that way.

Euelpides: Indeed, terrible things were done to us two, by that fellow of the
Birds—that bird-tray-selling, black-biled, nut Philocrates,
Who claimed that these two would point out, to us two,
Tereus[4] (He's that hoopoe-bird who became a bird from those birds.[5])—
And who sold this jackdaw son of Tharreleides[6]
For an obol, and this one here for three obols—

---

2. A "stade" is a length of about 600 feet.

3. An Athenian citizen who was apparently under a cloud of suspicion of having barbarian slave ancestry; also mentioned at 764 and 1527.

4. According to the myth dramatized by Sophocles in a play no longer extant, Tereus was a king transformed by the gods into a hoopoe bird.

5. Euelpides comically and momentarily breaks the dramatic illusion, reminding the audience who Tereus is.

6. Apparently some haplessly short and chattering fellow in Athens.

The two of them don't know anything else except how to bite!

20 And *now*, what are *you* gaping at? Is it among the rocks there,
That you are going to drag us again? For there isn't any path *here*!

PEISTHETAIROS: By Zeus, there isn't any straight path *here* either!

EUELPIDES: Doesn't the crow say *anything* about the route?

PEISTHETAIROS: By Zeus, she isn't croaking the same now as before!

EUELPIDES: Well what does she say about the route?

PEISTHETAIROS: What else does she say, except that by gnawing she'll eat
my fingers!

EUELPIDES: Isn't it simply awful that, when we need and
Are quite prepared to go to the crows,[7]
We can't find the way?

30 For we—Oh you men who are here witnesses to the account[8]—
Are ill, with an illness the opposite of that of Sacas.[9]
For he, not being a citizen, is forcing his way in,
While we, dignified by tribe and lineage,
Citizens among citizens, and on account of no scarecrow,
Have flown up and away from the fatherland with both feet:
Not because we hate that city herself,
As one which is not by nature great, and happy,
And a community for all—to spend their money, in fines and settlements!
For while the cicadas for a month or two only

40 Sing upon the branches, the Athenians *always*
Upon the lawsuits sing—their entire lives away!
That is why we are treading this path,
Carrying basket and pot and myrtle boughs,[10]
Wandering in search of a spot without busy troubles,
Where, having settled, we may dwell.
And our goal is Tereus,

---

7. An idiom equivalent to our modern "go to the dogs."

8. Again, Euelpides breaks the dramatic illusion to address the audience.

9. "Sacas" means "the Scythian," and was applied to the tragedian Acestor, a naturalized Athenian who apparently had some trouble with his citizenship (cf. *Wasps* 1221).

10. Implements for the sacrifice required at the founding of a new city.

The hoopoe, from whom we need to inquire
If he knows of some such city that he has flown over.

PEISTHETAIROS: Here!

EUELPIDES: What is it?

PEISTHETAIROS: The crow, once again,
Points upward!   50

EUELPIDES: And this jackdaw
Gapes up, as if showing me something;
It *must* be that there are birds here.
And we'll know at once, if we make a noise.

PEISTHETAIROS: But do you know what to do? Strike the rock with your leg![11]

EUELPIDES: Why don't you do it with your head, so as to make twice the
        noise!

PEISTHETAIROS: Look, take a stone and knock.

EUELPIDES: Sure, if so it's decided![12] Boy! Boy!

PEISTHETAIROS: What's this you're saying? You're calling the hoopoe "boy"?!
        Shouldn't you call, instead of "boy"—"hoo-po-e"?

EUELPIDES: Hoo-po-e! . . . You'll make me knock again. Hoo-po-e!

BIRD-SERVANT OF THE HOOPOE BIRD: Who are these? Who's the one   60
        shouting for the master?

EUELPIDES: Apollo shield us from this gaping beak!

SERVANT: Woe of woes! These two are bird hunters!

EUELPIDES: Isn't it terrible?! Not to speak more beautifully!

SERVANT: You two shall perish!

EUELPIDES: But we two are not humans!

SERVANT: What!?

EUELPIDES: I at any rate am a very frightened Libyan bird![13]

SERVANT: Nonsense!

---

11. There was a boys' saying: "Strike a rock with your leg and birds will fall down."

12. The formula for something passed by vote in the Assembly.

13. These birds were considered especially prone to defecate when frightened.

EUELPIDES: Well, just look at the stuff at my feet!

SERVANT: And this fellow—what bird is he? Can't you say?

PEISTHETAIROS: I for my part am a shitting Pheasant!

EUELPIDES: But, in the name of the gods, whatever sort of beast are YOU?!

70   **SERVANT**: I, for my part, am a slave-bird.

EUELPIDES: Defeated by some fighting cock?

SERVANT: No; but when my master
    Became a hoopoe, he then prayed that I might become
    A bird, so that he might have a servant following him.

EUELPIDES: So a bird also needs some servant?

SERVANT: This one does, at any rate: I think because he was previously
        a human.
    Sometimes he gets an erotic passion for eating Phalerian sardines;
    So, I run after the sardines, taking a bowl.
    He also desires soup, and he needs a ladle and a pot;
    So, I run after the ladle.

EUELPIDES: (We have here a running-bird [sandpiper].)
80   So, running-bird, you know what you're to do? Call your master for us!

SERVANT: But, by Zeus, he is just now taking a nap,
    Having gulped down myrtle and some fleas!

EUELPIDES: All the same, wake him up!

SERVANT: I know well that
    He'll be irritated—but I'll wake him for your sake. [Exit.]

PEISTHETAIROS: May you perish in foul fashion, for you frightened me
        to death!

EUELPIDES: Alas! Unhappy am I! I let the jackdaw get away
    In my terror!

PEISTHETAIROS: You most cowardly beast!
    Out of terror you let the jackdaw go?!

EUELPIDES: Tell me,
    Didn't you let go of the crow while you were shitting?

90   **PEISTHETAIROS**: By Zeus, not me!

EUELPIDES: So where is it?

PEISTHETAIROS: Flew away.

EUELPIDES: You didn't let it go? Oh-ho, good fellow, what a MAN you are!

TEREUS [having become a Hoopoe Bird]: Open the wood,[14] so that I may
then go out!

EUELPIDES: Heracles! What ever is *this* beast?
   What is this plumage? What is the fashion of this triple-cresting?

HOOPOE: Who are they who seek *me*?

EUELPIDES: It looks like the twelve gods[15] have afflicted you!

HOOPOE: You two mock me, seeing the plumage?! Strangers, *I was* a human!

EUELPIDES: We aren't laughing at *you*!

HOOPOE: Then at what?!

EUELPIDES: It's your beak: that's what appears ridiculous to us.

HOOPOE: It is in such ways that Sophocles abuses me,   100
   In his tragedies about Tereus!

EUELPIDES: YOU are Tereus?! Are you a bird, or a peacock?[16]

HOOPOE: I am a bird!

EUELPIDES: So then where are your feathers?

HOOPOE: They fell out.

EUELPIDES: On account of some illness?

HOOPOE: No, but in the winter, all birds
   Molt; and then we grow other feathers again.
   But tell me, who *you two* are.

EUELPIDES: Us two? Mortals.

HOOPOE: Of what stock?

EUELPIDES: From where there are the beautiful triremes.

HOOPOE: So you are jurymen?

---

14. There is a play here on the words for "wood" (*hylē*) and "gate" (*pylē*).

15. The twelve Olympians; a proverbial expression for terrible misfortune.

16. Used metaphorically for a ridiculous dandy (*Acharnians* 63).

EUELPIDES: Rather the contrary, NON-jurymen.

110   **HOOPOE:** Does such a seed get sown *there*?

EUELPIDES: If you search a bit you could get some from the countryside.[17]

HOOPOE: Out of need of what business do you two come here?

EUELPIDES: We wish to meet you.

HOOPOE: About what?

EUELPIDES: Because first, you were human, as we two are now,
      And you owed money, as we two do now,
      And you weren't pleased to pay it back, as we two aren't now;
      And then subsequently you have taken on the nature of birds,
      And have circled in flight above land and sea,
      And are prudent in all things that pertain to human or bird;
120   With these things in view, therefore, we two come now to you, as
      Suppliants, that you might point out to us some fleecy city,
      In which we might lie down, like some soft goat's-hair cloak.

HOOPOE: So then you seek a city greater than that of the Cranaeans?[18]

EUELPIDES: Not greater, but more suitable for us two.

HOOPOE: So, obviously you are looking for an aristocracy.

EUELPIDES: ME?!
      Least of all! I loathe the son of Scellius![19]

HOOPOE: Then in what sort of city would you most pleasantly dwell?

EUELPIDES: Where the most troubling business would be of the
         following sort:
      To my door, early in the morning, one of my friends would come,
130   Saying: "In the name of Olympian Zeus!
      You and your children, having festively bathed yourselves,
      Come early tomorrow to my place: for I am going to put on a wedding

---

17. The implication is that rural Athenians were less likely to spend time on juries.

18. Cranaus was one of the first mythic kings of Athens; when he ruled, the Athenians called themselves Cranaeans, and the city Cranae; from his daughter, Atthis, the land got its name Attica.

19. Aristocrates, son of Scellius, became a leader in the oligarchic regime that ruled Athens for a short while in 411 B.C., three years after the *Birds* was first produced.

Feast; now don't do anything else! If you don't come,
Then don't ever come to me at a time when I am faring *badly*!"

HOOPOE: By Zeus, you *do* have an erotic passion for affairs of misery!
And you?

PEISTHETAIROS: I too have an erotic passion for such things.

HOOPOE: For which?

PEISTHETAIROS: Where a father, having encountered me, blames me in
regards to
His blooming son, as if he's suffered an injustice, in the following
Terms: "A fine thing it is—you showoff!—when you encountered my
Son, coming away from the gymnasium, freshly bathed: 140
And you failed to kiss him, to speak with him, to put the make on
Him, to fondle his balls—you! who have been my ancestral friend!"

HOOPOE: Ah, you poor fellow! What ills you *do* have an erotic passion for!
But there is a city happy in the way you two say—
On the coast of the Red Sea!20

EUELPIDES: Egad, no! NOT on the sea coast, where the "Salaminia"21 will
show up,
Some early morning, carrying a herald!
Can't you point out to us some Greek city?

HOOPOE: Why don't you go dwell in Elis, at Lepreum?

EUELPIDES: Because, by the gods, though I haven't seen it,   150
I loathe "Lepreum," on account of Melanthius!22

HOOPOE: But there are others—the Opuntians in Locris—
Among whom you ought to settle.

EUELPIDES: But I at any rate would never become an Opuntius,23
Even for a mass of gold!
But, what's it like living with the birds?—
For you know with precision.

---

20. Equivalent to our "over the rainbow" (see also *Knights* 1088).
21. The ship the city sent out to catch those fleeing indictments.
22. A tragic poet who suffered from leprosy [*lepra*]; referred to also at *Peace* 1009.
23. A one-eyed fellow (see 1294 below) and a sycophant.

HOOPOE: It's not unpleasing, as time passes.
In the first place, you need to live without a purse.

EUELPIDES: That does away with a great deal of the dishonesty in life!

HOOPOE: And we graze the gardens for white sesame,
160   And myrtle, and poppy seeds, and mint.

EUELPIDES: So then you live the life of newlyweds![24]

PEISTHETAIROS: Whoa! Whoa! I have a great insight into a project for the
    race of birds,
And the power that would come about, if you would be persuaded by me!

HOOPOE: Persuaded by you in what?

PEISTHETAIROS: In *what* should you be persuaded?—First,
Don't fly around everywhere gaping!
For this is a dishonorable business. Among us,
If you were to ask about those who flit around,
"Who's this?" Teleas[25] will say as follows:
"The human's a bird—weightless, flighty,
170   Wavering, never staying put in any way."

HOOPOE: By Dionysus, in these respects your blame is on target!
So what *should* we do?

PEISTHETAIROS: Dwell in a *single city*.

HOOPOE: What sort of a *city* could we dwell in as *birds*?!

PEISTHETAIROS: Truly, "you have pronounced the most stupid utterance"[26]—
Look down below!

HOOPOE: I'm looking.

PEISTHETAIROS: Now look up!

HOOPOE: I'm looking.

PEISTHETAIROS: Turn your neck!

---

24. A cake containing the preceding ingredients was traditionally eaten by newlyweds.

25. Thought to be a wealthy political figure; also satirized in fragments of the comic poets Phrynicus and Plato; see also 1024–25 and *Peace* 1009. The joke of referring to him in this context has been lost.

26. A spoofing quotation or echo of some unknown tragic verse. For comic effect, Aristophanes mimics tragic diction as well as tragic scenes.

HOOPOE: By Zeus,
  I'll have enjoyment for sure, if I wrench my neck!

PEISTHETAIROS: Do you see anything?

HOOPOE: The clouds and the heaven.

PEISTHETAIROS: Well, is not this the vault [*polos*] of the birds?!

HOOPOE: "*Polos*?"—In what sense?   180

PEISTHETAIROS: Even as if someone would say "place."
  Because this "moves about" [*poletai*], and everything
  Proceeds on account of this, it is now called "*polos*."
  But if once you were to settle and fortify this,
  From being called "*polos*," it would become "*polis* [city]!"
  And the result would be, that you would rule over humans as [you do]
    over locusts,
  And the very gods you would destroy, with a Melian famine![27]

HOOPOE: How?

PEISTHETAIROS: Surely, the air is in between, in relation to the earth:
  And so, even as, when *we* wish to go to the Pythia [Delphic oracle],
  We have to request passage of the Boeotians,   190
  In the same way, when humans sacrifice to the gods,
  If the gods do not bring tribute to *you*,
  Then through the polis that does not belong to them, and the void,
  You will not let the savor of the thigh meat through!

HOOPOE: Hey! Wow! By Earth, by snares, by "Clouds,"[28] by nets!
  Never have I heard so elegant a conceit!
  So I would indeed found with you the city,
  If the other birds agree!

PEISTHETAIROS: So who will explain the affair to them?

---

27. A dual reference: 1) to the famous Athenian reduction of Melos by siege and starvation (see Thucydides 5.89–116), which occurred about a year before this play was first produced; and 2) also to philosophic atheism—Socrates is called "the Melian" in *Clouds* 830 because he is associated with the notorious atheistic philosopher "Diagoras the Melian" (referred to below at 1073); and in the *Clouds*, Socrates and his students are portrayed as starving ascetics.

28. "Cloud" was a term for a fine bird net; see also 528; but this is also one of many echoes of the *Clouds*.

HOOPOE: You! For I have taught them, who were previously barbarians,
200   To speak—having spent a lot of time with them.

PEISTHETAIROS: How do you call them together?

HOOPOE: Easily; for as soon as I step into the thicket here,
And then wake up my nightingale,
She and I will call them. And they, if they
Hear our two voices, will come running!

PEISTHETAIROS: Oh you dearest of birds! Now don't you delay!
But I beseech you, as quickly as possible
Go into the thicket and wake up the nightingale!

HOOPOE: Come, my mate, leave off sleeping,
210   And let loose the tunes of the sacred hymns,
By which you lament through your divine mouth
The much bewailed Itys, my [child] and yours—
Warbling with flowing songs
From your trilling mouth!
The pure echo proceeds, through the leafy
Yew, to the seats of Zeus,
Where golden-haired Phoebus [Apollo] hears;
And, in response to your elegies, plucks
Upon an ivory harp, to set in motion
220   The choruses of the gods! And from the immortal
Mouth there issues a divine resonance,
A cry of the blessed ones!

[A song is heard.]

PEISTHETAIROS [or **EUELPIDES**][29]: King Zeus! What a voice the bird has!—
Such as to pour honey over the entire thicket!

EUELPIDES [or **PEISTHETAIROS**]: Here he is!

PEISTHETAIROS [or **EUELPIDES**]:   What?

EUELPIDES [or **PEISTHETAIROS**]:   Won't you shut up?!

PEISTHETAIROS [or **EUELPIDES**]:   What's the matter?

---

29. The attribution of the lines here is disputed: the earliest printed edition has the attributions indicated in brackets, against the more authoritative manuscripts that we now have.

EUELPIDES [or **PEISTHETAIROS**]: The hoopoe is preparing to sing again!

HOOPOE: Epopoi! Popopopopopopoi!
    Ahoi! Ahoi! Come, come, come, come!
    Come here, who is of my feathered race!
    As many of you as upon the well-sown country fields   230
    Feed—ten thousand tribes of barley-eaters,
    And races of seed-pickers,
    Swift of flight, soft of voice;
    As many of you as frequently twitter around the furrow's clod,
    So light, in your pleasing voice.
    Tio! Tio! Tio! Tio! Tio! Tio! Tio! Tio!
    And you who upon the ivy shoots in gardens
    Have your grazing,
    And who upon the mountains eat wild olive berries,   240
    And arbutus—
    Complete your flight to my voice!
    Trioto! Trioto! Totobrix!
    You who seize the sharp-biting fleas near the marshy glens,
    And as many as possess
    The dewy places of the earth
    And the broad plain of Marathon:
    The motley-plumed bird—
    The Moorhen! The Moorhen!
    Let the tribes flying on the salty swell of the sea,   250
    With the Halcyons,
    Come hither to learn new things!
    For we are here gathering all tribes
    Of the birds with outstretched necks!
    For a certain sharp elder[30] has arrived,
    Of strange judgment,
    Who is taking in hand strange deeds!
    But come, everyone, to the discussions—
    Hither, hither, hither, hither!

---

30. The word translated as "elder" (*presbus*) can also mean "wren."

260 **CHORUS OF THE BIRDS:** Torotorotorotorotix!
Kikkabaw! kikkabaw!
Torotorotorotoroliliiix!

PEISTHETAIROS: Do you see any bird?

EUELPIDES: By Apollo! Not I!—
Yet I've looked up gaping into heaven!

PEISTHETAIROS: In vain, then, it looks like the Hoopoe went into
the thicket,
And clucked in imitation of the Lapwing![31]

A CERTAIN BIRD: Torotix! Torotix!

PEISTHETAIROS: But my good fellow, here's one bird coming now!

EUELPIDES: By Zeus, a bird indeed! What in the world sort? Surely not
a Peacock!

270 **PEISTHETAIROS:** This one here will himself explain to us: What IS
this bird?

HOOPOE: This is not one of the usual things you always see,
But, rather, a water bird.

EUELPIDES: Wow! Beautiful and purple!

HOOPOE: But of course: and its name is in fact "Purple-feathered."

EUELPIDES: Hey, psst, you there!

PEISTHETAIROS: Why are you yelling?

EUELPIDES: Here is another bird!

PEISTHETAIROS: By Zeus, another indeed, and "this one in a land that is
not its place!"[32]
Whatever is this out-of-place, mountain-treading "prophet-of-Muses?"[33]

HOOPOE: "Mede" is the name of this one.

PEISTHETAIROS: "Mede?!" Lord Heracles!
Then how, being a Mede, did it fly here without a camel?

---

31. A bird that, in order to decoy enemies, flies far from its nest and pretends to call its young
to it.

32. A spoofing quote from Sophocles' lost tragedy *Tyro*.

33. A spoofing quote from Aeschylus's lost tragedy *Edonians*.

EUELPIDES: Here is yet another bird, with a crest.

PEISTHETAIROS: What's this prodigy?! So you're NOT the only hoopoe, but 280
this is another?!

HOOPOE: This one is the son of Philocles the Hoopoe,[34]
And I'm his grandfather—even as you would say,
"Hipponicus the son of Callias," and "Callias son of Hipponicus."[35]

PEISTHETAIROS: So this bird is Callias?!—Look! He's shedding!

EUELPIDES: Yes, for since he is well born, he is plucked by the sycophants,
And the females as well come to pluck his feathers.

PEISTHETAIROS: Oh Poseidon!—what is this next dyed bird!
What ever is the name of this one?!

HOOPOE: This one is "Glutton."

PEISTHETAIROS: Is there another glutton besides Cleonymus?

EUELPIDES: How could he be Cleonymus, when he hasn't thrown away 290
his crest?![36]

PEISTHETAIROS: But why all this crest business among the birds?
Are they going to run the double-course [armored] race?

HOOPOE: It's like the Carians, my good man,
Who live on their mountain crests for security reasons.

PEISTHETAIROS: By Poseidon! Don't you see how much mischief is implied
in the
Birds' drawing around together?

EUELPIDES: Lord Apollo! What a cloud! Alas!
It is no longer possible to discern the *exits*[37] on account of them flying in!

PEISTHETAIROS: Here is a Partridge!

---

34. Philocles, whose nickname was apparently "Lark" (see 1295) was a tragedian who had also (like Sophocles) written a tragedy about Tereus.

35. A very wealthy and prominent Athenian, who figures in the Socratic writings of Xenophon and Plato.

36. A favorite butt of Aristophanes (*Acharnians* 88; *Knights* 958; *Wasps* 19; *Clouds* 353), who is referred to as a notorious coward and glutton, who threw away his shield at the battle of Delium; see also 1475. The joke turns on the two meanings of *lophos*, "crest of feathers on a bird" and "crest of horsehair on a war helmet."

37. Once again, Euelpides comically breaks the dramatic illusion.

EUELPIDES: And those, by Zeus, are Moorhens!

PEISTHETAIROS: And here's a Widgeon!

EUELPIDES: And there's a Halcyon!
What's this behind her?

PEISTHETAIROS: This? A Clipper.

300 **EUELPIDES:** Is a "Clipper" a bird?

PEISTHETAIROS: Well, isn't Sporgilus?[38]—and here's an owl.

EUELPIDES: What are you saying?! Who brought an owl here to Athens!?[39]

HOOPOE: Jay, Turtledove, Lark, Sedgebird, Thyme-finch, Ring-cove,
Rock-dove, Stock-dove, Cuckoo, Falcon, Fiery-crest, Willow-hen,
Lammergeyer, Porphyrion, Kestrel, Waxwing, Nuthatch, Water-hen.

PEISTHETAIROS: Egad! The birds! Double egad! The Blackbirds!
How they twitter, and run about shrieking!
Are they then threatening us? Alas! Their beaks are gaping
And they are staring at you and me!

EUELPIDES: That's how it seems to me too!

310 **CHORUS:** Popopopopopopopopopoi!
WHOooooooo then has summoned me?
In what place does he browse?

HOOPOE: Here I am, as of old, never far from my friends!

CHORUS: What? What? What-What-What-What-What-What?—
What speech then do you have to please me?

HOOPOE: One that is in common, and safe, and just, and pleasant, and
beneficial!
For a pair who are subtle men of reason have arrived at my place here!

CHORUS: Where? How? What do you mean?

320 **HOOPOE:** I am saying that two old men have arrived here from humans!
And they come having the root of a prodigious affair!

---

38. Apparently a well-known barber in Athens.

39. The owl was the sacred bird of Athena, and hence a proverb about bringing them to Athens, equivalent to "carrying coals to Newcastle." Once again Euelpides comically breaks the dramatic illusion.

CHORUS LEADER: Oh you greatest sinner of all my entire days!
What *are* you saying?!

HOOPOE: Now, now, don't be afraid of speech!

CHORUS LEADER: *What* have you done to me?

HOOPOE: I've welcomed two men, erotically passionate for intercourse
with us!

CHORUS LEADER: Have you really done this deed?!

HOOPOE: And I am pleased to have done it!

CHORUS LEADER: And are the two now somewhere among us?!

HOOPOE: If I am among you!

CHORUS: Ai Yi Yi! We are betrayed and suffer impious injuries!
He who was a friend and nourished together with us,
Who browsed the fields with us,   330
Has overstepped ancient laws,
Has overstepped the oaths of birds!
He summoned us into a trap, and has thrown me to
That impious species, which has, since the time it was born,
Against me waged war!
But we'll settle the account with this fellow later!
It is my judgment that these two old men will pay the just penalty
And be torn to pieces by us!

PEISTHETAIROS: So we are destroyed then!

EUELPIDES: You alone are to blame for these evils that now befall us!
For why did you draw me hither?!   340

PEISTHETAIROS: So that you would follow me!

EUELPIDES: Sure, so that I would weep to the utmost!

PEISTHETAIROS: In this you are an extreme babbler!
For how will you weep—once you have had your eyes gouged out?!

CHORUS: Hey! Hey!
Attack! Charge! Bear down with hostile,
Bloody assault, throw wings all around them,
And surround them!
For the two must both scream

And supply food for the beak!
For there does not exist a shady mountain, or ethereal cloud,
350   Or hoary sea that shall be a
Refuge of these two fleeing me!
But we will now not hesitate to pluck and to bite these two!
Where is the rank commander? Let him lead, on the right flank!

EUELPIDES: This is it! Where shall I flee in my wretchedness?

PEISTHETAIROS: Stand, won't you fellow?!

EUELPIDES: To be torn to pieces by these?!

PEISTHETAIROS: But how do you think you'll run away from 'em?!

EUELPIDES: I don't know how!

PEISTHETAIROS: But I am telling you,
We must make a stand, and fight, using the pots!

EUELPIDES: How are *pots* going to help us two?

PEISTHETAIROS: An owl will then never come near the two of us![40]

EUELPIDES: But what about these with the talons here?

PEISTHETAIROS: Snatch up a spit,
360   And then plant it before you!

EUELPIDES: What about these eyes of mine?

PEISTHETAIROS: Grab a vinegar cruet and hold it before them! Or a saucer!

EUELPIDES: Oh wisest one! You figured that out well, and like a general!
You outshoot Nicias[41] with your devices!

CHORUS: Hey! Hey! Hey! Advance with your beaks poised! No hesitations!
Draw! Pluck! Strike! Tear! First break the pot!

HOOPOE: Tell me, you worst of all beasts, why are you about to
Destroy these two men from whom you have suffered nothing,
And to slay these who are kin and tribesmen of my wife?![42]

---

40. Pots are frightening to birds because birds are cooked in them. Pots were understood to be under Athena's protection, as products of her inspiration of art and craft. Cf. *Acharnians* 284.

41. The famous Athenian general, who had won a victory (which proved to be short-lived) at Syracuse the autumn before the play was first presented (Thucydides 6.63–71).

42. Procne the wife of Tereus was of the ancient Athenian royal house before the gods transformed her into a bird along with her husband.

CHORUS LEADER: Are we to spare these any more than wolves?!
Whom would we punish who are more hostile than these? 370

HOOPOE: But what if, while in nature they are hostile, in mind they
   are friendly,
And have come hither to teach you something useful?

CHORUS LEADER: But how could these ever teach or communicate to us
Something useful—they who were enemies to our grandsires?

HOOPOE: But from enemies surely the wise learn many things.
For caution saves all things. From a friend,
You would not learn this; but an enemy compels you to do so at once.
Again, it is from men who are enemies, not friends, that cities learn
To labor at building high walls, and to acquire great ships;
And this sort of learning saves children, home, and property. 380

CHORUS LEADER: It is indeed useful, it seems to me, to hear first
   the speeches;
For one might learn something wise even from enemies.

PEISTHETAIROS: They are slackening the bridle of their rage. Move
   rearwards.

HOOPOE: And it is just; and you all ought to accord gratitude to me.

CHORUS: But we have not ever before opposed you in any other matter.

PEISTHETAIROS: They rather make peace, by Zeus! So let down the pot,
And the saucer.
But the spear—the spit—we must
Keep as we walk around,
Inside the weapons, looking out 390
Over the top rim of the pot.
For we two must not flee!

EUELPIDES: But really, if we should die,
Where in the earth will we be buried?

PEISTHETAIROS: The Cerameicus[43] will receive us.
For in order that we will receive public burial,

---

43. A suburb of Athens where was situated the cemetery for veterans who died in battle; also the potters' quarter in Athens.

We will declare to the generals
That we two died fighting the enemies
In Orneae.[44]

400   **CHORUS LEADER**: Fall back in ranks again to the same place,
And, bending, let down your spiritedness, next to your anger,
Like a hoplite![45]
And we will inquire from these the while who they might be, and
From whence they came,
And with what thought in mind.
Ahoy! Hoopoe, I call you!

HOOPOE: Do you call, in a mood to listen?

CHORUS LEADER: Who ever are these, and from whence?

HOOPOE: A pair of strangers, from wise Greece.

410   **CHORUS LEADER**: What fortune
Ever brings the pair
To come to the birds?

HOOPOE: An erotic passion for the way of life,
And for dwelling among you,
And having every sort of intercourse among you.

CHORUS LEADER: What are you saying? What speeches have they to say?

HOOPOE: Incredible and wild to hear.

CHORUS LEADER: Does he see some gain worth abiding here for,
Which he believes that he would make by being with me,
420   And by which he would overpower an enemy, or
Be able to benefit friends?

HOOPOE: He speaks of a great prosperity—
Unutterable and incredible!—he incites,
Saying how all things are yours,

---

44. A very ancient town in Argolis, whose name sounds like the Greek word for "bird" (*ornis*). In the year before the play was first presented, the town was taken by Sparta and then besieged, taken, and razed by Athens and her allies: there was no battle, and no one died, because the defenders slipped away.

45. There is here a parody of a standard hoplite maneuver.

What is here, and what is there, and
What is over there!

Chorus Leader: So he's crazy?

Hoopoe: Unspeakably prudent!

Chorus Leader: There's wisdom in his mind?

Hoopoe: The sharpest fox,   430
Sophist-like, a swindler, a trickster, thoroughly subtle.[46]

Chorus Leader: Bid him speak, speak to me!
For after hearing the things you say to me
I'm aflutter at the words!

Hoopoe: Come then, you! and you!—This weaponry
Hang back up again, with good fortune,
By the oven corner inside, near the trivet.
And you, as regards those speeches, concerning which I issued the
Summons, teach and expound to these.

Peisthetairos: By Apollo, I will not!—
Unless they contract with me the very covenant which   440
That ape—the swordmaker[47]—contracted with his wife: that these
Are neither to bite me, nor to yank my balls, nor to poke me in my—

Euelpides: You don't mean—

Peisthetairos: Not at all, no!—I'm speaking of the *eyes*.

Chorus Leader: I make the covenant.

Peisthetairos: Now swear these things to me!

Chorus Leader: I swear—but on the following conditions: that I'm judged
Victorious, by all the judges and all the spectators![48]

Peisthetairos: So it shall be!

Chorus: *And*, if I do breech the covenant, then I'm victorious if by only a
single judge's vote!

---

46. The terms for "trickster" and "subtle" recall the qualities that Socrates promises to educate Strepsiades in (*Clouds* 260).

47. A reference to a certain Panetius, who was short and ugly.

48. Here the chorus comically breaks the dramatic illusion.

HERALD: Listen to the people! The hoplites are now
To withdraw back homeward taking their weapons,
450 And are to watch to see what we post, in writing, on the bulletin boards!

CHORUS: Guileful always in every way
Is the human by nature. But still, speak to me.
For probably you may happen to express
Something worthy that you see in me; or
Some greater power,
Overlooked by my un-clever mind.
But speak to the community about what you have seen.
For whatever good you might happen
To provide for me, this will be shared in common with you.
460 Whatever business it is that you have come to persuade us of your
knowledge of,
Speak it out boldly. For we will not be the first to violate the treaty.

PEISTHETAIROS: Now I am impassioned, by Zeus! And a speech is
fermenting within me,
That I will not be stopped from kneading. Come, boy, the crowning
Wreath! Let someone quickly bring water to pour over my hands!

EUELPIDES: (Are we going to feast? or what?)[49]

PEISTHETAIROS: (By Zeus, no! I seek to speak some great, old, and fatted
word,
Such as will break down the soul of these!) How I *do* feel pain
For you all! Who once were kings—

CHORUS: US! Kings?! Over *what*?

PEISTHETAIROS: YOU were kings, of all that is—of me in the first place,
and of this
Fellow, and of Zeus Himself! More ancient than, and first before, Kronos
and Titans,
Did you come into being!—and before Earth as well!

---

49. A wreath of myrtle was worn by an orator as he spoke; the wreath was also worn at banquets. Hands were washed before dining, but also before any solemn affair.

Chorus: Earth as well?

Peisthetairos: Yes, by Apollo!

Chorus: Now this, by Zeus, I had never learned!   470

Peisthetairos: That's because you are by nature unlearned and overly
     busy, and
     Have not pondered Aesop: Who declares
     In speech that a bird, the crested lark, came into being first of all,
     Prior to Earth—and then her father fell ill, and died;
     And since Earth did not exist, his corpse laid out for five days; and that
          she, at a loss,
     And lacking devices, finally buried her father in her head!

Euelpides: (So then the father of the crested lark lies dead in the
     "Head-land?!"[50])

Peisthetairos: Now, are not those who came into being prior to Earth,
     and prior to gods,
     Since they are themselves eldest, correctly possessed of the kingship?

Euelpides: By Apollo! You had better tend your beak from now on!
     Zeus won't quickly surrender His scepter to an oak-pecker!   480

Peisthetairos: For, that of old it was *not* the *gods* who ruled over humans,
     But the *birds*, as monarchs, there is here much evidence.
     First, I point out to you the rooster, and how he tyrannized
     And ruled over the Persians, before all those Dariuses and Megabazuses,
     So that he is still called the "Persian bird" on account of that rule.[51]

Euelpides: (So that's why even now, like the great king,[52] he struts about
     And alone of the birds carries on his head the erect tiara!)

Peisthetairos: So mighty and very great was he once, that even now,
     On account of his strength at that time, when he merely sings the
     Dawn, everybody jumps up to their work—in bronze, in pottery,   490
          in tannery,

---

50. "Head," *Kephalē*, was an Attic district or *deme* where was situated a large cemetery.
51. Roosters, originating in India, were originally bought from Persian merchants.
52. I.e., the Persian emperor.

In shoemaking, as bath-attendant, as grain traders, in lyre and shield
    construction on the lathe;
While it's still night they run, putting on their sandals.

EUELPIDES: Just ask me!
For I lost my cloak of Phrygian wool on account of this, to that wicked
Fellow! For once, when I was invited to a child's tenth-day celebration[53]
    in the city, I drank too much,
And then went to sleep; and before the others had feasted, this one
    crowed;
And I, supposing it was dawn, headed for Halimus;[54] and, just as I
Am stooping outside the wall, a robber hits me on the back with a
Club! And I fall, and am about to cry out, but he's plucked off my cloak!

PEISTHETAIROS: And the kite then ruled as king over the Greeks!

500 **CHORUS:** Over the Greeks?!

PEISTHETAIROS: And that one, when he was first our king,
    Taught us to go down on our knees before kites.[55]

EUELPIDES: (By Dionysus, for my part
    I certainly got down on my knees when I saw a kite—and then, gaping
    Upward, I swallowed an obol![56] . . . And I dragged home an empty purse.)

PEISTHETAIROS: And the cuckoo was king over Egypt and all of Phoenicia;
    And when the cuckoo said "cuckoo!" it was then that all the
    Phoenicians harvested the wheat and barley, in their fields.[57]

EUELPIDES: (So that's why the proverb is truly spoken: "Cuckoo! To the
    fields, with stiff peckers!")

PEISTHETAIROS: And such a rule did they exercise, that if someone ruled
    as king

---

53. Children were named in a celebration on the tenth day after birth.

54. A district or *deme* about four miles outside of Athens; apparently a home of Euelpides, who is thus identified as a rural character (see also 585 and 645—where Euelpides is said to come from another rural *deme*).

55. The kite reappeared in Greece each year as a harbinger of Spring, and the Greeks therefore went down on their knees at the sight of one at that time of year.

56. Lacking pockets in their cloaks, Greeks often carried small coins in their mouths.

57. To understand the following response of Euelpides: the word "barley" means in slang an erect phallus (after the shape and appearance of the stalk), and the word "field," associated with "plowing," means a woman's genitals.

In the cities of the Greeks—an Agamemnon or a Menelaus—
A bird used to perch on their scepters, to partake of whatever gifts   510
 they received!

EUELPIDES: (This I did not know! And indeed I've been struck with
 amazement,
Whenever, in the tragedies, some Priam has come out, with a bird;
It must be that the latter perches there to watch out for what gifts
 Lysicrates[58] received!)

PEISTHETAIROS: And, what is most awesome of all, Zeus, the present king,
Stands having the eagle-bird perched on His head as emblem of kingship;
And His daughter, again, has an owl; and Apollo, being a servant, has
 a falcon!

EUELPIDES: By Demeter! You speak these things well! But what's the point
 of their having these?

PEISTHETAIROS: In order that, when someone is sacrificing, and puts into
 the hand of the gods, according to law,
The innards, *these* may take the innards, *before* Zeus does!
Besides, no human used to swear by a god, but all swore by birds.   520
And Lampon still now swears by the goose, whenever he practices
 a deception.[59]
SO: everyone previously believed *you* to be great and hallowed,
But now—slaves, simpletons, nobodies![60]
Now, as if you were insane,
They pelt you; and in the temples,
Everyone is a bird-catcher of you,
Setting up nooses, traps, sticks,
Snares, "clouds," nets, cages;
And when they take you, they sell you in flocks;
And those who buy you feel you up!   530
And they don't stop, if they feel like doing it,
At cooking and serving you up.

---

58. A notoriously corrupt general, according to the scholia.

59. Lampon was a prominent authority on oracles and religious ritual; the word for "goose," *chēna*, differs by only one letter from the word for Zeus, *zēna*.

60. Literally, "Maneses"—a common name for a slave.

But they grate cheese, add oil,
Silphium, and vinegar, and, whipping up
A sauce that is sweet and oily,
They then pour this, heated,
Over you—
As if you were so much carrion!

CHORUS: Far, far the harshest of accounts[61]
540   Have you brought, Oh human! How I weep
At the vice of my fathers, who,
Having such honors as these handed down from their ancestors,
Squandered them for me!
But you, in accordance with a divinity and a good, lucky coincidence,
Have come to me as a savior!
For I will live having offered up to you
My nestlings and myself!

CHORUS LEADER: But whatever it is that ought to be done, you stay and
teach: for we hold life
Not worth living, if we do not obtain our kingship in every respect!

550 **PEISTHETAIROS:** Now, my teaching is that, in the first place, there is to be a
single city of the birds,
And then, that all the air around, and this entire middle part,
Is to be surrounded with a wall made of great baked bricks, like Babylon.

EUELPIDES: Oh Cebrione and Porphyrion![62] How terrible is this city
fortification!

PEISTHETAIROS: And then, when this has been set up, demand back the
rule from Zeus!
And if he refuses, and is unwilling, and fails to submit immediately,
A Holy War proclaim against Him, and forbid the gods
From traversing your territory with erections,
As they have in the past, descending for adulteries with their Alcmenes,

---

61. This line looks like a parody of line 442 of Euripides' tragedy *Alcestis*.

62. Two of the Giants who were leaders in the war with the Olympian gods; porphyrion is also the name of a water fowl—see lines 707, 882. At line 1249, Peisthetairos tells Iris that he will send six hundred porphyriones through the air to attack Zeus if Zeus troubles him further.

And Alopes, and Semeles.[63] And if they do try to traverse, you'll clap a
    seal around

Their erections, rendering them unable to fuck the girls in the future!   560

And to humans, I urge that another bird be sent as herald, with the
    word that,

From here on, they are to sacrifice to birds, since the birds are the kings,

And to gods only afterwards. And they are to apportion in a fitting way

Birds to the gods, whichever bird is most in accord with each:

If it is to Aphrodite that one is going to sacrifice, then sacrifice barley
    grains[64] to the "*Phall*-eris" bird;

If one is going to sacrifice a sheep to Poseidon, let him consecrate wheat
    grains to a duck;

If one is going to sacrifice something to Heracles, let him sacrifice
    kneaded honey cakes to a gull;[65]

And, if one is going to sacrifice a ram to Zeus the king, let the king be the
    kinglet-wren,[66]

To whom one must, prior to Zeus Himself, slaughter an ant—equipped
    with balls!

EUELPIDES: I get a kick out of that slaughtered ant: Thunder away, Oh   570
    great Zan![67]

CHORUS: And how will humans ever believe us to be gods, and not
    jackdaws—

We who fly and have wings?

PEISTHETAIROS: You're driveling! By Zeus, Hermes at any rate,

Being a god, flies and has wings!—As do very many other gods!

---

63. Mortal women: Alcmene and Semele had intercourse with Zeus and bore, respectively,
the hero Heracles and the god Dionysus; Alope bore the hero Hippothoon to Poseidon.

64. Slang for the erect phallus. It is enough in the following lines to note the comic links
between bird and god; the additional wordplay is difficult to follow.

65. The gull was proverbially voracious, as was Heracles, in comedy. See 1583–90 and 1685–
92 and *Frogs* 62.

66. The name used for this bird is obscure and has the same root as the slang term for testi-
cles used in the next line; there seems to be here a reference to a fable in Aesop where the wren
becomes king of the birds by the test of which can fly higher: when the eagle appeared at first to
win by soaring to its maximum height, the clever wren, who had hidden in the eagle's feathers,
took off and soared even higher.

67. Euelpides uses the Doric word for "Zeus."

Victory, for instance, flies with golden wings! And also Eros, by Zeus!
And Homer says that Iris resembles "a timorous wild pigeon."[68]

EUELPIDES: But won't Zeus thunder, and send winged lightning down
on us?!

PEISTHETAIROS: And if they still, out of ignorance, believe you to
be nothing,
And the gods to be these who are on Olympus, then it will be necessary
for a united cloud of sparrows,
And seed-pluckers, to gobble up their seeds from the fields;
580 And then let Demeter measure out grain to them in their starvation!

EUELPIDES: By Zeus, She won't be willing, but you'll see her coming up
with excuses!

PEISTHETAIROS: And again: the crows shall pluck out the eyes of the
oxen, with
Which they plough the earth, and of their sheep—as proof of your power!
And then let Apollo, who is the Healer, heal them; and earn his fee!

EUELPIDES: No!—not until I've sold my own two little oxen!

PEISTHETAIROS: But: If they hold YOU to be God, you Life, you Earth, you
Kronos, you Poseidon,
Every good thing shall be theirs!

CHORUS LEADER [or **HOOPOE**][69]: Tell me one of the good things.

PEISTHETAIROS: First, the locusts will not eat up their grape-flowers,
But instead, a single regiment of owls and kestrels will bear down upon
the locusts!
590 And then, the bugs and mites will not always eat up the figs,
But instead, a single flock of thrushes will pick the figs all clean!

HOOPOE: But from what source will we make them wealthy? For this is what
especially their erotic passion is for!

PEISTHETAIROS: When they come to seek divinatory advice, these will give
to them mines of worth;

---

68. In the Homeric *Hymn to Delian Apollo* 114.

69. The major manuscripts differ on the attribution of the lines here and as indicated in what
follows.

And they will inform the seer about profitable voyages of trade,
So that no ship owner will be destroyed.

HOOPOE [or **CHORUS LEADER**]: How will none be destroyed?

PEISTHETAIROS: One of the birds will always warn the one seeking
    divinatory advice concerning the sailing:
"Now is not the time to sail, a storm is coming!"; "sail now, there'll
    be profit!"

EUELPIDES: I'm going to buy a merchant ship and become a ship owner! I'm
    not going to stay with you folks!

PEISTHETAIROS: And they will point out to them the treasures of money
    that people
Have previously buried. For these know. Everyone says: 600
"No one knows where my treasure is, unless it's a little birdy!"

EUELPIDES: I'm selling the merchant ship! I'm going to buy a shovel, and
    dig up the urns!

HOOPOE: But how will they give them health, which is in the lap of the gods?

PEISTHETAIROS: If they prosper, is this not great health? Know clearly,
    That a human whose affairs are going badly is simply not one who's in
    good health!

CHORUS LEADER: But how will they ever make it to old age? For this is in
    the hands of Olympus—
Or must they die in childhood?

PEISTHETAIROS: By Zeus, No! But three hundred additional years will
The birds add to their lifespan!

CHORUS LEADER: From where?

PEISTHETAIROS: From where? From themselves!
Don't you know that "five human generations lives the cawing crow?"[70]

EUELPIDES: Wow! These are by far mightier kings for us than Zeus! 610

PEISTHETAIROS: For is it not so, by far?

---

70. From a speech by the Nymphs, in a poem of Hesiod's of which we possess only a fragment containing this line, quoted by Plutarch (*On the Obsolescence of Oracles* 415c) to show that according to Hesiod even the Nymphs and other demigods are mortal.

First, no temple
Need we build for them, of stones,
Nor gated with golden gates,
But instead in thickets and small trees
They will dwell. And again, for the august among
The birds, the olive tree
Will be the temple! And neither to Delphi
Nor to Ammon will we go to
620   Sacrifice, but among the arbutus trees
And the wild olives we will stand, holding
Barley grains and wheat, praying to them
With outstretched hands
To give us a portion of the good things; and these things will
At once be given to us,
When we cast down a few wheat grains!

Chorus Leader: Oh you dearest one to me by far of elders, who has
changed from being most hated!
It is not possible that I should ever again voluntarily depart from
your judgment!

Chorus: Exulting at your words,
630   I threaten and I swear, that
If you, after having established with me
Words of like-minded agreement,
That are just, guileless, and pious,[71]
Go to confront the gods, united with me
In judgment, then, in not much time
The gods will no longer abuse my scepter!

Chorus Leader: But for whatever things it is necessary to do with
strength, we are arrayed in order;
And for whatever things it is necessary to deliberate upon with judgment,
all these are left up to you.

---

71. A traditional formula in treaties (cf. *Lysistrata* 168; Thucydides 4.18.3, 9).

HOOPOE: And now, by Zeus, it is no time for us to slumber any more,
Nor for Nicias-delay,[72]
But action must be as swift as possible. But first,
Come into my nest
Among my wool-bits and twigs here,
And tell us your names.

PEISTHETAIROS: But that's easy:
My name is Peisthetairos; and this fellow here
Is Euelpides of the Deme of Crioa.

HOOPOE: Well, welcome to you both!

PEISTHETAIROS: We accept your welcome.

HOOPOE: Come in here.

PEISTHETAIROS: Let's go . . . you lead us in.

HOOPOE: Come.

PEISTHETAIROS: Wait! Egad! Back water!
Look here, explain to us two, how I and this fellow will
Consort with you who are winged, when we are wingless?

HOOPOE: In a fine fashion.

PEISTHETAIROS: But look how, in the writings of Aesop,
Something is said about a fox, as to how
He once fared badly in a partnership with an eagle.[73]

HOOPOE: There's nothing to be afraid of: for there is a certain root,
Which if you chew will make you two winged.

PEISTHETAIROS: On this basis let's go in. Come, Xanthias
And Manodorus: bring the baggage.

CHORUS LEADER: Hey you! I'm calling you, I say, you!

640

650

---

72. A word coined in reference to the delay Nicias as general advocated before, and exhibited during, the Sicilian expedition.

73. An eagle violated its friendship with a fox by helping its young to feed on the fox's cubs. Later, however, the eagle also suffers, for it ignites its nest with hot meat stolen from an altar; and the eaglets perish.

HOOPOE: What are you calling about?

CHORUS LEADER: You take these with you
   To a good meal. But the sweet-voiced nightingale who sings with
     the Muses,
660   Send out and leave with us, so that we can fool around with her!

PEISTHETAIROS: By Zeus, obey their request!
   Send the little bird out from the flowering rush!

EUELPIDES: In the name of the gods, send her out here, so that
   We two also may see the nightingale!

HOOPOE: But if that is what you two wish, it ought to be done.—Procne!
   Come out and show yourself to the guests!

PEISTHETAIROS: Oh much-honored Zeus! How beautiful is the little bird!
   How soft! How white!

EUELPIDES: Then do you know how much
   I would enjoy spreading her thighs?

670 **PEISTHETAIROS:** How much gold she is wearing! Like a virgin!

EUELPIDES: I think I'd also like to kiss her!

PEISTHETAIROS: But you ill-starred fool, she has a beak like two spits!

EUELPIDES: But, by Zeus, you have to peel the shell from her head, like
     an egg,
   And then in that way kiss!

HOOPOE: Let's go!

PEISTHETAIROS: You lead us two, with good fortune.

[Peisthetairos, Euelpides, and Tereus exit into the latter's nest.]

CHORUS: Oh dear one, Oh tawny-throat!
   Oh dearest of all birds,
   Sharer in my songs,
   Nightingale who is my fellow nursling!
680   You have come! You have come!—Displayed,
   Bringing to me your sweet voice!
   You, who elicit from the beautiful voice of
   The flute the songs of spring—
   Begin the anapests!

CHORUS LEADER: Come, ye men, who by nature live a life in darkness,[74]
  like to the race of leaves—
Accomplishing little, formed out of mud, tribes shadowy and feeble
  in form,
Wingless creatures of a day, miserable mortal men resembling dreams!
Turn your mind to us immortals who exist forever:
The ethereal ones, who never grow old and who ponder deathlessly;
So that, after having heard a correct account from us of everything
  concerning matters aloft,
Knowing correctly the nature of the birds, and the coming into being of
  the gods, and of the rivers, and of Erebus[75] and Void,
You can tell Prodicus,[76] from me, to go hoot!
First, there was Void and Night and dark Erebus, and broad Tartarus,[77]
But there was not Earth or Air or Heaven. In the limitless bosoms
  of Erebus,
Night the dark-winged bore, at the very first, a wind-egg,
From which, as the seasons revolved, longing Eros,
His back glistening with golden wings, grew—like to windy vortices!
And he, mingling with winged, dark Void upon broad Tartarus
Hatched our race, and first drew it up into the light.
There was no prior race of immortals, before Eros mixed together
  all things.
But, other things being mixed with others, there came into existence
  Heaven, and Ocean,
And Earth, and the undying race of all the blessed gods. So, WE are
By far the oldest of all the blessed ones; and that we are of Eros,
Is evident from many things. For we fly, and we spend time with lovers.
And in the case of many beautiful boys, who have sworn against it
  throughout the bloom of their youth,

690

700

---

74. Scholia suggest an alternative reading: "an ephemeral life."

75. The personified underworld, born from Void [*Chaos*]—which was the primeval emptiness that at first "came into being" according to Hesiod (*Theogony* 116ff).

76. A preeminent sophist, contemporary with Socrates (see *Clouds* 361); he taught that gods were personifications of things beneficial to humans (Cicero, *On the Nature of the Gods* 1.118).

77. The personified region far beneath the Underworld; "broad Tartarus" is a Hesiodic formula: *Theogony* 868.

Male lovers have through our force spread their thighs—
One giving the gift of a quail, another a porphyrion, another a goose,
  another a Persian bird.
And all the greatest things come to mortals through us birds!
In the first place, we signal the seasons—spring, winter, and fall.
710 It's time to sow, when the whooping crane moves to Libya;[78]
And it announces, to the ship's captain, to hang up his oar and to go
  to bed,
And to Orestes,[79] to weave a cloak, so that he won't be chilled when he's
  stripping others!
And after this, the kite in turn appears to signal another season—
The season to fleece the sheep; and then, the swallow:
When it is time to sell your cloak and buy something lighter.
And we are your Ammon, Delphi, Dodona, Phoebus Apollo.[80]
For you go first to a bird, no matter what you turn to,
Whether it be trade, or acquisition of livelihood, or a man's marriage.
And you regard as a bird every matter that is decisively divinatory:[81]
720 An ominous statement is for you a bird, a sneeze you call a bird,
A coincidence is a bird, a voice is a bird, a servant is a bird, an ass is
  a bird;
So, is it not manifest that we are for you Apollo's oracle?

If therefore you hold us to be gods,
You will have at your disposal Muses as prophets—
Breezes, seasons, winter, summer,
Heat that is within measure; and we won't run off
To sit solemnly above,
Beyond the clouds, as does Zeus;
Instead, remaining in your presence we will give to you—
730 To yourselves, to your children, to your children's children,
Wealth in health, life, peace,

---

78. Announcing the coming winter; Hesiod, *Works and Days* 448–50.

79. Apparently a famous highwayman.

80. The sites of the most famous oracles.

81. The word for "bird" was also used for any omen, because birds were considered especially auspicious.

Youth, laughter, choruses, festivities,
And the milk of birds! The result will be that
So wealthy will you all become!

CHORUS: Woodland Muse—
Tio tio tio tio tio tio tiotinx!—
Versatile in song, with whom I,
In the vales and on the peaks of the mountains— 740
Tio tio tiotinx!—
Perch upon the leafy headed ash—
Tio tio tio tiotinx!—
Singing through my trilling throat,
Bringing forth sacred songs for Pan,
And solemn choral dances for the mountain Mother[82]—
Totototototototix—
From where, like the honeybee,
Phrynicus[83] consumed the fruit
Of ambrosial tunes, always 750
Bearing his own sweet song—
Tio tio tio tiotinx!

CHORUS LEADER: If someone among you, Oh spectators, wishes with
    the birds
To weave the rest of life in pleasure—let him come to us!
For as many things as are around here repressed, as being shameful by
    lawful convention,
All these things are, among us birds, noble!
For if around here it is shameful by lawful convention to beat one's father,
This very thing is here noble among us—if someone, running at
    his father,
Should strike him, saying, "Raise your spur, if you want to fight!"
And, if one of you should happen to be branded on the forehead as a 760
    runaway slave,

---

82. Probably Cybele, a mother-nature goddess whose cult entered Athens from Asia Minor
during the Persian wars.
83. An early tragedian whose beautiful songs remained popular especially among the older
generation (*Wasps* 220, 268–69, 1490; *Frogs* 910, 1300).

This one shall be called a spotted francolin bird among us!
And if someone should happen to be a Phrygian no less than Spintharos,
Here he may be a Phrygian linnet-bird, of the family of Philemon![84]
And if he is a slave and a Carian like Execestides,[85]
Let him puff up grandfathers among us, and they will appear as
    fellow tribesmen!
And if the son of Peisius wishes to betray the gates to dishonored men,
Let him become a partridge, a chick of his father!—
Since among us there is nothing shameful in partridge-flight.
Such things the swans—
770   Tio tio tio tiotinx!—
With mingled cry, and in unison
Beating wings, shouted to Apollo—
Tio tio tio tiotinx!—
Sitting on the bank by the Hebrus River.[86]—
Tio tio tio tiotinx!—
And through the ethereal cloud went the cry,
And the varied tribes of wild beasts quaked in fear,
And the windless ether quelled the waves—
Totototototototototinx!—
780   And all Olympus rang!
And astonishment seized the leaders;
And the Olympian Graces,[87]
Together with the Muses, took up the tune—
Tio tio tio tiotinx!

CHORUS LEADER: Nothing is better or more pleasant than to grow wings!
If one of you spectators were winged,
When he was hungry and irritated at the tragic choruses,
He could take flight and go home for a meal;
And then, being filled, he could fly back to us here again!

---

84. The joke is unclear.

85. The Carian slave who became an Athenian citizen, mentioned at 11 and 1527.

86. Probably an echo of a famous paean by Alcaeus describing Apollo's flight from the Hyperboreans to Delphi in a swan-drawn chariot.

87. The Graces were daughters of Zeus and attendants of Aphrodite. Hesiod, *Theogeny* 907–11.

And if some Patrocleides[88] among you happened to be shitting, 790
He wouldn't ooze in his cloak, but would fly up,
And having farted and caught his second wind, fly back again!
And if one of you happens to be an adulterer,
And sees the husband of the woman in the Council seats,[89]
He could spread his wings and fly up away from you,
And then, having fucked, could fly back here again!
So: isn't it worth everything to become winged?
Dietrephes[90] at least, having only flask wings,
Was elected Tribe-commander, and then cavalry commander, and then, from nothing,
He did great things; and is now a twittering cock-horse![91] 800

[Peisthetairos and Euelpides reemerge, with wings.]

PEISTHETAIROS: So be it. —By Zeus, I have never
Seen a more ridiculous affair!

EUELPIDES: What are you laughing at?

PEISTHETAIROS: At your wings!
You know what you most resemble in those wings?
A cheap painting of a gander!

EUELPIDES: And you, a blackbird plucked like a bowl-head![92]

PEISTHETAIROS: In this way we make comparisons illustrating the line
of Aeschylus—
"Not by others' but by our own plumes."[93]

CHORUS LEADER: Come, what are we to do?

---

88. A political leader known for his flatulence, according to the scholia.

89. A block of seats in the front was reserved for members of the Council (cf. *Peace* 887, 906).

90. According to the scholia, Dietriphes became rich selling wine flasks, the wicker handles of which were called "wings"; he is mentioned in Thucydides (7.29–30, 8.64) as a commander and an oligarch.

91. The "cock-horse" was a mythic winged creature, used to characterize pompous leaders also at *Peace* 1177.

92. Peisthetairos is evidently bald; in the *Clouds* and *Peace*, Aristophanes makes fun of his own baldness.

93. A famous line from Aeschylus's lost tragedy *Myrmidons* which became proverbial as an expression meaning "the eagle shot by an arrow of eagle feathers," apparently like the English "hoisted by his own petard."

PEISTHETAIROS: First, for the city
810   Establish some great and glorious name; then,
        After this, sacrifice to the gods.

EUELPIDES: These things meet also with my approval.

PEISTHETAIROS: Look here, what will be our name for the city?
        Do you wish one that is great, and shall we not call it by
        The Lacedaimonian name of Sparta?

EUELPIDES: Heracles!—Me, establish *Sparta* as the name of MY city?!
        Not for my bedstead, even if I had the mattress![94]

PEISTHETAIROS: Well, what name shall we establish for it?

EUELPIDES: From the clouds here and the regions aloft,
        Something gaping.

PEISTHETAIROS: Do you want "Cloudcuckooia?"

HOOPOE: Hey! Wow!
820   You have invented a simply beautiful and great name!

EUELPIDES: Then is this Cloudcuckooia itself,
        Where there is the great wealth of Theogenes,
        And everything belonging to Aeschines?[95]

PEISTHETAIROS: And it is best that
        This be the plain of Phlegra,[96] where the gods
        Outshot in boastfulness the Earthborn [Giants].

HOOPOE: Shining is this affair of the city! So what god will be
        The guardian of the citadel? For whom shall we weave the Peplos?[97]

EUELPIDES: Why not let it be Athena, Guardian of the city?

PEISTHETAIROS: And how would a city ever become well ordered,
830   Where the god is a woman, who
        Stands fully armed, while Cleisthenes[98] holds the spindle?

---

94. The word "sparta" meant also the cords used to support the mattress of a bed.

95. Two notorious boasters about their vague or cloudy wealth; see below 1127 and *Wasps* 324, 459, 1243.

96. Where the rebellion of the Giants was crushed by the Olympians led by Zeus.

97. An embroidered robe offered at the great festival to Athena.

98. A notorious effeminate.

EUELPIDES: So who will hold the Stork Wall[99] of the city?

HOOPOE: A bird from our Persian breed,
Who is everywhere said to be the most fierce
Offspring of Ares.

EUELPIDES: O master offspring!
How the god is suited to dwell on the rocks!

PEISTHETAIROS: Come now, you go up in the air
And serve to help the builders—
Bring rubble, strip and mix clay,
Carry up the hod, fall off the ladder,   840
Set up guards, keep the fire always banked,
Make the rounds bearing the alarm bell, and sleep there.
And send a herald up to the gods,
And another herald down to the humans,
And from there back to me.

EUELPIDES: And you, staying here,
Can go hang!

PEISTHETAIROS: Good fellow, go where I send you!
For nothing of what I say will be accomplished without you!
[Exit Euelpides.]
And I, so that I may sacrifice to the new gods,
Shall summon the priest to conduct the sacrifices.
Boy! Boy! Take the basket and the basin.   850

CHORUS: I row with you,[100] I agree with you,
I join in approving
The approach to the gods with great and solemn songs,
And moreover at the same time the sacrifice of some lamb, to curry favor.
Go! Go! Shout the Pythian cry to the god!
And let Chaeris[101] accompany the song!

---

99. The "Pelargicon," the ancient wall around the acropolis in Athens.

100. According to the scholia, these lines are modeled on a chorus in Sophocles' lost *Peleus*.

101. A notoriously bad flute player, who used to show up and play uninvited (see *Acharnians* 16, 866; *Peace* 951).

PEISTHETAIROS: You! Cease that puffing! —Heracles! What is this?

860   By Zeus, I've seen many awful things, but this![102]

I've never yet seen a mouth-band-wearing[103] crow!

[Enter a priest, with a sacrificed goat.]

PEISTHETAIROS: Priest, it's your job: sacrifice to the new gods!

PRIEST: I will do these things. But where is the one who has the basket?
Let us pray; to Hestia[104]—of the birds, and to the Kite who keeps
    the Hearth,
And to all the Olympian Birds and all the Olympian Birdesses . . .

870   **PEISTHETAIROS:** Hail Sounium Hawk, Sea-stork Lord![105]

PRIEST: And to the Pythian and the Delian Swan, and to the
    Quail-mother Leto, and to Artemis the Goldfinch . . .

PEISTHETAIROS: No longer Colainis,[106] but Goldfinch!

PRIEST: And to Sabazius[107] the Finch, and to the Great Ostrich
    Mother of gods and of humans . . .

PEISTHETAIROS: Mistress Cybele, the ostrich mother of Cleocritus![108]

PRIEST: Grant health and salvation to these Cloudcuckooians—and also to
    the Chians . . .

880   **PEISTHETAIROS:** It delights me to have the Chians always tacked on![109]

PRIEST: And to the birds who are heroes and children of heroes—to the
    Porphyrion and the White Pelican and the Grey Pelican and the Red
    Hawk and the Grouse and the Peacock and the Sedge Warbler and the

---

102. The line-numbering here and in what immediately follows varies in the most authoritative editions.

103. A leather muzzle used by flute players to modulate the flow of breathing.

104. The goddess of the hearth, center of household worship and also of the civic worship at the communal hearth.

105. Sounium is the cape south of Athens where stands a famous temple to Poseidon; the hawk is here saluted as replacing Poseidon, and in what follows various birds supplant the traditional divinities.

106. A traditional epithet for Artemis.

107. A Phrygian god, worshipped by the Greeks as Bacchus.

108. A fat fellow notorious for resembling an ostrich: *Frogs* 1437.

109. At official prayers, the Athenians always invoked blessing also for the Chians, who were the only subject-allies who had never revolted against them.

Teal and the Harrier and the Heron and the Gannet and the Black Tit
and the Titmouse and . . .

PEISTHETAIROS: Stop! Go to the crows! Stop calling! Egad!
To what sacred victim, you ill-starred fool, are you calling   890
Vultures and Sea-eagles!? Don't you see, that
One single kite would snatch and fly away with the meat?!
Get away from us, you with your garlands!
For I by myself alone shall perform this sacrifice!

[Priest exits, leaving the goat.]

CHORUS: Once again, then, for you
Must I raise a second pious and reverent song
For the ablution, and invoke
The Blessed Ones—or rather some one alone,
If you have even enough meat offering for that!   900
For the offerings here are nothing but
A [goat's] beard and horns!

PEISTHETAIROS: As we sacrifice we shall pray to the winged gods.

POET [entering]: Cloudcuckooia the Happy!
Salute Her, Oh Muse, in singing hymns![110]

PEISTHETAIROS: Where did this come from?! Tell me, WHO are you?

POET: I, giving forth song of "honey-tongued" lyrics,
Am a "nimble servant" of the Muses,
As Homer says.[111]   910

PEISTHETAIROS: A slave, but you wear your hair that long?![112]

POET: No! Rather, WE are all the EDUCATORS—
And *thus* "nimble servants of the Muses,"
As Homer says.

PEISTHETAIROS: Surely that is why you are wearing such a "nimble," cheap,
little cloak!
Look, poet, why have you come here—for your ruin?

---

110. The line-numbering here and in what immediately follows varies in the most authoritative editions.

111. *Iliad* 1.249 has the phrase "honey tongued" and 1.321 "nimble servant."

112. Only free men wore their hair long.

POET: Because I have made for your Cloudcuckooia
Many beautiful dithyrambs,
And songs for maiden choruses, and also in the manner of Simonides![113]

920 **PEISTHETAIROS**: When did you write this poetry? Starting when?

POET: From of old! From of old do I celebrate this city!

PEISTHETAIROS: Didn't I just make the tenth-day sacrifice,
And just now give the name, as to a baby?

POET: But the word of the Muses is fleet,
Like the sparkle of horses!
But you, "founding father of Aetna,
Synonymous with the very divine temples,"[114]
Give to me whatever
With a nod of your head you will,
930 Giving of thine to me!

PEISTHETAIROS: (This fellow is going to give us troubles,
If we don't escape this fellow's clutches by giving him something!)
You there, who have a leather jacket over an under-cloak!
Take it off and give it to this wise poet! . . .
Here, you can have the leather jacket;
You seem altogether chilly to me.

POET: This with not unwilling affection
The Muse accepts as her gift.
Now you may learn with your mind a little word of Pindar's.

940 **PEISTHETAIROS**: (This fellow is not going to depart from us!)

POET: "For among the Scythian nomads,
Wanders, away from the hosts, he
Who of a woven cloak is not possessed;

---

113. A poet famous for his love of money.

114. According to the scholia, this is a quotation from a (lost) poem of Pindar (fragment 105) in honor of the Syracusan tyrant Hiero, who had refounded Catana in Sicily under the name "Aetna."

Inglorious he goes in a leather jacket without underwear!"[115]
Cogitate upon what I am saying.

PEISTHETAIROS: (I cogitate that he wants to take the underwear!)
Okay you, Strip! For one must help the poet!
—Now take this and go!

POET: I depart;
And to the city, after I depart, I shall make the following poetry:
"Celebrate, Oh golden-throned one,[116]   950
The shivering and icy place!
To the snow-struck plain of numerous paths
I came: La-la-la!"

PEISTHETAIROS: By Zeus! You have surely escaped these
Shivers by taking that underwear! . . .
By Zeus, I never expected this evil—
That so quickly this fellow would learn about the city!
You! Go around once again taking the basin for ablutions!
Let auspicious speech be observed!

ORACLE-COLLECTOR: *Do not start the sacrifice of the goat!*

PEISTHETAIROS: And who are YOU?   960

ORACLE-COLLECTOR: Who? A collector of oracles!

PEISTHETAIROS: Go hang!

ORACLE-COLLECTOR: Oh you daimonic one! Do not treat vulgarly the
divine things!
For there is an oracle of Bacis[117] that speaks plainly
About the Cloudcuckooians!

PEISTHETAIROS: So then how come you did not report this oracle before I
Founded this city?

---

115. Another comically altered quotation from the proceeding poem of Pindar, with which the poet asked for a chariot, to go with mules that the tyrant had already given as a gift.

116. Pindar speaks of the "golden-throned Muse": *Pythian Odes* 4.464; *Nemian Odes* 1.57.

117. An ancient Boeotian prophet, whose prophecies were compiled in books and enjoyed wide respect during the Peloponnesian War. Cf. *Knights* 123–24, 1003–4; *Peace* 1070.

ORACLE-COLLECTOR: The divine within prevented me.

PEISTHETAIROS: Well, there's nothing like hearing the verses!

ORACLE-COLLECTOR: "But when wolves and hoary crows will dwell in the same spot betwixt Corinth and Sicyon . . ."

PEISTHETAIROS: What in the world concerning Corinth pertains to ME?!

970 **ORACLE-COLLECTOR:** Bacis utters this as a riddle in regard to the air!
"First, to Pandora[118] sacrifice a white-haired lamb;
And he who shall come as the first prophetic expounder of my words,
To him give a clean cloak and new sandals . . ."

PEISTHETAIROS: *Sandals* are in there?

ORACLE-COLLECTOR: Here, take the book!
"And give also a cup, and fill his hands with the entrails! . . ."

PEISTHETAIROS: And giving the *entrails* is in there?

ORACLE-COLLECTOR: Here, take the book!
"And, if, Oh divinely inspired youth, thou shalt do as I command,
Thou shalt become an eagle in the clouds! But, if thou givest not,
Thou shalt become neither dove nor eagle nor oak-woodpecker! . . ."

980 **PEISTHETAIROS:** These things too are in there?

ORACLE-COLLECTOR: Here, take the book!

PEISTHETAIROS: Well, the oracle is not at all the same as this one,
Which I took down as dictation from Apollo!—
"Now if ever an uninvited boasting human should arrive,
Troubling the sacrifices and desiring the entrails,
Then indeed one must beat him in the middle of his ribs . . ."
[Striking the oracle-collector]

ORACLE-COLLECTOR: I think you are talking nonsense!

PEISTHETAIROS: Here, take the book!
"And spare nothing, not even if he be an eagle in the clouds,
Or Lampon, or even the great Diopeithes!"[119]

---

118. An earth-goddess, whose name means "Giver of all gifts."
119. Well-known soothsayers: for Lampon, see 521 and *Clouds* 332; for Diopeithes (a prosecutor of atheists), *Knights* 1085 and *Wasps* 580.

ORACLE-COLLECTOR: These things are in there?!

PEISTHETAIROS: Here, take the book!
Won't you exit? —to the crows!   990

ORACLE-COLLECTOR: Woe is me! I *am* a coward!

PEISTHETAIROS: Will you not run off, to deliver oracles elsewhere!?

METON[120]: I come among you . . .

PEISTHETAIROS: YET ANOTHER foul fellow here!
So what are YOU doing? What's your form of project?
What's the conceit, what's afoot?

METON: I wish to measure the air geometrically
For you, and measure it out in proportion to the earth.

PEISTHETAIROS: In the name of the gods!
Who ARE you among men?

METON: Who am I?
I'm *Meton*! Whom Hellas and Colonus know![121]

PEISTHETAIROS: Tell me,
What are these things of yours?

METON: Air-measurers.
For air is in its form as a whole   1000
Very much like an oven.[122] So I apply
The measuring ruler, and from above I insert this bent
Compass[123]—you do understand?

PEISTHETAIROS: I do NOT understand!

METON: I shall measure by applying the straight measuring stick, so that
The circle will become for you squared, and in the middle

---

120. A famous scientist, astronomer, and mathematician; his proposed reform of the calendar may be referred to by the chorus of Clouds in *Clouds* 615.

121. Meton had recently erected a water clock in a part of Athens named Colonus.

122. The same analogy is ascribed to Socrates and his followers by Strepsiades in *Clouds* 96, except that Strepsiades supposes that the doctrine is that the air is literally a stove.

123. The "bent compass" appears in *Clouds* 178 as the instrument which Socrates is reported by his student to have been pretending to use to lay out a geometric problem while actually using it to snare and filch a cloak to pay for supper.

Will be the agora, with roads leading straight into
The middle of it—even as from a star,
Itself being circular, in every direction
Shine forth straight rays.

PEISTHETAIROS: This human is a Thales![124] —Meton!

1010   **METON:** What is it?

PEISTHETAIROS: You know how much I love you;
 So, be persuaded by me, and slip away down the road.

METON: What's so terrible a danger?

PEISTHETAIROS: As in Sparta,
 Certain people are driven out as strangers;[125]
 There are many beatings throughout the city.

METON: So you have civil strife?

PEISTHETAIROS: By Zeus, no indeed!

METON: Well then what?

PEISTHETAIROS: It is agreed by all, united in spirit, to crush all boasters.

METON: Then I should be on my way!

PEISTHETAIROS: By Zeus, I don't know whether
 You'll be quick enough! For they have come very near!

METON: Alas! I am ill starred!

PEISTHETAIROS: Did I not long ago warn you?

1020   Won't you go away and measure yourself?!

INSPECTOR: Where are the consuls?

PEISTHETAIROS: Who's THIS Sardanapalus?[126]

INSPECTOR: I come hither as Inspector, having been chosen by the lot,
 To the Cloudcuckooians.

PEISTHETAIROS: Inspector?!
 Who sent you here?

---

124. Thales is renowned as the first recorded philosopher. In *Clouds* 180 Strepsiades, having
heard of Socrates' feat with the bent compass, asks, "So why do we wonder at Thales?"
125. Sparta kept aliens out to prevent corruption of the citizenry.
126. The proverbially luxurious last king of Assyria.

INSPECTOR: A paltry bill of Teleas.[127]

PEISTHETAIROS: What?! Look, do you want to get paid,
And go away without having trouble?

INSPECTOR: Yes, by the gods! I need to be busy in the Assembly at
home, anyway.
For I have to do business for Pharnaces.[128]

PEISTHETAIROS: Take it and leave: here's the payoff [striking him]!

INSPECTOR: What's this?!   1030

PEISTHETAIROS: It's an Assembly about that Pharnaces!

INSPECTOR: I call to witness that I, an Inspector, am being beaten!

PEISTHETAIROS: Will you not get out? Will you not take away your twin
voting urns?[129]
[Inspector exits.]
—Isn't this terrible? They're sending inspectors
To the city, before the gods have had their sacrifices!

SELLER OF DECREES: *"and if the Cloudcuckooians do injustice to an
Athenian . . ."*

PEISTHETAIROS: Now what evil is THIS—this scroll?!

SELLER OF DECREES: A seller of decrees am I, and new laws
I come hither to sell to you!

PEISTHETAIROS: With regard to WHAT?!

SELLER OF DECREES: *"Cloudcuckooia is to employ the same*   1040
measurements and
Weights and decrees as the Olophyxians."[130]

PEISTHETAIROS: And you will soon have to use the same as the Ototyxians!

SELLER OF DECREES: Look fellow, what is your problem?

---

127. See note 25.

128. A Persian satrap or proconsul (the implication is of treasonous dealings with the Persians, inveterate enemies of the Greeks).

129. The Athenian inspector has brought the equipment for democratic politics.

130. The city Olophyxus has a name that sounds like the Greek word for "lament," *ototozein*, upon which the pun is made in the following line.

PEISTHETAIROS: Will you not take away your laws?!
   Bitter are the laws I shall show you today!

[Inspector re-enters.]

INSPECTOR: I summon Peisthetairos
   On a charge of hubris,
   To appear in the month of Munychion![131]

PEISTHETAIROS: Are you for real? Are you *still* here!?

1050 **SELLER OF DECREES:** *"If someone should drive out the officials and not receive them*
   In accordance with the treaty . . ."

PEISTHETAIROS: Egad, am I ill starred! Are YOU still here too?

INSPECTOR: I'll destroy you and I'll indict you for a penalty of ten thousand drachmas!

PEISTHETAIROS: And I'll smash your twin voting urns!

[Inspector exits, on the run.]

SELLER OF DECREES: Do you remember those evenings when you used to crap on the monument?!

PEISTHETAIROS: Egad! Someone seize him! [Seller of Decrees flees.] So, you aren't staying?
   Let's get away from here as quickly as possible,
   And go inside in order to sacrifice the goat to the gods.

[Exit Peisthetairos and slaves with goat.]

CHORUS: Now it is to Me, the All-seeing
   And All-ruling, that all mortals
1060   Will sacrifice with votive prayers.
   For I watch over the entire earth,
   And I preserve the blooming crops
   By killing the breed of many tribes
   Of wild beasts, who with omnivorous jaws
   Devour everything on earth that grows from the pod
   And the fruit on the branches on which they sit;

---

131. Roughly, April, when lawsuits involving non-Athenians were heard.

And I kill those who the fragrant fruits
Destroy with most hateful pollutions—
Snakes and biting insects, all
Perish in deaths beneath my wing! 1070

CHORUS LEADER: On this very day it was announced,
That if any one of you slays Diagoras the Melian,[132]
He will receive as reward a talent; and if someone slays one of
The dead tyrants,[133] he will receive a talent![134]
Now, it is our wish that here also we proclaim the very same things.
If any one of you slays Philocrates the Sparrovian,[135]
Let him take a talent, and if he captures him living, four!
For he strings up finches and sells them for seven obols;
And then, having inflated the thrushes, he displays them and does 1080
    outrage upon them;
He sticks feathers up the noses of the blackbirds;
He similarly holds captive pigeons that he has taken,
Whom he compels to serve as decoys bound in a net!
These things we wish to announce; and if someone among you
Is raising birds that he keeps in the courtyard, we charge him to let
    them go!
And if you do not obey, you will be captured by the birds
And in turn *you* will be bound as decoys by *us*!

CHORUS: Happy race of winged
Birds, who in winter
Do not clothe themselves in wool! 1090
Nor again in the stifling heat does
The far-flashing ray heat us:
But I dwell in the bosoms of
Flowery, leafy meadows
When the divine sharp song of the grasshopper,

---

132. See 186.
133. The last tyrant of Athens was expelled in 510 B.C., but the fear of tyrants was constantly whipped up by demagogues.
134. A substantial measure of money.
135. See 14.

Crazed by the sun, shouts out in the noonday heat!
And I winter in hollow caves
Playing with mountain Nymphs!
And in spring we feed on virgin
1100 White young myrtle and the garden herbs of the Graces![136]

To the judges we wish to say something about the victory:
How many good things we will give to all of them, if they judge for us,
So that they will get greater gifts by far than from those of Alexander.[137]
For in the first place, what every judge especially aims for—
You will never lack Laureian owls;[138]
But they'll dwell with you, and in your purses
Build nests, where they will hatch little coins!
And then in addition, you will dwell as if in temples:
1110 For we will roof your homes with gables that look like eagles!
And if you obtain a little office and wish to engage in a bit of corruption,
We'll put a sharp little hawk in your hands!
And if you are dining somewhere, we'll send you some bird gizzards!
BUT: if you do NOT judge us first, then build bronze moon-shaped shields to carry
As if you were statues![139] For whoever of you doesn't have a "moon,"
Then, when you are wearing a white dress cloak especially, you will
Pay the just punishment through us, being crapped on by all the birds!

PEISTHETAIROS: The divine omens are all fine for us, Oh birds!
But no messenger has come from the wall,
1120 From whom we might learn about affairs there.
But here comes running one with Alphian panting![140]

FIRST MESSENGER: Where, where is he? Where, where, where is he?
Where, where, where is he? Oh where,
Where, is Peisthetairos the ruler?

---

136. The line-numbering here and in what immediately follows varies in the most authoritative editions.

137. A name of Paris, who was offered gifts by the goddesses among whom he was asked to judge a beauty contest.

138. The coins of Athens, from silver mined at Laureium and stamped with the figure of an owl, the bird sacred to Athena.

139. The scholia says that little cups were put over statues to protect them from bird droppings.

140. I.e., like someone running in the Olympics. (The Alpheus river flows to Olympia.)

PEISTHETAIROS: Here!

FIRST MESSENGER: Your wall has been built!

PEISTHETAIROS: You speak well!

FIRST MESSENGER: A most beautiful and most magnificent work!
Such in width that Proxenides of the loud-mouth district
And Theogenes[141] could with two chariots
Drawn by horses as big as the Trojan,
Pass one another!

PEISTHETAIROS: Heracles!

FIRST MESSENGER: And the height, since I measured it myself,   1130
Is one hundred spans![142]

PEISTHETAIROS: Oh Poseidon, how great!
Who built it so big?

FIRST MESSENGER: Birds, no one else: not an Egyptian
Bricklayer, not a stonemason, not a carpenter was present;
But with their own hands, so that it amazed me.
For from Libya there came about thirty thousand
Cranes, having swallowed foundation stones.[143]
These the crakes fashioned with their beaks.
Ten thousand other storks carried the bricks up;
And water the lapwings and other water birds   1140
Carried from below up into the air.

PEISTHETAIROS: Who carried the mortar up to them?

FIRST MESSENGER: Herons, in hods.

PEISTHETAIROS: How did they pour the mortar in?

FIRST MESSENGER: This, my good fellow, was devised in the wisest fashion!
The geese, digging down as if with shovels,
Got it into the hods for them with their feet!

PEISTHETAIROS: What, indeed, would feet not accomplish!?[144]

---

141. See 822.
142. A span was the length of the outstretched arms, or about six feet.
143. Cranes were believed to swallow stones for ballast when flying; see also 1429.
144. The proverb was, "What indeed would hands not accomplish?"

FIRST MESSENGER: And, by Zeus, the ducks carried
The bricks in girdles around the waist!
1150 And the swallows flew up carrying the trowel
Behind, even as a child carries the mud against his stomach!

PEISTHETAIROS: Why indeed would anyone pay hired workers still?
Come, look: what about this: who fashioned the wooden beams for
The wall?

FIRST MESSENGER: Birds were the carpenters:
Most wise woodpeckers, who with their beaks
Pecked the gates. And there was a noise
While they were hewing as in a shipyard.
Now everything is gated with gates,
And fastened and guarded in a circle,
1160 The rounds are being made, the alarm bell carried, everywhere
Guards are established and watch-fires
In towers. But I'm running off
To wash up. You yourself do the other things now.

CHORUS LEADER: Look here, what are you doing? Are you astounded that
The wall has thus been built so swiftly?

PEISTHETAIROS: I am, by the gods! And I deserve to be!
For it truly appears to me to be equivalent to lies!
But here is a guard as messenger from the ones there
Running toward us looking like a war-dancer!

1170 **SECOND MESSENGER**: Yi! Yi! Yi! Yi! Yi! Yi!

PEISTHETAIROS What's the matter?

SECOND MESSENGER: We have suffered the most terrible things!
For one of the gods from Zeus has just
Flown through the gates into the air,
Escaping the notice of the jackdaw day-sentinels!

PEISTHETAIROS: Oh what a terrible deed, and what a scoundrel to have
done it!
Which of the gods was it?

SECOND MESSENGER: We don't know; but that it had wings,
This we know.

PEISTHETAIROS: Should you not have sent the city guards after him
In hot pursuit?

SECOND MESSENGER: But we did send
Thirty thousand falcons as mounted archers,
And every one went with talons curved,   1180
Hawk, buzzard, vulture, owl, eagle!
With the rush and the wings and the whirring
The ether vibrates as the god is sought!
And the god's not far away, but already somewhere around here,
Presumably.

PEISTHETAIROS: Then we should take up slings
And bows! Every servant run hither!
Take up the bow! Strike! Someone give me a sling!

CHORUS: War is raised! An unspeakable war
Between me and the gods!   1190
But guard the entire
Cloud-wrapped air,
That Erebus bore,
Lest some god
Escape your notice going by here!
Everyone gather in a circle looking out,
Because nearby is audible the sound
Of the winged whir of some divinity aloft!

PEISTHETAIROS: Here, you! Where, where, where are you flying to?
Stay calm,
Hold, unflinching! Stand here! Hold back from running!   1200
. . . Who are you? From where? You must say where in the world
you're from!

IRIS[145]: *I* am from the Olympian Gods!

PEISTHETAIROS: Your name: what is it? Sail or head?[146]

---

145. The messenger-goddess Rainbow, daughter of Wonder and Electra. Winged, she dressed in thin silk that in sunlight had all the colors seen in the rainbow.

146. The question is apparently prompted by her appearance onstage—her dress and wings look like sails, and her headdress is equally striking.

IRIS: Iris the swift!

PEISTHETAIROS: The Paralus or the Salaminia?[147]

IRIS: What's that?!

PEISTHETAIROS: Why doesn't some three-balled buzzard fly up and
    grab her?

IRIS: Seize ME?!—
    What in the world is this evil?

PEISTHETAIROS: You'll suffer in a big way!

IRIS: This is a very strange business!

PEISTHETAIROS: Through which gates
    Did you get in through the wall, you most vile one?

1210 **IRIS**: By Zeus, *I* do not know which gates!

PEISTHETAIROS: You hear how ironic she's being?
    Did you go after the jackdaw sentinels?—Aren't you going to say?
    Do you have a pass from the storks?

IRIS: What is this evil?!

PEISTHETAIROS: So you didn't get one!?

IRIS: Are you sane?

PEISTHETAIROS: Nor did any bird official stick on you a pass-badge?

IRIS: By Zeus, fellow, no one stuck anything on ME!

PEISTHETAIROS: Aha! So then you flew silently
    Through a foreign city and the void?

IRIS: For in what other way *should* the GODS fly?!

1220 **PEISTHETAIROS**: By Zeus, I don't know; but not in THIS way!
    You are now committing injustice. SO: do you know this, that
    It would be most just for you, of all Irises, being caught,
    To die—if you got what you deserve?

IRIS: But I'm deathless!

PEISTHETAIROS: But all the same, you are to die.

---

147. The two swiftest Athenian ships, sent out on special missions.

For we'll be undergoing terrible things, in my opinion,
If we rule over the others, but if you gods
Are unrestrained, and still do not know that
You must pay heed in your turn to the stronger!
But tell me, where are you navigating to with those wings?

IRIS: I? I fly to human beings from the Father, 1230
Announcing that they are to sacrifice to the Olympian gods
With sheep-slaughter on sacrificial hearths
Filling the street with savor.

PEISTHETAIROS: What are you saying? —To WHICH gods?

IRIS: WHICH? . . . US! The gods in heaven!

PEISTHETAIROS: YOU are gods?!

IRIS: For who ELSE is a god?

PEISTHETAIROS: The birds are now gods for humans,
And sacrifice is to be made to them; but, by Zeus! NOT to Zeus!

IRIS: You fool! You fool!—do not stir up the awful thoughts of gods,
Lest Justice wreak destruction upon your entire race
With the spade of Zeus, 1240
And by fire, your body, and the enfolding walls of your house,
Incinerate with Licymnian bolts![148]

PEISTHETAIROS: Listen, you! Cease these bombastic sputterings!
(And you there: stand fast without trembling!)—Now, look here:
Do you think I'm a Lydian, or a Phrygian,[149] whom you are going to
    spook by talking this way?
Don't you know that if Zeus gives me too much grief,
His roof and halls of Amphion[150]
I shall incinerate, using fire-bearing eagles?!
And I shall send into heaven against him porphyrion birds
Clad in leopard skins, 1250

---

148. The *Licymnius* is a lost tragedy of Euripides; the phraseology here is taken from tragedy.
149. Civilized non-Greek or "barbarian" peoples in the Persian empire; the phrase is from Euripides' *Alcestis* 675.
150. Spoofing a line from the lost *Niobe* of Aeschylus.

More than six hundred in number! —And indeed there was an occasion
When a single Porphyrion gave him trouble![151]
And you: if you give me grief in some way, I'll spread
The thighs of His chief serving girl, and screw
This Iris here, so that you'll be astonished
How, though I am an old man, I can show an erection as big as three
    ships' prows!

IRIS: May you be split, fellow, for these utterances!

PEISTHETAIROS: Will you not scat?! Quickly! . . . Shoo! Shoo!

IRIS: MY FATHER will put a stop to your hybris!

1260 **PEISTHETAIROS**: Alas! Alas! —Won't you please fly somewhere else
And "incinerate"[152] one of the younger fellows?

[Exit Iris.]

CHORUS: We have shut out the Zeus-born gods
From ever again passing through my city,
Nor ever again shall there be sent through here, from mortals on
    the plain,
Some smoke dedicated to the gods!

PEISTHETAIROS: It is frightening, if the herald who
Went to the mortals
1270 Will never again return home.

HERALD: Oh Peisthetairos! Oh blessed one! Oh wisest one!
Oh most glorious one! Oh wisest one! Oh most subtle one!
Oh thrice blessed! Oh (—give the cue!)[153]

PEISTHETAIROS: What are you saying?

HERALD: With this golden crown, on account of your wisdom,
All the peoples crown and honor you!

PEISTHETAIROS: I accept. But why do the peoples honor thus me?

---

151. Porphyrion was a leader of the Giants who warred with the Olympians led by Zeus.
See 553.

152. With an obscene double entendre.

153. The actor playing the Herald here comically breaks the dramatic illusion.

HERALD: Oh you who founded the most glorious ethereal city,
 Don't you know how much honor you have from humans,
 How many passionate lovers you have of this land!
 For before you founded this city,   1280
 All humans had become, at that time, crazed with Spartan ways:
 They wore long hair, they starved themselves, they lived in filth,
  they Socratized,
 They carried Spartan message-scrolls around; but now, revolutionizing,
 They learn to be birds, and do everything for the sake of pleasure—
 In which they imitate the birds!
 In the first place, together they all from bed straightway
 Fly at dawn, as we do, up to the law/pasture;[154]
 And then together they brood upon archival books;
 And then graze upon decrees.
 They have become so manifestly bird-crazed that   1290
 Many have been given birds' names.
 "Partridge" one lame merchant is named,
 And Menippus[155] is called "Swallow,"
 Opuntius[156] "One-eyed Raven,"
 Philocles[157] "Crested Lark," Theogenes[158] "Sheldrake,"
 Lycurgus "Ibis," Chaerephon[159] "Vampire-bat,"
 Syracosius[160] "Jay." And Meidias is there
 Called "Quail"—for he is like a quail
 Flipped on its head by a quail-flipper.[161]

---

154. A play on the word *nomos*, which means both "pasture" and "law."

155. A horse-breeder and blacksmith: the word for the hollow of a horse's foot sounded like the word for "swallow."

156. An obnoxious, one-eyed informer: see 153.

157. See 281.

158. See 822.

159. The student and associate of Socrates in the *Clouds*; see also *Wasps* 1408. He is likened to a bat apparently because of his gaunt, death-like appearance.

160. An orator ridiculed for his croaking speech who, according to the scholia, got a decree passed restraining the liberty of speech of comic poets and in particular outlawing reference in plays to citizens by their real names.

161. Referring to a curious sport of the time, in which a human contestant tried to make a quail back off using his finger.

1300 And on account of love of birds all are singing a song,
In which some swallow is in the lyrics,
Or a wild duck, or some goose, or a ring-dove,
Or wings, or even some small part of a feather!
So much about things down there. But one thing I tell you:
There are coming here, from there, more than ten thousand
In need of wings and taloned characteristics.
So you have to get wings from somewhere for the arrivals!

PEISTHETAIROS: Then, by Zeus, our work can't be delayed!
But, as quickly as possible, you run in and
1310 Fill the crates and baskets with wings;
Let Manes bring the wings to me at the gate;
And I shall receive those who are coming for them.

[Manes the slave rushes off, soon returning with baskets; during the
following lines he is reviled and beaten intermittently.]

CHORUS: Soon "many-manned" is what
This city will be called by a human!

PEISTHETAIROS: If only fortune is favorable!

CHORUS: Passionate lovers of my city are pouring in!

PEISTHETAIROS [to slaves]: I command you, move faster!

CHORUS: For what, that is noble for a real man,
Does not dwell in this city?—
1320 Wisdom, Longing, the immortal Graces,
And the cheerful countenance of kindly
Tranquility![162]

PEISTHETAIROS [to slaves]: How slackly you serve!
Can't you comply more quickly?

CHORUS: Someone quickly bring the basket of wings!
You, goad them on!

PEISTHETAIROS: By beating this fellow, THUS!

CHORUS: Yes, for he's as slow as some donkey!

---

162. Wisdom, Longing, and Tranquility are personified deities.

PEISTHETAIROS: For Manes is an unmanly one.

CHORUS: And you, first   1330
  Set out the wings in order, thus:
  The musical ones together, and the prophetic, and
  The seafaring. And next look to see that, in a prudent fashion,
  You apply the wings to each man.

PEISTHETAIROS: By the kestrels! I'll not hold back anymore from you,
  When I see you being so unmanly and slow!
  [Beats Manes.]

A FATHER-BEATER: Would that I might become a high-flying eagle,
  So that I might fly up over the swell
  Of the barren, shining sea!¹⁶³

PEISTHETAIROS: It's likely that the messenger was not false in his message;   1340
  For here comes someone singing of eagles.

FATHER-BEATER: Hey!
  There is nothing sweeter than to be winged!
  I am bird-crazy, and I fly and I wish
  To dwell with you; and I desire *your* lawful conventions!

PEISTHETAIROS: Which lawful conventions?! For there are many lawful
  conventions of the birds.

FATHER-BEATER: All of 'em! But especially that it is conventionally held to
  be noble
  Among birds to choke and bite one's father!

PEISTHETAIROS: Yes, by Zeus, he is lawfully held by us to be very manly,
  Whoever as a chick has beaten his father!   1350

FATHER-BEATER: These are the reasons why I have emigrated hither,
  Desiring to strangle my father, and to have everything!

PEISTHETAIROS: But there is an ancient lawful convention among us birds,
  Inscribed on the tablets of the storks:
  "When the father stork has

---

163. The language mixes Homeric and other famous poetic echoes, and is partly borrowed, according to the scholia, from the lost *Oenomaus* of Sophocles.

Nourished all the little storklings to the point where they are
Fledged, the offspring must in turn nourish the father."

FATHER-BEATER: Then much have I gained to enjoy, by Zeus, by
    coming hither,
If my father's going to feed off me!!!

1360 **PEISTHETAIROS**: No matter: for since, fellow, you have come
Well disposed, I shall make you winged as if you were an orphan bird.[164]
And you, young man, I shall not ill advise,
But I'll give you the very advice I learned when I was a boy; for you
Must not beat your father; taking this
Wing and this spur, each in one of your hands,
Believe, in accordance with convention, that you have here this crest of
    a rooster:
Stand guard, campaign as a soldier, support yourself as a mercenary,
Let your father live; but when you are in the mood for a fight,
Fly away to affairs in Thrace, and fight there!

1370 **FATHER-BEATER**: By Dionysus, in my opinion you speak well,[165]
And I shall be persuaded by you!

PEISTHETAIROS: And then, by Zeus, you'll have intelligence!

KINESIAS[166] [singing]: I fly up toward Olympus on light wings![167]
And I fly a path of different melodies at different times—

PEISTHETAIROS: This business is in need of a weight of wings!

KINESIAS: —With fearless mind and body ascending the new path—

PEISTHETAIROS: We greet scrawny Kinesias!
Why have you circled in your circling dances with your lame foot hither?

1380 **KINESIAS** [sings]: I wish to become a bird, a clear-voiced nightingale.

---

164. In Athens, orphaned sons of citizens who died in battle were maintained in honor by the city.

165. The line-numbering here and in what immediately follows varies in the most authoritative editions.

166. A dithyrambic poet, unusually thin, involved in writing for certain characteristic sacred circle-dances of choruses in festivals.

167. Spoofing a line from the lyric poet Anacreon, according to the scholia.

PEISTHETAIROS: Stop singing, and *tell* me what you are saying!

KINESIAS: After having been made winged by you, I wish to fly aloft
    And pluck from the Clouds new
    Air-soaring and snow-beaten preludes!

PEISTHETAIROS: From the Clouds you would pluck preludes?

KINESIAS: Yes, for our art is derived from thence.[168]
    For the bright things in dithyrambs
    Are airy and misty and darkly gleaming
    And soaring on wings; but as you listen, you will soon know:

1390

PEISTHETAIROS: No! Not I!

KINESIAS: Yes, by Heracles, you!
    For you, I shall go through EVERYTHING about air:
    [Singing] Images of winged,
    Ether-treading,
    Slender-necked birds!—

PEISTHETAIROS: Whoa!

KINESIAS: —Bounding along the saltwater path,
    I would go on the streams of the winds!—

PEISTHETAIROS: By Zeus, *I* shall stop your wind! [Lunges for him.]

KINESIAS [eluding Peisthetairos]:—At times striking off on a southern path,
    At times, again, northward my body bending,
    Cutting a harborless furrow of ether!—

1400

    [Here apparently Peisthetairos gooses him.]
    [No longer singing] Very gracefully, old fellow, you act the sophist
    With these wise tricks!

PEISTHETAIROS: So you aren't grateful to become "soaring on wings?"

KINESIAS: You have done thus to the Teacher-producer of the circle dances?!
    To ME, over whom the tribes always fight?![169]

---

168. This and what follows echo *Clouds* 331–38.

169. The ten tribes of the Athenian citizenry competed in dithyrambic contests, and for the best producers.

PEISTHETAIROS: Do you wish, then, to stay with us and teach
　　For Leotriphides[170] a chorus of winged birds
　　Of the Crake-tribe?

KINESIAS:　　　　　You are ridiculing me, it's obvious!
　　But then I for my part shall *not* stop, know well,
　　Until winged I run through the air!

[Exit Kinesias.]

1410　**IMPOVERISHED "SYCOPHANT"** [singing]: Who are these birds of
　　　　varied wing,
　　Possessing nothing?—
　　You long-winged one, of varied-hue, you swallow![171]

PEISTHETAIROS: This is no paltry evil that has broken out!
　　This fellow has come hither, warbling in his turn!

SYCOPHANT: Again I address you, long-winged one, of varied-hue!

PEISTHETAIROS: (It seems to me that the song he sings refers to his cloak,
　　But it's likely he'll need more than a few swallows!)[172]

SYCOPHANT: Who's the one here who puts wings on those who arrive?

PEISTHETAIROS: Here he is; but you need to say what it is you want.

1420　**SYCOPHANT**: Wings, wings are wanted![173] Don't inquire twice!

PEISTHETAIROS: So do you intend to fly straight to Pellene?[174]

SYCOPHANT: No, by Zeus! I am an island summons-server,
　　And sycophant, . . .

PEISTHETAIROS:　　Bless you for your art!

SYCOPHANT: And pettifogger. So I need to take wings
　　In order to go around bothering cities with summonses.

---

170. Another very thin fellow, like the poet Kinesias.

171. Spoofingly adapted from the poet Alcaeus.

172. Meaning, his cloak is so threadbare that it evokes swallows to signal the return of Spring, referring to the ancient Greek proverb, "one swallow does not Spring make."

173. According to the scholia, a spoofing play on a famous line in the lost *Myrmidons* of Aeschylus: "weapons, weapons, are wanted!"

174. Where victors in chariot races received thick honorary cloaks.

PEISTHETAIROS: With wings you'll be wiser in some way at
    summons-serving?

SYCOPHANT: No, by Zeus, but the pirates won't give me grief,
    And I'll come back with the cranes,
    Having swallowed many lawsuits for ballast.

PEISTHETAIROS: So is this really the work you perform? Tell me,   1430
    Do you, a young man, play the sycophant with foreigners?

SYCOPHANT: For what am I to do? I don't know how to shovel!

PEISTHETAIROS: But there are other moderate jobs, by Zeus!
    —From which a man of your size ought to make his livelihood,
    In a way so much more just than contriving lawsuits!

SYCOPHANT: Give me wings, not advice, you divinely possessed fellow!

PEISTHETAIROS: I am now giving you wings, through speech.

SYCOPHANT: And how through speeches
    Would you make a man winged?

PEISTHETAIROS: All are through speeches
    Made aflutter.[175]

SYCOPHANT: All?

PEISTHETAIROS: Have you not heard,
    When fathers on occasion say   1440
    About their lads, in the barbershops, the following things:
    "It's terrible how Dieitrephes[176] with his talk has
    My lad flying about chariot-driving."
    And another will say of his, that it's tragedy
    About which he's flying—and that his thinking has "flown away."

SYCOPHANT: So then they are winged through speeches?

PEISTHETAIROS: So I assert.
    For by speeches the mind is raised aloft
    And the human being is elevated. And thus I

---

175. An idiom, meaning "stirred up."
176. See 798.

Wish to set you flying, with worthy speeches,
1450   That exhort to lawful work.

SYCOPHANT: But I don't wish it!

PEISTHETAIROS: But what will you do?

SYCOPHANT: I'll not disgrace my lineage!
To be a sycophant is for me an ancestral calling of my grandfather.
But give me swift and light wings—
Of a falcon, or a kestrel, so that, on foreigners
Having served summonses,
I can then get a judgment here,
And then fly back there again!

PEISTHETAIROS: I understand.
What you are saying is this—so that the foreigner may lose the
Lawsuit here, before he has even arrived!

SYCOPHANT: You have understood entirely.

PEISTHETAIROS: And then while he is sailing here, you can fly there again,
1460   To rob him of his property!

SYCOPHANT: You've got it entirely—
No different from a spinning top!

PEISTHETAIROS: I understand—
Tops, uh-huh. . . . And by Zeus, I have
Such very beautiful *Corcyraean*[177] wings for this!

SYCOPHANT: Egad! Alas! You've got a whip!

PEISTHETAIROS: This is a pair of wings,
With which I shall make you spin like a top this day!

SYCOPHANT: Alas! Alas!

PEISTHETAIROS: Will you not fly from here?
Will you not drop off into destruction, you most evil one?
You shall swiftly see bitter evil-working-twisting-of-justice!
[To slaves] Let's gather up the wings and depart!

---

177. Corcyra was famous for making double-thonged whips, and for troops armed with whips (Thucydides 4.47).

CHORUS: Many and strange and   1470
  Wonderful are the things over which we have flown, and
  Terrible are the affairs we have seen!
  For there is a tree, by nature
  Cleonymus[178]—
  Worthless, and otherwise
  Cowardly and large.
  It always in the springtime
  Grows and plays the sycophant,
  And in winter once again   1480
  Throws off shields like leaves.

  There is, again, a certain far-off land
  Near darkness itself,
  Bereft of lights,
  Where humans with heroes
  Dine, and
  Mingle until evening;
  Then no longer
  Is the encounter safe.
  For if one of the mortals encounters the hero   1490
  Orestes[179] at night,
  He would be stripped and paralyzed by him
  On the right side.

PROMETHEUS: Alas! Alas! Oh that Zeus may not see me!
  Where is Peisthetairos?

PEISTHETAIROS: Here, what's this?
  Who's the fellow wrapped up?

PROMETHEUS: Do you see any of the gods
  Behind me there?

PEISTHETAIROS: By Zeus, I do not!
  But who are YOU?   1500

PROMETHEUS: How late is it in the day?

---

178. See note 36.
179. The hero of Aeschylus's trilogy, the *Oresteia*, but also the famous robber referred to at 712.

PEISTHETAIROS: How late? A little after noon.
But WHO ARE you?

PROMETHEUS: Is it Ox-loosing time, or later in the day?

PEISTHETAIROS: Egad! You're reducing me to idiocy!

PROMETHEUS: What's Zeus doing?
Dispersing the clouds, or gathering them?

PEISTHETAIROS: Go hang high!

PROMETHEUS: Here; I'll uncover myself!

PEISTHETAIROS: PROMETHEUS, my friend!!

PROMETHEUS: SHHH! Stop! Don't shout!

PEISTHETAIROS: What is it?

PROMETHEUS: Silence! Do not call my name!
For you will be my destruction, if Zeus sees me here!
But, so that I might inform you of all the affairs above,
Take this parasol of mine and hold it up
Over, so that the gods won't see me.

1510 **PEISTHETAIROS**: Hey! Wow!
That is good thinking, and very "Promethean"![180]
Get under it quick, and then be bold to tell me.

PROMETHEUS: Now listen—

PEISTHETAIROS: Talk, I'm listening!

PROMETHEUS: Zeus is destroyed!

PEISTHETAIROS: Since when is he destroyed?

PROMETHEUS: Since when you settled in the air.
For no one of the humans still sacrifices anything
To the gods, and no savor of thigh meat
Come up to us since that time,
But we fast as at the Thesmophoria,[181]
1520   Without burnt offerings. And the barbarian gods,
Who are starving and screeching like Illyrians,

---

180. The word means "thinking ahead."
181. An Athenian women's festival in honor of Demeter, which included one day of fasting.

Declare that they will start a military campaign from above
    against Zeus,[182]
If he doesn't get the markets reopened,
So that chopped innards can be introduced again!

PEISTHETAIROS: So there are some other, barbarian gods
    Above you?!

PROMETHEUS: Aren't there barbarian ones,
    Among whom is the ancestral deity of Execestides?[183]

PEISTHETAIROS: And the name of these barbarian gods—
    What is it?

PROMETHEUS: What is it?—"Triballians."[184]

PEISTHETAIROS: I understand: isn't that where "rub yourself off!" has   1530
    come from?

PROMETHEUS: Most of all! But one thing I tell you plainly:
    Envoys will be coming here to negotiate—
    From Zeus and from the Triballians up beyond.
    You should not make peace, unless Zeus hands
    The scepter over again to these birds,
    And gives Basileia to you to have as wife.[185]

PEISTHETAIROS: Who is Basileia?

PROMETHEUS: The most beautiful girl,
    Who keeps the thunderbolt of Zeus
    And everything else together—good counsel,
    Good lawful rule, moderation, dock arsenals,   1540
    Invective, the judicial paymaster, the three-obol payments.[186]

PEISTHETAIROS: So she keeps everything for him?

---

182. The barbarian gods are being compared to the barbarians from the interior, who could attack the Greek cities on the coast of Illyria.

183. The citizen whose dubious ancestry makes him a special butt of this play; see 11 and 764.

184. The name of a fierce Thracian tribe allied with Athens; the name also connotes male sexual arousal and energetic or excessive sexual activity, to which savage barbarians were conceived as highly prone; Greek words with the root for "rub" (*tribō*) are charged with connotations of chafing the genitals to arousal.

185. "Basileia" means both "Queen" and "royal power."

186. The daily pay for a juror's service.

PROMETHEUS: So I declare.
    And if you take her from him, you'll have everything!
    That's why I came hither, to explain to you.
    For I am always well disposed in mind to humans!

PEISTHETAIROS: For it is on account of you alone among gods that we cook
    over coals!

PROMETHEUS: And I hate all the gods, as you know!

PEISTHETAIROS: By Zeus, you were indeed always by nature a hater of gods!

PROMETHEUS: A pure Timon![187] But, so that I can run away again,
1550   Hold the parasol, so that if Zeus should see me
    From above, I will look like I am following the basket bearer.[188]

PEISTHETAIROS: And take this stool here,[189] and be the stool-carrier!

CHORUS: And then near the Shadefoots[190] there is
    A certain marshy lake, where the unwashed
    Socrates leads souls;
    And there Peisander came,[191]
    Begging to see the soul which
    Departed from him early while he was still alive,
    Having a baby camel as sacrificial victim—
1560   Whose throat he cut,
    Like Odysseus did,[192] and went away,
    While behind him there came up from below
    To the blood of the camel
    The vampire bat Chaerephon.

[Enter Poseidon, Heracles, and a barbarian god, Triballian.]

---

187. Timon was an Athenian proverbial for the hatred he bore his fellow Athenians.

188. In the Panathenaic processions, maidens from the best families had the honor of carrying the baskets, each followed by a maiden of a non-citizen resident family carrying a stool, and attended by a parasol bearer.

189. The word was euphemistically used for a trivet on which a chamber pot sat.

190. A mythic people inhabiting the Atlantic coast of Africa; they had feet so large that they used them for shade.

191. A democratic, and then later an oligarchic politician often lampooned for cowardice.

192. This is all a parodic reference to Odysseus's visit to the underworld (*Odyssey* 11.35ff.; dramatized in the lost *Soul Leaders* of Aeschylus), where he summoned and inquired of the souls of the dead by pouring blood in a trench for them to drink.

POSEIDON: The city of Cloudcuckooia
  Is here visible, the destination of our embassy.
  [To Triballian] You, whatever *are* you doing? You're wearing your cloak
    on the left!?!?[193]
  Won't you change it to the right?!
  You ill-starred one! What are you by nature—a Laispodias?[194]
  Oh Democracy! Where will you ever take us,   1570
  If the gods are going to choose by vote such a one as this!
  Will you hold still?! [Trying to adjust Triballian's cloak] Go hang! You are
    really the most
  Barbarian of all gods I have ever seen!
  Look here, what are we going to do, Heracles?

HERACLES: You have heard
  From me, at any rate, that I wish to throttle the human,
  Whoever it was, that once walled out the gods!

POSEIDON: But my good fellow, we have been elected envoys for *negotiations*!

HERACLES: So throttle him twice over, in my opinion!

PEISTHETAIROS: Somebody give me the grater! Bring the silphium spice!
  Somebody bring the cheese! Stir up the coals!   1580

POSEIDON: We three gods bid greeting to the man!

PEISTHETAIROS: But I'm busy grating the silphium spice now.

HERACLES: What's this meat the flesh of?

PEISTHETAIROS: Some birds,
  Having risen up against the people's party of the birds,
  Were judged to have committed injustice.

HERACLES: So first you grate
  Silphium over them?

PEISTHETAIROS: Oh, hello there, Heracles! What's afoot?

POSEIDON: We have come as envoys
  From the gods to negotiate an end to the war.

---

193. A cardinal sin of upper class decorum: wrongly draping one's cloak.
194. A politician who apparently had an unsightly leg which he concealed by awkwardly draping his cloak.

Peisthetairos: Hey, there's no olive oil in the flask!

1590 **Heracles:** Yeah, and bird-meat ought to be well oiled!

Poseidon: For we do not gain from warring;
And you, if you were to have friendly relations with us gods,
Would have rain water in your pools
And Halcyon days you would reap always!
We come invested with full authority in all these matters.

Peisthetairos: But we never began
To make war before you did; and now we are willing—if so it is decided,
If only you are now willing to do something just—
To make a peace treaty. And the just things are the following:
1600 Zeus is to give back to us birds the scepter;
AND, if we come to an agreement
On these terms, . . . I'll invite the ambassadors to dine!

Heracles: For me these things suit, and I vote for it.

Poseidon: What, you ill-starred fool! You are a simpleton and just
a stomach!
You would deprive your own father of the tyranny?!

Peisthetairos: Is that true? Won't you gods in fact have MORE
Strength, if the birds rule below?
Because now, hidden by the clouds,
The mortals skulk and falsify their oaths;
1610 But, if you have the birds as allies,
When someone swears by the crow and by Zeus,
The crow in stealth will come by that false swearer,
And, flying upon him, will by striking pluck out his eyes!

Poseidon: By Poseidon, these things are beautifully said!

Heracles: Seems so to me too.

Peisthetairos: So what do YOU say?

Triballian: Nabaisatreu.[195]

Heracles: You see? This one too praises it.

---

195. Gibberish, but the beginning (Na) sounds like Greek for "yes" (*nai*).

PEISTHETAIROS: And now in still another way
You will hear how much good we will do you.
If one of the humans to one of the gods
Should in prayer vow a sacrificial victim, and then sophistically say,
"The gods are patient"—not giving it back out of greed, 1620
We'll undo also these things.

POSEIDON: Come, show—in what way?

PEISTHETAIROS: When this human happens to be counting his money,
Or to be sitting in his bath,
A kite will stealthily fly down and seize
The price of two sheep, which he will bring up to the god!

HERACLES: I again vote to give back the scepter to these!

POSEIDON: And the Triballian—let him now speak.

HERACLES: Triballian, is it your decision to cry out in pain? [Raising
his club.]

TRIBALLIAN: Younoclubit!

HERACLES: He declares that I speak very well.

POSEIDON: Oh well, if you both agree to these things, then so do I. 1630

HERACLES: Listen you, it has been decided to do these things concerning
the scepter!

PEISTHETAIROS: By Zeus, there is another thing I've just happened
to remember!
I give up Hera to Zeus,
But: that girl who's Queen [Basileia] is to be given to me as my wife.

POSEIDON: Your erotic passion is not for reconciliation!
Let's go back home!

PEISTHETAIROS: A lot I care!
Cook! You need to make the sauce sweet!

HERACLES: Poseidon, you-divinely possessed human! Where are you going!
Are we going to fight a war over one woman?[196]

---

196. The Trojan War was fought over one woman (Helen): the gods here lack respectful memory of the greatest Greek war.

1640   **POSEIDON**: Well what *are* we to do?

    HERACLES: What?! Come to terms!

    POSEIDON: You dumbell! Don't you know you've been cheated?
      You are hurting yourself! For if Zeus dies,
      And hands the tyranny down to these,
      You'll be impoverished! For all the wealth becomes yours—
      As much as Zeus leaves when he dies!

    PEISTHETAIROS: Ai yi-yi, how he is sophistically lying to you!
      Come aside here, so that I can explain something to you.
      Your uncle's deceiving you, wretch!
      For not a bit of your patrimony is yours,
1650   According to the laws: for you are a bastard, and not legitimate!

    HERACLES: ME?! A *bastard*? What are you saying?

    PEISTHETAIROS: By Zeus, you
      Are the child of a foreign woman![197] Or how else
      Would Athena ever be the heiress, do you suppose,
      When she is a daughter, if there were *legitimate* brothers?!

    HERACLES: Well, but what if my father gives me the money
      After he has died, as a legacy to a bastard?

    PEISTHETAIROS: The law won't allow it.
      This Poseidon here, who now excites you on, will be the first
      To wrest from you the patrimonial funds,
      Claiming that he is a legitimate brother!
1660   But I will read out to you the Solonic law:
      "To a bastard
      There is not to be
      Rights of close kinship,
      Where there are legitimate children.
      And if there should not be legitimate children,
      The money is to be shared by the nearest of kin."[198]

    HERACLES: I get no share of the patrimonial property?

---

197. The mother of Heracles was the mortal human Alcmene, wife of Amphitryon.
198. Not in meter; an actual quotation from the law (also quoted in Demosthenes 43.51).

PEISTHETAIROS: NO, by Zeus! —And tell me,
Has your father already introduced you to his *phratry*[199] brothers?

HERACLES: Not me, no. . . . And indeed, I've been wondering about that, for 1670
quite a while.

PEISTHETAIROS: Why indeed are you gaping up?—to look for a fight?
But if you are with us, I, having set you up as
Tyrant, will provide you with birds' milk!

HERACLES: In my opinion, you speak things of long-standing justice.
As regards the girl, and for my part, I let you have her!

PEISTHETAIROS: So what do YOU say?

POSEIDON: I vote the contrary!

PEISTHETAIROS: So the whole matter is up to the Triballian. What do you say?

TRIBALLIAN: Bootiful girl and great queen
Bird I give!

HERACLES: He says to hand her over!

POSEIDON: By Zeus, this fellow does NOT say to hand her over! 1680
He twitters away like the swallows!

PEISTHETAIROS: So he says give her to the swallows!

POSEIDON: You two negotiate and come to terms;
I, if you two agree, shall remain silent!

HERACLES: Everything you say is agreeable to us.
But come with us yourself into heaven,
So that you may take the queen [Basileia] and all things there.

PEISTHETAIROS: Well then, these were slaughtered just in time
For the wedding festivities!

HERACLES: You want me
To stay here and cook the meat meanwhile? You all go ahead! 1690

POSEIDON: YOU are going to cook the meat? You mean, to do a lot of
gobbling!
You're going with us, right?!

---

199. The religious guild, descended from a common ancestor, to which every legitimate Athenian male needed to be formally presented in order to gain citizenship.

HERACLES: But I would have done it so well!

PEISTHETAIROS: Someone bring me a wedding robe!

CHORUS: And there is in Phanae, near
   The water-clock,[200] a rascally
   Race that fills-its-belly-with-its-tongue[201]—
   Who reap and sow,
   And gather grapes (and figs[202])
   With their tongues.
1700   Barbarians are this race,
   Gorgiases and Phillips.[203]
   And from the belly-fillers-with-the-tongue,
   These Phillips,
   Everywhere in Attica,
   The tongue is cut away![204]

HERALD: Oh you doers of all good things, greater than can be spoken!
   Oh thrice-blessed winged race of birds,
   Welcome the tyrant to the prosperous halls!
   For he approaches, shining as no all-blazing
1710   Star has ever been approaching its golden-rayed home!
   The incandescence of the rays of the far-shining sun
   Has not been so bright as his coming,
   Possessed of a wife whose beauty is beyond utterance,
   And wielding the thunderbolt, the winged shaft of Zeus!
   An ineffable fragrance ascends to the depth of the sphere above,
   Beautiful to behold; and breezes
   Blow away the wreath of smoke from the incense!
   And here he is, himself! Let the divine
   Muse open Her sacred and auspicious mouth [to sing]:

---

200. A water clock was used to time the speeches in lawsuits; "Phanae" was a town in Chios, whose name sounds like a word that can mean "to denounce" or "to indict" (*phainein*).

201. A word invented to play on a common term of scorn for laborers—a race "that fills-its-belly-with-its-hands."

202. The word has the same root as the word "sycophant."

203. Gorgias is the famous teacher of rhetoric; Phillip was one of his Athenian students (*Wasps* 421).

204. The custom in sacrifices was to cut the tongue out of the victim.

CHORUS: Move back! Make way! Draw together! Stand aside! 1720
  Fly around
  The blessed one with his blessed fortune!
  Oh, wow! Wow!
  The bloom, the beauty!
  Oh You who have entered into a marriage most blessed for this city!

CHORUS LEADER: Great, great fortune has overtaken
  The race of birds
  Through this man! But
  Welcome with wedding songs and nuptial songs—
  Him and his Queen! 1730

CHORUS: Once with Olympian Hera
  Of the lofty thrones
  The great ruler of the gods
  Was conducted by the Fates
  On that wedding day!
  Hymen, Oh Hymenaeus!
  Hymen, Oh Hymenaeus![205]

  And Eros, flourishing on all sides,
  Golden-winged,
  Steered straight with his bridle stretched back,
  The best-man driver of the chariot at the marriage of Zeus 1740
  And the happy Hera.
  Hymen, Oh Hymenaeus!
  Hymen, Oh Hymenaeus!

PEISTHETAIROS: I am charmed by the hymns, I am charmed by the songs;
  And I delight in the words. Come now,
  Celebrate also his earth-echoing thunder,
  And fiery lightning of Zeus,
  And terrible white-hot bolt![206]

CHORUS: Oh great light of golden lightning!
  Oh immortal fire-bearing spear of Zeus!

---

205. Two names of the god of marriage.
206. The line is Homeric: *Iliad* 8.133.

1750 Oh heavily groaning, earth-echoing,
And—simultaneously—rain-bearing thunders,
With which *this* one *now* shakes the earth!
Having entirely overpowered Zeus,
He possesses also the Queen [Basileia] who sat beside Zeus![207]
Hymen, Oh Hymenaeus!

PEISTHETAIROS: Follow now the wedding party, Oh
All you tribes of flocking
Feathered ones—up to the floor of Zeus
And to the marriage bed!
Extend, Oh blessed one, your
1760 Hand, and taking my wings,
Dance with me!
And I shall take you and lightly lift you up!

CHORUS: Ala-lal-lai! raise the Paean—
Taenella! Most noble of victors![208]
Oh highest of the divinities!

---

207. According to poetic tradition, it was the goddess Justice who sat beside Zeus: Hesiod *Works and Days* 256ff.; Pindar *Olympian Odes* 8.28; Sophocles *Oedipus at Colonus* 1267, 1382; see also Demosthenes 25.11. Basileia is an invention of Aristophanes. The replacement of Justice by Basileia is both a radical theological innovation by Aristophanes, and an indication that justice has been eclipsed by royal sway in the regime of Peisthetairos.

208. "Taenella" is a word invented by the poet Archilochus (frag. 119) to imitate the sound of the twanged string at the beginning of the traditional triumphal song to Heracles with which victors in the games were saluted; hence this line ("Taenella! Most noble of victors!") became formulaic.

PEACE

DRAMATIS PERSONAE[1]

TWO SERVANTS OF TRYGAEUS
TRYGAEUS[2]
DAUGHTER OF TRYGAEUS
HERMES
WAR
BATTLE-DIN
CHORUS OF FARMERS[3] [and its LEADER]
HIEROCLES [a seer and oracle-monger]
SICKLE-MAKER
ARMS-MERCHANT
[CREST-MAKER
BREASTPLATE-SELLER
TRUMPET-MAKER
HELMET-MAKER
SPEAR-MAKER]
SON OF LAMACHUS
SON OF CLEONYMUS

[Mute Characters:
PEACE
OPORA[4]
THEORIA[5]]

---

1. Bracketed material lacks manuscript authority; it is intended only to facilitate a first reading of the play. Line numbers are borrowed from the Greek texts of the plays; they will not always be sequential in English.

2. Derived from the verb *trugaō*, which means "to harvest" or "bring in the vintage," but it also reminds of *trugōidia*, a term Aristophanes uses to refer to comedy, as at *Acharnians* 499–500. Cf. *Clouds* 296.

3. The Aldine edition has "Chorus of Athmonian farmers," thus limiting membership to men of Trygaeus's deme or township in Athens. The actual composition of the chorus appears to change, as it seems to include Greeks of many cities and occupations during the excavation of Peace (459–507) but to be limited to Athenian or Athmonian farmers later.

4. *Opōra* designates autumn, the harvest, fruit, or, metaphorically, youthful ripeness.

5. *Theōria* has a wide range of meanings. In other contexts it can refer to an embassy, to being a spectator at games or the theater, to a sight or spectacle, or to theory or contemplation. Its main meaning here is "festival" or "festivity."

SERVANT A: Grab one! Grab me a cake for the dung beetle[6] as quick as
    you can!

SERVANT B: There! Give it to him! May he be doomed to perish in the
    worst way,
    And may he never eat another cake more pleasant than this one!

SERVANT A: Give me another cake, one formed from donkey dung.

SERVANT B: Take another. But where is the one which you took for him
    just now?
    He didn't eat it, did he?

SERVANT A: By Zeus, he seized it,
    Rolled it with his two feet, and scarfed it down whole.
    Now as quickly as you can, knead lots more—solid ones!

SERVANT B [to the Audience]: You dung collectors! Join in, by the gods,
    Unless you wish to watch me suffocate!   10

SERVANT A: Gimme another one! And another! One from a boy prostitute,
    For he says he desires one well compacted.

SERVANT B: Here!
    [To the audience] I think I'm in the clear, men, of at least one charge:
    No one would say that I eat any of what I knead!

SERVANT A: Yuck! Bring me yet another, and another;
    And keep kneading more.

SERVANT B: No, by Apollo, I won't;
    For I am no longer able to keep above the rising bilge waters.

SERVANT A: Then I'll pick it up, and carry in the entire tub of bilge.

SERVANT B: Carry it to the crows,[7] by Zeus, and yourself as well!
    [To the audience] Now, if any of you knows where I might buy a nose   20
    without holes,

---

6. *Kantharos*, "dung beetle," was also the name of a familiar comic poet, to whom the original audience would have seen a reference.

7. Since crows feed voraciously on carrion, going "to the crows" was a horrible fate. The general meaning here is "go to the dogs."

Tell me!
For there is no more wretched work
Than constantly kneading food for a dung beetle.
For whatever someone shits, a pig or a dog goes at it vigorously;
But this one bears himself haughtily with high thoughts and does not
    deign to eat,
Unless I spend the whole day working to serve to him, as to a lady,
A cake rounded by kneading.
But I'll take a look—opening the door a little bit, so he doesn't see me—
30   to see whether he has quit his feeding.
[To the beetle] Go to it: don't ever cease from your eating
Until, unaware, you blow yourself up.
How this accursed creature eats! Bending down like a wrestler,
Exposing its molars! And this while rotating its head
And its two hands, rather like this,
Just like those who plait the hawsers
For the heavy merchant ships!
The beast is unclean, foul-smelling, and gluttonous.
From whichever of the divinities we owe this visitation, I do not know.
40   It sure does not seem to me to be from Aphrodite,
Nor again from the Graces![8]

SERVANT A: Then from whom?

SERVANT B: There's no way that this wonder is not from Zeus the
    Descender.[9]

SERVANT A: Then if one of the spectators—a young man
Who considers himself wise—would say, "What's going on?
What's the point of the dung beetle?" Then some Ionian man
Seated beside him would say,

---

8. The Graces were daughters of Zeus and attendants of Aphrodite. Hesiod, *Theogony* 907–11.

9. Rather than *kataibatou*, "descender with lightning bolts," some MSS. read *skataibatou*, which would yield "dungwalker" or "dungmounter" and which would suggest homosexual relations. This would have been heard, even if it was not written.

"I think it's a riddle about Cleon,[10]
Since he shamelessly devours diarrhea."
I'm going to go in and give the beetle something to drink.[11]

SERVANT B: Then I will explain the argument to the boys, 50
To the half-men, to the men,
To the highest men, and
Especially to the men who think themselves beyond men:
My master is mad in a very new way,
Not the way you are, but in a very new and different way.
Throughout the day he looks toward heaven,
Gaping like this, and reviles Zeus, saying,
"O Zeus, whatever do you wish to do?
Put down your broom; do not sweep Greece clean!"
Shh! Shh!! Be silent! 60
I think I hear his voice.

TRYGAEUS: O Zeus, whatever are you trying to do to our people?
You will gut our cities without realizing it.

SERVANT B: This is the very evil of which I was speaking;
For you are hearing the very pattern of his ravings.
Learn what he first said when his madness began.
For he said to himself right here:
"How could I ever go straight to Zeus?"
Then he made light little ladders
And on them he kept trying to scramble up to heaven, 70
Until he fell down and broke his head.
Then after this, yesterday, he vanished I know not where,
And brought back an enormous Aetna dung beetle,
And then he compelled me to groom it like a horse,

---

10. The most powerful leader in Athens after the death of Pericles. He favored vigorous prosecution of Athens' war with Sparta and was a favorite target for attack in the first five of Aristophanes' eleven surviving comedies. He died in the year preceding this play, which in Aristophanes' view helped make possible the peace achieved in this play. See 261–73 for Cleon as a pestle with which War would mash up the Greeks.

11. Presumably by urinating.

And he himself stroked it like a pony,
Saying, "My little Pegasus, my well-born winged one,
See to it that you take me up and fly straight to Zeus."[12]
But I will see what he is doing if I stoop and peep in. . . .
Oh! Woe of woes! Come here, neighbors, come here!

80 For in midair my master is rising
Up into the air on the dung beetle as if he were riding a horse!

TRYGAEUS: Calmly, calmly, easy does it, my pack-ass.
Do not take off too violently at the start,
Trusting in your strength;
Wait until you work up a sweat and loosen up
The tendons of your joints by the rush of your wings.
And do not breathe your bad breath on me, I beg you!
If you are going to do this, just stay here,
At our house.

90 **SERVANT B**: Master, lord, how demented you are!

TRYGAEUS: Quiet! Quiet!

SERVANT B: So why are you fruitlessly thrashing about in midair?

TRYGAEUS: I am flying for and over all the Greeks,
Having contrived a new and daring plan!

SERVANT B: Why are you flying? Why are you insane to no purpose?

TRYGAEUS: You must keep an auspicious silence,
Blabber no foolishness but raise a cheerful prayer.
Tell human beings to be silent,
And to wall off with new bricks

100 Their latrines and sewers,
And put their assholes under lock and key.

SERVANT B: There is no way I'll be silent, unless you tell me where you
intend to try to fly.

TRYGAEUS: Where else than to Zeus, to heaven!

---

12. In Euripides' lost *Bellerophon*, the hero rides Pegasus up to the gods to complain of their mismanagement of the world.

Servant B: With what in mind?

Trygaeus: In order to ask him what he is planning to do
Concerning the Greeks, all of them.

Servant B: And if he does not announce this to you?

Trygaeus: I will indict him for betraying Greece to the Medes.[13]

Servant B: No, by Dionysius, not while I am alive!

Trygaeus: There is no other way.   110

Servant B: Alas! Alas! Alas!
Little children, your father is leaving you all alone
And going off secretly to heaven!
So plead with your father, you ill-starred little things.

Little Child[14]: Father, father, then is the report which has reached
Our domicile a true one,
That you have abandoned me
And will go windborne[15] to the crows, keeping company with birds?
Is any of this true? Speak, father, if you love me at all.

Trygaeus: As it is possible to infer, girls, I am really grieved in your regard:
whenever you ask
Me for bread and call me "Papa,"   120
There is not even a tiny bit of silver inside, none at all.
But if I fare well and come back again, you will have
At the proper time a great treat and some knuckle sauce to go with it.

Little Child: In what way will you travel there?
For no ship will conduct you on this voyage.[16]

Trygaeus: A winged colt will convey me. I will not go by ship.

Little Child: What are you thinking, that you
Have bridled a beetle and intend to ride to the gods, daddy?

---

13. By allowing war among the Greeks to continue, Zeus makes them vulnerable to the Medes (Persians).

14. For comic effect, Aristophanes mimics tragic diction as well as tragic scenes. According to the scholia, the mimicry here is based on Euripides' lost *Aeolus*.

15. This word also means, "in vain," "without effect."

16. The scholia note that these exchanges parody Euripides' *Bellerophon*.

TRYGAEUS: In the words of Aesop, this alone has been found
130   To reach the gods on wings.[17]

LITTLE CHILD: Father, father, you have spoken an unbelievable myth,
That a foul-smelling beast made it to the gods!

TRYGAEUS: Once upon a time long ago, one got there on account
Of his hatred for the eagle, and rolled down its eggs out of revenge.

LITTLE CHILD: Then shouldn't you have bridled up winged Pegasus
So your appearance to the gods would be more tragic?

TRYGAEUS: But then, my dear, I'd need twice the provisions;
Whereas this way whatever provisions I myself gobble down,
With these I will furnish him fodder.

140   **LITTLE CHILD:** But what if he falls into the deep wet sea?
How will he be able to escape with his wings wet?

TRYGAEUS: I got an oar on purpose, which I will use,[18]
And my boat will be a Naxian-made beetle-boat.[19]

LITTLE CHILD: But what harbor will receive you as you are tossed
by storms?

TRYGAEUS: The Piraeus of course has its Beetle Harbor.

LITTLE CHILD: Be careful not to slip and fall off, and then—
As a cripple—offer up a story for Euripides
And become a tragedy.[20]

TRYGAEUS: That's for me to worry about; so, farewell!
150   [To the audience] But you, on whose behalf I undertake these labors,
Do not fart or shit for three days.
For if he smells it once he is up in midair,
He will throw me head first and head for his pasture.

---

17. This seems to refer to Aesop's fable of the eagle and the snail, but see also *Wasps* 1448.

18. By "oar" Trygaeus means the comic phallus with which male characters were outfitted.

19. The Greek word for "dung beetle" also referred to a kind of light boat (as well as to a large drinking vessel). It was also the name for one of the three harbors in the Piraeus, as the next lines indicate.

20. For Aristophanes' spoofing slander that Euripides preferred crippled heroes, see also *Acharnians* 411, 455, 1214–15; *Women at the Thesmophoria* 22–24; *Frogs* 846.

But come, Pegasus, advance and take your leave,
Setting off with your bright ears
That rattling of the curb chains on your bridle.
What are you doing? What are you doing? Which way are you inclining
Your nostrils? Toward the sewers!
Throw yourself confidently away from earth,
And then extend your swift wings   160
And head straight for Zeus's halls,
Keeping your nose pointed away from poop
And from your routine foods.
You there, human being, what are you doing? You—the one shitting
In the Piraeus near the whores,
You will destroy me! You will destroy me! Will you not bury it,
And put a lot of earth over it,
And plant thyme on top
And pour on scented oil? Because if I fall from here
And get hurt, the city of the Chians   170
Will owe five talents for my death,
All on account of your asshole.
Oh! Oh! How afraid I am, and now I am no longer joking!
Crane operator,[21] keep your mind on me,
For a bit of gas is already churning near my navel,
And if you are not careful, I'll be furnishing fodder for the beetle.
But I think I'm near the gods,
And in fact I spy Zeus's house.
Who is it that waits upon Zeus's doors? Won't you open up?!

HERMES: Whence am I assaulted by a mortal's. . . . Lord Heracles!   180
    What is this foul thing?

TRYGAEUS: A beetle-horse.

HERMES: You disgusting, audacious, shameless
    Loser,—total loser, and biggest loser!

---

21. Greek drama employed a crane that could raise or lower actors, usually gods, to ten feet or so above the stage. In calling out to the crane operator to be careful, Trygaeus speaks as a fearful actor and breaks the dramatic illusion that he is riding a flying beetle.

How did you get up here, you biggest loser of all losers?
What's your name? Won't you speak?

TRYGAEUS: Biggest loser.

HERMES: Where's your kin from? Tell me.

TRYGAEUS: Biggest loser.[22]

HERMES: Who's your father?

TRYGAEUS: Biggest loser.

HERMES: There is no way you will not die—by Earth!—
If you do not tell me your name, whatever it is.

190 **TRYGAEUS:** Trygaeus, from Athmonon, a clever pruner of grape vines,
No sycophant, and no lover of troubles.[23]

HERMES: What have you come for?

TRYGAEUS: To bring you this meat.

HERMES: How can you have gotten here, you poor little thing!

TRYGAEUS: You greedy little thing,
Do you see that I no longer seem to you to be the biggest loser?
Come, now, call Zeus for me.

HERMES: Ha, ha!
You're not even going to get near the gods,
For they're gone: they moved out yesterday.

TRYGAEUS: Where on earth to?

HERMES: "Earth," you say?

TRYGAEUS: But where?

HERMES: Very far. Simply put, under the very dome of heaven.

---

22. Although it is even less likely that a place be called "biggest loser" than a person, the very inappropriateness of the response might add to the humor. Hermes' questions are the usual way for one Greek to identify another: name, paternity, and place of origin.

23. The Greek word *pragmata* suggests meddling, as by way of legal disputes, including those with which sycophants harassed others. It may here allude also to the troubles that come from the war, as it does at 293, 352, and 1297. Trygaeus is from the township in Athens called Athmonon.

Trygaeus: Then how is it that you have been left here alone?   200

Hermes: I am watching over the gods' utensils that were left behind,
Little cups, bowls, and wine jars.

Trygaeus: Why did the gods move out?

Hermes: They became angry at the Greeks. Thus they settled
War here, where they had been,
Allowing him to do to you whatever he wishes.
They themselves moved up higher, as high as possible,
So they don't have to keep looking upon your fighting
And won't hear your pleas.

Trygaeus: Why did they do this to us? Tell me.   210

Hermes: Because you many times chose to make war,[24] even though they
were trying
To bring about a truce. And if the Spartans
Got the upper hand, they would speak as follows:
"By the two gods, now Attica will pay the price!"[25]
But if, on the other hand, you of Attica would succeed in something,
And the Spartans would come asking about peace,
You would directly say, "We are being tricked,
By Athena! By Zeus, we must not heed them!
They will come again, if we keep Pylos."[26]

Trygaeus: The character of this remark, at least, sure sounds like us.   220

Hermes: I thus don't know if in the future you'll ever see Peace again.

Trygaeus: But where has she gone?

---

24. Compare Homer, *Odyssey* 1.32–43, where Zeus assigns directly to human beings the responsibility for their misery. Trygaeus's effort to place the blame on Zeus goes against at least part of the tradition.

25. The Spartans often swore to the twin hero gods Castor and Pollux, also called the Dioscuri. (See 285.)

26. The Athenians won the Battle of Pylos, kept possession of the area and its fort, and took as prisoners about 120 members of the Spartan ruling class. This huge victory strengthened Cleon's hand and inclined the Athenians to exploit their advantage rather than seek peace. (As Thucydides put it, the Athenians "kept grasping for more," 4.41.4.) On the Spartan prisoners, see 479–80.

HERMES: War threw her into a deep cave.

TRYGAEUS: Which one?

HERMES: The one down here. And then
You see how many stones he put on top,
In order that you *never* get her.

TRYGAEUS: Tell me, what is he preparing to do to us?

HERMES: The only thing I know is that last evening
He brought in a mortar of preternatural size.

230 **TRYGAEUS**: What use will he make of this mortar?

HERMES: He wishes to grind up your cities in it.
But I'm leaving, for in my opinion he's about to come out;
At least he's making a racket inside. [Exit Hermes.]

TRYGAEUS: O, woe is me—frightened me! I'll run away from him: I think I
too heard
The sound of a mortar of war.

WAR: Alas for you, mortals, mortals, mortals with much to endure,
How severely your jaws will ache with pain any moment now!

TRYGAEUS: Lord Apollo, the breadth of that mortar!
How great an evil it is! And that look of War!
240   So is this the one we've been trying to escape,
The terrible one, the one who always has a shield, the one who [sends
shit] down our legs?

WAR: Alas, Prasiae, thrice wretched![27] No, five times
And many tens wretched, how you will perish on this very day.

TRYGAEUS: This, men, is not yet a problem for us;
For this evil belongs to Sparta.

WAR: Megara, Megara: how you will be ground
Into a perfect paste, all of you.

---

27. Located in the Peloponnese, Prasiae had already been sacked by Athens (Thucydides
2.56), but War will add new woes to those already suffered, plausibly if Sparta had occupied it
(Thucydides 6.105). The comic reason for picking on Prasiae is that it makes a pun with "leeks,"
which War adds as he grinds up his tasty paste.

TRYGAEUS: My, my, what great and bitter tears
  He's tossed in for the Megarians![28]

WAR: Alas, Sicily, how you too are being destroyed!   250

TRYGAEUS: What a city, now to be wretched, will be grated away!

WAR: Okay, let me now pour in also this honey, Attic honey.

TRYGAEUS: Hey, I advise you to use another honey;
  This one costs four obols. Spare the one from Attica.

WAR: Boy, Boy, Battle-din!

BATTLE-DIN: Why are you calling me?

WAR: You're
  Going to weep big time! Have you been standing around not working?
    Here's a knuckle for you! [Beats him.]

BATTLE-DIN: That was bitter! O, woe of woes, master.
  You didn't put any garlic on that knuckle, did you?

WAR: Run and fetch a pestle.

BATTLE-DIN: But, sir, we don't have one. We moved in just yesterday.   260

WAR: Won't you run fast and get one from the Athenians?

BATTLE-DIN: I will, by Zeus. (If I don't, it means tears.)

TRYGAEUS [to audience]: Now what shall we do, you poor little humans?
  You see how great our danger is,
  For if he comes back with the pestle,
  War will sit down and mash up our cities with it.
  But, Dionysius,[29] may he perish and not bring it back!

WAR: Hey!

BATTLE-DIN: What?

WAR: Didn't you bring it?

---

28. The word for "tears" sounds loosely similar to "garlic," which could also in this paste-making context have been modified by "great and bitter."

29. The god of the theater, of whom there was a statue in the theater, which might be addressed here.

BATTLE-DIN: Well. . . . The Athenians' pestle is lost and gone,
270   That leather-seller, who stirred up Greece.[30]

TRYGAEUS: Revered Lady, Mistress Athena, he did well in dying, at least,
And precisely when the city needed it,
Before he[31] poured the paste on us.

WAR: Then won't you go fetch another from Sparta, and fast?

BATTLE-DIN: I will, master.

WAR: Be back soon!

TRYGAEUS: Men, what will we suffer? Now our crisis is great indeed!
But if one of you happens to have been initiated in Samothrace,[32]
Now is a fine time to pray that the two feet
Of the one who is running this errand be turned aside and twisted back.

280   **BATTLE-DIN:** Woe is me, and woe indeed, and then, especially: Woe!

WAR: What is it? You didn't fail to bring it, did you?

BATTLE-DIN: The Spartans'
Pestle is also lost and gone.

WAR: What, you rascal?

BATTLE-DIN: They loaned it to others
In the lands up toward Thrace, and then they lost it.

TRYGAEUS: They did well, Dioscuri, well indeed.
Perhaps things just might go well: take heart, mortals!

WAR: Gather up and carry this gear back again.
I'm going inside to make a pestle.

TRYGAEUS: So here we now are: here's that song of Datis,[33]
290   The one which he used to sing while jerking off around noon,

---

30. The Athenian pestle is Cleon; the Spartan pestle is Brasidas (lines 274–84). Both these generals died the year before this play in the battle of Amphipolis, thus improving radically the prospects for peace. See line 47 and Thucydides 5.10.

31. Presumably War but possibly Cleon.

32. Those initiated into the religious mystery cult in Samothrace were believed to be more likely to receive favorable responses to their prayers, though it is not known what gods were associated with the cult.

33. Datis was the name of a commander of the Persian army defeated by the Athenians at Marathon.

"How pleased am I, what joy I'm given, what delight I feel!"
Now's a fine time for us, Greek men,
To free ourselves of woes and battles
And to drag out Peace, who's dear to all,
Before some other pestle prevents it.
But, farmers, traders, carpenters,
Craftsmen, resident aliens, foreigners,
And islanders, come here, all peoples,
And as quickly as possible get shovels, levers, and ropes;
For now it's possible for us to take hold of "the Good Divinity."[34]   300

CHORUS LEADER: Come here, everyone, and come eagerly, straight for
    salvation!
    Let's give aid, all of you Greeks, if ever we did,
    And free ourselves from battle-ranks and cowardly crimson uniforms.[35]
    For this day shines out as one hostile to Lamachus.[36]
    Tell us, therefore, if something needs doing, and be our foreman.
    For there is no way I intend to be tired today,
    Until with levers and other tools I drag up into the light
    The greatest of all goddesses and the one most friendly to grapevines.

TRYGAEUS: Won't you be quiet, so that in being overly overjoyed at
    this event
    You don't enflame War in there with your shouting!   310

CHORUS LEADER: But we're joyful at having heard a proclamation like this,
    Instead of "Come with rations for three days."

TRYGAEUS: Watch out now for that Cerberus down below,[37]
    Lest by his spluttering and shouting, as he used to do when he was up here,
    He prevent us from dragging out the goddess.

---

34. The first libation after a banquet and to begin a drinking party would often be offered to "the Good Divinity." It was offered with undiluted wine, and the divinity in question may have been Dionysius, the god of wine.

35. The word translated "cowardly" means more generally "bad" or "evil." The leaders of the army, who wore these crimson uniforms, are charged with cowardice also at 1172–78.

36. An Athenian general and Aristophanes' preferred example of one too fond of war. As the play concludes Trygaeus scolds a young boy who insists on singing about war and discovers that the child is the "son of Lamachus" (1289–92).

37. For Cleon as Cerberus, see also *Knights* 1017, 1030.

CHORUS LEADER: None of them will take her away now,
If I get my hands on her just once. Hurrah! Hurrah!

TRYGAEUS: You will destroy me, men, if you don't stop shouting,
For he will run out and throw all our efforts into confusion with his feet.[38]

320   **CHORUS LEADER**: So let him stir up and trample on everything, and throw
it into confusion!
We would not cease rejoicing today.

TRYGAEUS: What is this evil? What's wrong with you, men? By the gods,
Don't let your dancing destroy this most noble project!

CHORUS LEADER: But I don't wish to dance! Yet even though I'm not trying
to move my legs,
They are dancing of their own accord from sheer pleasure.

TRYGAEUS: Not now! No longer! But stop, stop your dancing!

CHORUS LEADER: Okay. Look: I have stopped.

TRYGAEUS: So you say, but you have not yet stopped!

CHORUS LEADER: Let me do just this one step—then no more.

TRYGAEUS: Okay, just this one, but then you will dance no more—not at all!

330   **CHORUS LEADER**: We'll stop dancing, if it helps you at all.

TRYGAEUS: But look, you have not yet stopped!

CHORUS LEADER: After we kick out our right legs here, by Zeus, we
will conclude.

TRYGAEUS: I'll grant you this, on the condition you'll cause me no
more pain.

CHORUS LEADER: But it's necessary that I kick out my left leg too!
For I'm filled with pleasure, I rejoice, I fart, and I laugh
Even more from tossing my shield than if I'd given old age the slip.

TRYGAEUS: No you don't: don't rejoice now, at least; for you don't yet know
for sure.
But when once we've gotten her, then rejoice
And shout and laugh;

---

38. "He" might refer to War or perhaps to Cleon. Neither appears, though Hermes soon will.

Then you'll be able   340
To sail away, to stay at home, to screw, to sleep,
To go and see the great festivals,
To feast, to play drinking games,
To be sybaritic,
To shout "Hurrah! Hurrah!"

CHORUS: Oh, if it should be that I see this day!
    For I've endured many woes and camp beds
    Which Phormio provided.[39]
    And you'd no longer find me a bitter or peevish juryman,
    Nor, of course, harsh in my ways, as I was before,   350
    But you'd see me gentle and much younger,
    If I were free of these woes.
    For long enough have we been ruined and worn down,
    Wandering, with spear and shield
    To and from the Lyceum.[40]
    But, come tell us, by doing what in particular will we gratify you?
    For a certain good fortune chose you as our leader.   360

TRYGAEUS: Come, let me see, where shall we carry off these stones to?

[Hermes enters.]

HERMES: Bold wretch! What do you think you're doing?

TRYGAEUS: Nothing wicked; just what Cillicon[41] did.

HERMES: You're done for, you wretched fool!

TRYGAEUS: Yes indeed, if that's my lot. For since you are Hermes,
    I know you'll hold a *lot*-tery.[42]

HERMES: You're done for; you're really done for.

TRYGAEUS: Oh? On what day?

---

39. An Athenian general in the early years of the war with Sparta who was especially successful in naval campaigns.

40. A public exercise area where troops may also have mustered.

41. A notorious villain and perhaps also a traitor.

42. Hermes was thought to preside over lotteries. The scholia say that at Athens on any given day only a single person could be executed—chosen by lot if there were more than one condemned to death at that time.

HERMES: Right now!

TRYGAEUS: But I haven't yet made the purchases, neither of grain nor of
Dried cheese, of one who is about to perish.[43]

HERMES: Yet you will be rubbed out![44]

370 **TRYGAEUS:** And why didn't I notice that I was getting so great a good?

HERMES: Don't you know that Zeus proclaimed death for anyone who
        should be caught trying to
    Dig her up?

TRYGAEUS: So, then, there is every necessity that I die now?

HERMES: Know it well!

TRYGAEUS: Loan me now three drachmas for a piglet;
    For I must be initiated before I die.[45]

HERMES: O Zeus, sender of the thunder and lightning bolt!

TRYGAEUS: By the gods, do not denounce us, I beg you, master.

HERMES: I couldn't stay silent!

TRYGAEUS: By the meats that I eagerly came to bring you, do!

380 **HERMES:** But, sir, I'll be pulverized by Zeus
    If I don't shriek this out and howl about it.

TRYGAEUS: Don't howl about it, I entreat you, dear little Hermes.[46]
    Tell me, what's up with you, men? You stand there dumbstruck.
    Rascals, don't remain silent! If you do, he'll howl.

CHORUS: Don't do it, master Hermes, don't don't don't.
    If you are aware of having gobbled down a gratifying piglet from me,
    Do not believe it negligible as regards this present issue.

TRYGAEUS: Don't you hear how they fawn upon you, lord and master?

---

43. Since these were foods that soldiers took on campaigns, the joke is not about a traditional last meal but about the perils of military service.

44. The verb may also mean "fucked," in which case Trygaeus's response might not be ironic.

45. Piglets were sacrificed when initiates entered into the Eleusinian Mysteries, which promised a happy afterlife.

46. Trygaeus uses an endearing or coaxing diminutive of Hermes' name. At 416 he says "dear Hermes" literally.

CHORUS: Don't be hostile and thus keep us from getting her. 390
　But be gracious to us,
　You who among the divinities are
　The most loving of human beings and the greatest giver of gifts,
　If you are ever disgusted by the helmet crests and furrowed brows
　　of Peisander.[47]
　We will glorify you on every occasion, master,
　And for all time, with holy rites of sacrifice
　And great processions.

TRYGAEUS: Come, I entreat you, pity their call, 400
　Since they are honoring you more than before.[48]

HERMES: Because they are now more thievish than ever before.[49]

TRYGAEUS: And let me tell you a great and terrible matter,
　Which is being plotted against all gods.

HERMES: Come, then, out with it; for perhaps you would persuade me.

TRYGAEUS: The Moon and the Sun (who stops at nothing)
　Have been plotting against you for a long time already
　And are betraying Greece to the barbarians.

HERMES: For what end do they do this?

TRYGAEUS: Because, by Zeus, 410
　We sacrifice to you, while the barbarians sacrifice to them.
　They therefore would of course wish us all to be destroyed,
　So that they themselves might seize control of the rites of the gods.

HERMES: So this is why they've for a long time been filching days and
　Nibbling their own circles by trickery.[50]

---

47. As emphasized here, Peisander was among those who urged support for the war. His democratic credentials also showed in his selection as a lead prosecutor of people accused of the mutilation of the Herms. Nevertheless, he later joined an oligarchic conspiracy in 412 B.C. He is referred to as cowardly at *Birds* 1557.

48. Hermes was the beneficiary of no major festivals or sacrificial rites at Athens.

49. Hermes was the patron deity of trickery and, hence, of thievery. See *Wealth* 1157–59, for example. Scholars hotly debate the authenticity of this line, and some attribute it to Trygaeus.

50. Or "cycles." Hermes seems to refer to difficulties in keeping the lunar calendar correct. Cf. *Clouds* 615–16.

Trygaeus: Yes, by Zeus! Therefore, dear Hermes,
Help us with her eagerly and join in pulling her out,
And it will be to you that we celebrate the Great Panathenaic Festival
And all the other rites of the gods:
420   The Mysteries, the Dipolieia, the Adonia—all for Hermes.
And other cities, gaining rest from evils,
Will everywhere sacrifice to Hermes the Averter of Evils,
And you will obtain still other goods. As a first gift
I offer you this bowl for use in libations.

Hermes: Oh, my, how prone to pity I have always been for golden vessels.
It's your job from here on out, men. Go on in with your shovels,
And drag those stones out as quickly as possible.

Chorus Leader: We'll do it. But you, wisest of the gods, since you have
taken charge,
Tell us as a craftsman would what we must do.
430   As for the rest, you'll find that we are not bad at working under direction.

Trygaeus [to Hermes]: Come, hold the bowl, and quickly,
So we can pray to the gods and get to work.

Hermes: Libation! Libation! Holy silence! Holy silence!
As we pour this libation let us pray that this day
Is the beginning of many good things for all the Greeks,
And that whatever man helps eagerly with the ropes
May never need take up a shield.

Trygaeus: No, by Zeus, but may he live his life in peace
440   Stoking the coals of a hot girlfriend.

Hermes: But whoever wishes that there be war instead, may he never, Lord
Dionysius, cease—

Trygaeus: —picking arrowheads out of his elbows!

Hermes: And if someone, out of the desire to be a leader of soldiers,
Resists your coming up into the light again, Revered Lady,[51] may he in
these battles—

---

51. Trygaeus refers to Peace, whereas he had before used this adjective, *potnia*, to refer to Athena (271).

TRYGAEUS: —suffer just what Cleonymus did![52]

HERMES: And if any spear-maker or shield-huckster
Desires battles so he can sell at a better price—

TRYGAEUS: —may he be captured by raiders and eat only barley-corns!

HERMES: And if someone does not join in helping   450
Because he wishes to be a general or is a slave getting ready to
run away[53]—

TRYGAEUS: —may he be drawn out on the torture wheel and whipped.

HERMES: And may good things come to us! Hurrah! Strike up the Paean!
Hurrah!

TRYGAEUS: Take away the "strike"; just say "Hurrah!"

HERMES: Hurrah! Hurrah! I say only "Hurrah!"

TRYGAEUS: To Hermes, to the Graces, to the Seasons, to Aphrodite,
to Yearning![54]

HERMES: But not to Ares!

TRYGAEUS: No!

HERMES: Nor even to Enyalius?

TRYGAEUS: No!

TRYGAEUS: Then let everyone get to it and haul on the ropes.

CHORUS: Heave!

HERMES: Heave hard!   460

CHORUS: Heave!

HERMES: Heave really hard!

CHORUS: Heave! Heave!

---

52. Cleonymus is a frequent butt of jokes in Aristophanes for a variety of weaknesses but especially for cowardice. See also *Birds* 289–90.

53. The war made it easier for slaves to run away, especially since Athens' enemies offered refuge.

54. The Seasons (*Horai*) were daughters of Zeus and Themis. Yearning (*Pothos*) appears as a son of Aphrodite in one source, as a son of Eros in another. Enyalios (below) was either an epithet of Ares or a god of war distinct from Ares. On the Graces, see line 41 and note.

TRYGAEUS: But the men aren't pulling equally.
Won't you join in helping? What airs you put on!
You Boeotians will be sorry for this![55]

HERMES: Now heave!

TRYGAEUS: Heave!

CHORUS LEADER: Come on, you two, join with us in the pulling![56]

470 **TRYGAEUS**: Am I not pulling, putting my weight into it,
And working in earnest?

CHORUS LEADER: Then why is the work not going forward?

TRYGAEUS: Lamachus, you're being unjust by sitting and blocking us.
We have no need of your shield, mister.[57]

HERMES: Nor have these Argives been pulling, not for a long time!
Instead they mock those who work and suffer, while
Getting paid in fine barley from both sides.[58]

HERMES: But the Spartans, good fellow, are pulling in manly fashion.

TRYGAEUS: Don't you know that it's only the ones in the stocks who
are eager,

480 And the bronze-smith is restraining them.[59]

HERMES: Nor are the Megarians accomplishing anything,[60]
Although they are pulling relentlessly, like puppies—

TRYGAEUS: —yet they are all but destroyed by hunger, by Zeus.[61]

---

55. The Boeotians opposed the Peace of Nicias.

56. This accusation is presumably directed against Hermes and Trygaeus, the two supervisors.

57. "Mister" here translates *anthrōpos*, the Greek word for human being, which denies any special title or status to Lamachus; and "shield" is for "Mormo," a Gorgon-like monster featured on the emblem of Lamachus's shield. See *Acharnians* 572 ff.

58. Argos's opposition to the peace may also have stemmed from fear that shared rule between Athens and Sparta would have made it more difficult for cities like theirs to enjoy independence.

59. The Greek here is not clear but seems to say that only the Spartan prisoners from Pylos were eager for peace, while their guards keep them from having any effect.

60. The Megarians refused to sign the Peace of Nicias.

61. There are once again major disagreements over which characters speak which lines in this section.

HERMES: We're not accomplishing anything, men.
　　Let's all join in, once again in full accord.

CHORUS: Heave!

HERMES: Heave hard!

CHORUS: Heave!

HERMES: Heave, by Zeus!

CHORUS LEADER: We're moving it a little at least.　　　　　　490

TRYGAEUS: This "little" is no surprise, since
　　Some are straining one way; others are pulling the opposite way.
　　You'll be beaten, you Argives!

HERMES: Now heave!

TRYGAEUS: Heave!

CHORUS: How malevolent some of us are!

TRYGAEUS: At least you who long for peace,
　　Pull in manly fashion!

CHORUS: But there are others who are preventing us!

HERMES: Men of Megara, won't you go to the crows?　　　　500
　　For when she remembers you, the goddess hates you;
　　For you were the first—you anointed her with garlic!
　　To you Athenians I say stop pulling
　　With the grip you are using now,
　　For you are doing nothing but disputing like jurors.
　　If you desire to drag her out,
　　Withdraw a little more toward the sea.[62]

CHORUS LEADER: Come, men, let us farmers grab hold all by ourselves!

HERMES: This business is advancing much more with you, men.

CHORUS LEADER: He says the business is advancing. Let every man　　510
　　be eager.

TRYGAEUS: The farmers alone are advancing the work, and no one else!

---

62. That is to say, Athens should be satisfied with its maritime empire and not seek land in addition.

CHORUS: Come on now, come on everyone!

HERMES: Look, now it's close by!

CHORUS: Let's not ease up now, but
  Let's exert ourselves more manfully.

HERMES: That's it!

CHORUS: Now heave; everyone heave!
  Heave, heave, heave, heave, heave, heave!
  Heave, heave, heave, heave, heave, everyone.

[Peace emerges, as do Opora and Theoria.]

520 **TRYGAEUS**: Revered Lady, Giver of Grapes, with what words may I
      address you?
  Where could I find a 10,000 gallon phrase
  To address you with? I don't have one of my own.
  Welcome, Opora, and you too Theoria.
  O Theoria, what a face!
  How pleasant is your breath to my heart!
  It's the sweetest, like perfume and the cessation of hostilities.

HERMES: Not at all like the aroma of a soldier's pack, is it!

TRYGAEUS: "I spurn of a hateful mortal his most hateful knapsack."[63]
  It reeks of acidic onion belches,
530 While she smells of harvest, hospitality, festivals of Dionysius,
  Flutes, tragic actors, lyrics of Sophocles, thrushes to dine on,
  Scraps of verses of Euripides—

HERMES: You'll shed tears for having told that lie at her expense:
  For she takes no pleasure in a poet of contentious verses.

TRYGAEUS: —and of ivy, wine strainers, bleating sheep,
  The breasts of women running to the field,
  A drunken slave girl, an overturned pitcher,
  And many other good things.

---

63. The scholia indicate that this line is a parody of line 727 of Euripides' lost *Telephus*. Aristophanes substitutes "knapsack" for "child."

HERMES: Come now: look how the cities now reconciled
    Chatter with each other and laugh with gladness—   540

TRYGAEUS: —and yet they all have daemonically black eyes and
    Are using eye-cups.[64]

HERMES: —and take a look at the faces of
    These spectators here, so you can recognize their trades.

TRYGAEUS: Yuck!

HERMES: Don't you see that maker of helmet crests, tearing at his hair?

TRYGAEUS: Right, but the hoe-maker just farted at that sword-maker!

HERMES: And don't you see how pleased the scythe-maker is?

TRYGAEUS: And how he gave the spear-maker the finger?

HERMES: Come now, tell the farmers to depart.   550

TRYGAEUS: Hearken, people! Let the farmers take
    Their farming implements and go back to their fields as quickly
        as possible,
    Without spear, sword, and javelin,
    Since everything here is now full of ripe old peace.
    After singing the paean, let everyone go to work in the fields.

CHORUS LEADER: O day yearned for by the just and farmers,
    I am glad to see you and wish to give a greeting to my vines;
    And as for the fig trees I planted when I was younger,
    It's our heart's desire to hug them fondly after so long a time.

TRYGAEUS: But now, men, let us first pray to the goddess,   560
    Who eliminated those helmet crests and Gorgon-studded shields;
    Then we'll hurry to our fields,
    After having bought some good salt-fish for the farm.

HERMES: Poseidon, how noble do their ranks appear,
    Close-packed and intimidating, like cakes and the scene at full-
        bore parties!

---

64. Some sort of heated cup was used in treating black eyes.

TRYGAEUS: Yes, by Zeus, for the clod-mallet gleams brightly, having been
    primed for battle,
And the pitchforks flash in the sun.
Nobly they will set free [from weeds] the soil between the plants.
So I too now desire to go into the fields
570   And again, after so long, start working my little plot of earth with
    my mattock.
But men, after recalling
The old way of life
Which she herself[65] once provided us—
Those cakes of fruit,
The figs and myrtle berries,
The sweet new wine,
The patches of violets beside the well,
And the olive trees,
For which we yearn—
580   In return for all these things,
Now address the goddess.

CHORUS: Welcome! Welcome! You have come to us who are so glad,
    dearest one.
I am overcome with yearning for you
And have a daemonic wish to go back to the fields.
For you—you whom we yearn for—were the greatest gain
For all of us who pounded out a life of farming,
590   Since you alone would benefit us.
Once before, in your time, we experienced many things
That were at once sweet, free of charge, and dear.
For us rustics in the fields,
You were our wheat and our salvation.
Thus the little grape vines, young fig saplings,
And whatever other plants there are
600   Will greet you gladly and with smiles of joy.
But when she was away from us this long time, wherever was she?
Teach us this, you most benevolent of the gods.

---

65. Here and through line 705, Peace is often addressed and referred to without being named.

HERMES: Wisest farmers, attend to my words,
  If you wish to hear how she perished.
  First of all, Phidias started the disaster when he got into trouble.[66]
  Then Pericles became afraid that he might share in Phidias's misfortune.
  Fearing your natures and your ferocious character,
  Before he suffered anything terrible himself,
  He enflamed the city by tossing in a small spark of a Megarian decree,[67]
  And he fanned it into a war big enough that its smoke   610
  Could make all Greeks cry, both those over there and the ones here.
  Although unwilling in the
  Beginning, a grape vine burned loudly,
  And on being struck, a storage jar kicked back in anger at another
      storage jar,
  And since there was no longer anyone to stop it, she then vanished.

TRYGAEUS: By Apollo, I hadn't learned this from anyone,
  Nor had I heard how Phidias was related to her.

CHORUS LEADER: Nor had I, until now. So this is why she's got such a
      lovely face,
  Since she is related to him. Many things escape our notice!

HERMES: And then, when the cities you ruled came to know that
  You were angry with one another and were baring your fangs,   620
  Out of fear for their tribute payments they contrived every measure they
      could against you, and
  They tried to win over the greatest of the Spartans with cold cash.[68]
  And they, since they seek gain shamefully and are thoroughly dishonest
      with foreigners,

---

66. Phidias, the great sculptor, was accused of embezzling gold when creating the monumental statue of Athena Parthenos on the Acropolis, but he fled before his trial. The beauty of his sculpture is again alluded to in comic fashion at line 618. For another Aristophanean account of the origins of the war, see *Acharnians* 509–56.

67. An Athenian act barring Megara from all Athenian-controlled ports and markets. Sparta objected, Pericles persuaded the Athenians to ignore the Spartan complaint, and the war began soon after (Thucydides 1.144–45).

68. Athens was the head of a large maritime empire, and required tribute from all subject states. A Spartan invasion of Athenian territory might make it easier for such subjects to revolt, but the war also tempted Athens to increase their tribute payments.

Shamefully tossed her out and snatched up War.
And their gains were evils for the farmers.
For the triremes sent forth from here would take revenge
And swallow down the figs of blameless men.

TRYGAEUS: Our response was just, since they cut down that black fig tree
   of mine,
Which I planted and reared.[69]

630 **CHORUS LEADER**: Yes, by Zeus, it was just indeed, sir, since they
   Hurled a rock and destroyed my eight-bushel storage bin!

HERMES: And then, when the working people came in from the field,[70]
   They did not realize they were being bought and sold in the
      same manner,[71]
   But since they were lacking in raisins and longing for dried figs,
   They turned to the orators. But these,
   Who knew quite well that the poor were growing weak and were
      without barley,
   Shoved this goddess away with their threatening cries—
   Even though she often appeared because of her yearning for this land,
   And they shook down the fat and wealthy ones among the allies,
640   Trotting out the charge that they were plotting with Brasidas.
   And then like little dogs you would tear at the accused;
   For the city then was pale and crouching in fear,
   And she ate up with great pleasure whatever slanders anyone offered her.
   When the allies saw the beatings they were taking,
   They stuffed the mouths of those doing it with gold,
   Which made them rich; but even if Greece were completely depopulated,
   You would not have noticed. The one behind all this was a
      leather salesman.[72]

---

69. A parody, by the substitution of a fig tree for children, of Euripides' *Medea* 1349.

70. Hermes refers to 431 B.C., when the outlying population was forced by the Spartan invasion to come within the shelter of Athens' walls (Thucydides 2.14–17).

71. In the same manner as the farmers of Sparta (622–27).

72. That is, Cleon, who is now dead, as Trygaeus will indicate in his next speech. Another reference to Cleon and leather is just below, at 669.

TRYGAEUS: Stop! Stop, Master Hermes, do not speak,
But let that man stay down below, right where he is.
For the man no longer belongs to us, but to you.[73]
So whatever you might say about him—
Even if he was one who would stop at nothing when he was alive,
And a loudmouth and a sycophant,
And a tool for stirring things up and for throwing them into confusion—
You would now be bad-mouthing your own
To say any of these things at all.
But tell me, Revered Lady, why you are silent.

HERMES: She would not speak, at least to these spectators.
For she is still very angry with them for what she suffered.

TRYGAEUS: Well, then, let her whisper to you alone.

HERMES: Tell me what you are thinking about them, dearest.
Come, you who among women most hates shields.
[Peace appears to whisper to Hermes, here and below.]
Yes. I am listening. These are your complaints? I understand.
Listen, all of you, to why she blames you.
She says that when she came here on her own initiative after the events
    at Pylos
And brought a chest full of treaties for the city,
She was thrice voted down in the Assembly.[74]

TRYGAEUS: In this we were wrong, but be forgiving.
For our mind was then in our leather.

HERMES: Come, now, and hear what she just asked me:
Who was especially malevolent to her here,
And who was her friend and was earnest that there be no battles?

TRYGAEUS: The most well disposed by far was Cleonymus.

650

660

670

---

73. Hermes bore some responsibility for the dead in part because of his role as conductor of souls to Hades.

74. The Athenians won a great victory at Pylos in the summer of 425, thus leading the Spartans to seek peace. See also Thucydides 4.41 and note 26 above.

HERMES: How did this Cleonymus seem to be
As regards warfare?

TRYGAEUS: He was best in soul, except that
He did not descend from the father he said he did.
For if ever he went out as a soldier,
The first thing he did was to discard his weapons.

HERMES: Hear now another thing she asked me just now:

680 Who is now the master of the rock on the Pnyx?[75]

TRYGAEUS: Hyperbolos now holds this place.[76]
[To Peace] But what are you doing? Why are you turning your head away?

HERMES: She is turning away from the people, outraged because
They chose so wicked a leader.

TRYGAEUS: Yes, but we won't use him any more for anything.
The people just now being at a loss for a guardian, and naked,
Clad themselves with him just for the moment.

HERMES: She asks how this will be advantageous for the city.

TRYGAEUS: We will become better at deliberating.

HERMES: In what way?

690 **TRYGAEUS:** Because he happens to be a lamp-maker. Before this we
Groped in the dark to solve our problems,
But now we will deliberate about everything in lamplight.

HERMES: Oh, oh, she just bade me ask you about something else.

TRYGAEUS: About what?

HERMES: About many ancient matters which she left behind back then.
First, she asked how Sophocles is doing.

TRYGAEUS: He's happy. But he's undergoing something wondrous.

HERMES: What?

TRYGAEUS: Having been Sophocles, he's now becoming Simonides!

---

75. The Pnyx was a rocky hill on which the Athenian Assembly met.

76. After the death of Cleon, Hyperbolos was for four years the leading demagogue. See 921 and 1319 below, as well as *Clouds* 561.

HERMES: Simonides? How so?

TRYGAEUS: Because although he is old and worn out,
He'd go sailing on a wicker mat for the sake of gain.[77]

HERMES: What about the wise Cratinus, is he alive?[78]

TRYGAEUS: He died when the Spartans invaded.

HERMES: From what?

TRYGAEUS: From what? He just fainted away, for he couldn't stand seeing
A full wine jar get broken. And can you think how many other things
Have happened in the city!
Thus, Mistress,[79] we will never let go of you again.

HERMES: Come, now, on these terms take Opora here
To be your wife, and then dwelling together with her
In the countryside, beget for yourself litters of grapes.

TRYGAEUS: Come here, dearest, and let me kiss you!
Does it seem to you, Master Hermes, that it would
Do me any harm after all this time to thrust into Opora?

HERMES: No, not if you then drank a little pennyroyal.[80]
But take Theoria here and lead her as quickly as possible
To the Council, to whom she once belonged.[81]

TRYGAEUS: Council, blessedly happy in your Theoria,
How much broth you will gulp down in the next three days!
And how much boiled sausage and meat you will devour!
But, dear Hermes, hearty farewell.

---

77. Simonides was known for his old age and especially for his love of money. Sophocles was now about 75; what evidence there may have been for calling him greedy is unclear.

78. Cratinus was the great Athenian comic poet of the previous generation, the chief originator of the Old Comedy as we find it in Aristophanes. His last known play, *Wine Flask*, was produced in 423 B.C. Here and in *Acharnians* (848–53, 1173) and *Knights* (400, 526–36), Aristophanes mocks him for his love of drinking.

79. *Despoina* is the feminine form of the word for "master," *despotēs*, which Trygaeus uses of Hermes at 710 and elsewhere. It does not suggest any erotic relationship. It is used of Athena at 271 and twice again of Peace at 976.

80. Pennyroyal was a kind of mint drink. Pliny wrote that it was effective as a cure for nausea.

81. Before the war, the Council sent festivity delegations to Delphi and to Delos.

HERMES: And you, human being, farewell: go, and remember me!

720 **TRYGAEUS:** Let's fly home, Dung Beetle, home!

HERMES: He's not here, good fellow.

TRYGAEUS: Where has he gone?

HERMES: He has gone off harnessed to Zeus's chariot, and he bears his lightning.[82]

TRYGAEUS: How then will the poor wretch get his food up here?

HERMES: He will dine on the "ambrosia" of Ganymede.[83]

TRYGAEUS: Then how will I descend?

HERMES: Take heart. You'll do it in fine fashion. Go this way, past the goddess herself.

TRYGAEUS: Come here, Maidens. Follow along with me quickly, because
Many yearn for you greatly and are waiting fully erect.

[Exit all but the Chorus.]

CHORUS LEADER: Go, and farewell. Meanwhile, let's give our gear[84]
730   To our attendants to keep safe, for lots of thieves are especially
Accustomed to lurk around this stage and do evil.
So guard these things courageously; while as for us,
Let's tell these spectators the path of our words and what's on our mind.
The ushers ought to beat any comic poet who comes forward in
    the anapests
Of the parabasis[85] and praises himself in the front of the theater.

---

82. This line is from Euripides' *Bellerophon* (fr. 312) describing how the winged horse who flew to heaven, Pegasus, remained in heaven and bore Zeus's lightning.

83. A beautiful young mortal carried off by Zeus to be his cup bearer and beloved.

84. The Chorus came on stage equipped with tools used in the excavation of the goddess, so it is probably these which they now ask attendants to guard courageously.

85. A feature of Old Comedy in which only the chorus would remain on stage. In most cases the chorus would give up its dramatic role in the play and speak directly to the audience about other matters, such as the insufficiently-recognized excellences of the author of the play. The parabasis was thus a sort of interlude. Since the heart of the parabasis was written in anapests, it could be referred to by this meter, as here and at *Birds* 684. *Peace* has a second parabasis at 1127–90. See note on 1127.

But if, Daughter of Zeus,[86] it is fitting to honor someone who among
    human beings is
The best comic producer and has become most famous,
Our producer declares that he's the one who deserves great praise.[87]
For in the first place, he alone among human beings stopped his
    rivals from
Always cracking jokes about rags and from making war on lice;   740
And with regard to those stage Heracleses who knead bread and yet go
    hungry[88]—the ones who
Run away, attempt deception, and intentionally get themselves beaten—
    he was the first to strip
Away their civic honors and drive them into exile; and he dismissed those
    slaves whom others
Always bring onto the stage in tears, as well as those whom they bring
    on only
So a fellow slave can make jokes about being beaten and then ask,
"Hey, unhappy one, what happened to your skin? Did the whip attack you
    with repeated blows to
Your sides, and did it ravage your back?"
By removing such evils, vulgarity, and low-class buffoonery,
He made our art great and built it high as a tower, fortifying it
With great verses, thoughts, and jokes far from commonplace.   750
Not mocking the lesser human beings of ordinary life, nor women,
But with the anger of Heracles he set upon the greatest,
Facing the terrible smells of curing leather[89] and muck-minded threats.
First of all, I did battle with the sharp-fanged one himself,[90]

---

86. The Muses were daughters of Zeus.

87. This comic producer was Aristophanes himself. In going on to claim that he avoided all commonplace jokes, he must have been joking.

88. Mocking a satyr drama of Euripides, *Syleus*.

89. Another reference to Cleon, who traded in leather. This passage is almost identical to *Wasps* 1029–37.

90. The image is of Cleon as Cerberus, the canine guard of Hades, whom Heracles had dragged to the surface. In the next line, the reference is to Cynna, an Athenian prostitute. Her name and the word for female dog are closely related; thus Aristophanes gets to call Cleon both the hell-hound Cerberus and the whore, Cynna.

From whose eyes Cynna's rays flashed most terribly,

And one hundred heads of cursed flatterers licked in a circle all around
his head,

And he had the voice of a mountain torrent in full surge, a deadly one,

And the smell of a seal, the unwashed balls of a Lamia,[91] and the asshole
of a camel.[92]

Yet on seeing such a monster, I did not become afraid, but I went to war
on your behalf,

760   And for the islands, and I always stood my ground.

It is now therefore fitting that you repay me with gratitude and remember
me. For previously,

When I fared as I had intended,[93] I did not go looking for boys at the
wrestling schools, I took

My gear and promptly went on my way, after having afforded little pain
and much pleasure,

Furnishing everything needful.

Thus both the men

And the boys ought to be on my side.

And we exhort all the baldies[94]

To join me in being zealous for my victory,

For if I am victorious, everyone will say

770   Both over dinner and over drinks,

"Bring goodies for baldy! Give goodies to baldy!

Don't stint with the man who has the high forehead,

The noblest[95] of our poets."

CHORUS: Muse, having rejected wars, dance with me, your friend,

Celebrating the wedding feasts of gods,

The banquets of men,

---

91. A monster of lewdness who ate men and children, Lamia had the breasts of a woman and
the lower parts of a donkey.

92. Aristophanes often mocked passive homosexuals by commenting on the expansion of
their anal openings.

93. Aristophanes won the prize for his *Acharnians* in 425 and for his *Knights* in 424 at the
Lenaia festivals.

94. Aristophanes makes fun of his own baldness. See also *Knights* 550.

95. *Gennaios*, which may refer to one's family or lineage in particular.

And the festivals for the blest,
For these have been your concerns since the beginning.   780
But if Carcinus comes and
Entreats you to dance with his children,[96]
Do not heed him
Or become his assistant,
But believe them all
To be home-bred quails,
Scraggy-necked dancers,
Dwarfish in nature, scraps of goat-turd,   790
Famished for new stunts.
For their father claimed that,
Although beyond his every hope
He had a play,
A weasel did away with it last night.
The wise poet must sing
Such public songs
Of the Graces
With their beautiful hair,
When in spring the perching swallow sings,   800
And Morsimus[97] does not get a chorus—
Nor Melanthios[98] either,
Whom I
Heard singing out
In a most bitter voice
When he and his brother
Obtained a tragic chorus,
Both of them being
Dainty-devouring Gorgons,   810
Skate-craving Harpies,
Foul hag-lovers, fish-gulpers
With armpits rank as goats.

---

96. Carcinus was a tragic poet whose three sons were dancers. They are teased also in the conclusion of the *Wasps*, 1497–1537.

97. A tragic poet and great-nephew of Aeschylus.

98. A tragic poet and perhaps a tragic actor. See also 1009–15 and *Birds* 151.

Hock up and spit a fat luger on them, Muse Divine,
And play with me at my festival.

[Now back on Earth, Trygaeus reenters the stage with Opora and Theoria.]

TRYGAEUS: How difficult it was to go straight to the gods!

820   I've completely worn out my two legs.
[Addressing the audience] You were tiny to behold from up there.
You appeared from heaven, at least to me,
To be of pretty bad character,
But from here you seem of much worse character by far!

SERVANT: Master, you have come!

TRYGAEUS: So I have heard from someone.

SERVANT: What happened to you?

TRYGAEUS: I got a sore pair of legs on the long road I've traveled.

SERVANT: Come now: tell me—

TRYGAEUS: What?

SERVANT: Did you see any other man wandering in the air besides yourself?

TRYGAEUS: No, unless one considers two or three souls of
        dithyrambic poets.

830 **SERVANT**: What were they doing?

TRYGAEUS: They were flying about, collecting some
        Musical preludes that were floating in the fair-weather airy breezes.

SERVANT: So what they say is not the case,
        That we become stars in the air, when one dies?

TRYGAEUS: But it is!

SERVANT: Who is a star there now?

TRYGAEUS: Ion, from Chios, who once long ago composed
        Here on earth "The Dawn Star."
        And when he went up, they all called him the dawn star right away.

SERVANT: Who are the shooting stars,
        The ones that burn as they race along?

840 **TRYGAEUS**: These are some of the rich stars
        Who are walking away after dinner with lanterns, with fire in
            the lanterns.

[Gesturing toward Opora] But take her in as quickly as possible,
Wash out the tub, heat water,
Strew the marriage bed for her and me.
When you have done all this, come back here again.
[Gesturing toward Theoria] Meanwhile, I will give this girl to the Council.

SERVANT: Where did you get them?

TRYGAEUS: Where? From heaven.

SERVANT: I would not give three obols for the gods
If they deal in whores just as we mortals do.

TRYGAEUS: No, they don't . . . but even there some do make a living off   850
of them.
Come now, let's go.

SERVANT: Tell me, shall I give her something to eat?

TRYGAEUS: Not at all. For she won't be willing to eat
Either bread or cake, since she's always been accustomed
To lick ambrosia up there beside the gods.

SERVANT: Then we must get something ready for her to lick down here too!

CHORUS: The old man fares happily now,
At least as far as one can see.

TRYGAEUS: What then will you say when you see me
As a radiant bridegroom!

CHORUS: You will be envied, old man,   860
For being young again,
Anointed with scented oil.

TRYGAEUS: I think so! And what will you say when we're together, and I'm
holding her tits!

CHORUS: You will seem even happier than the whirling tops of Carcinus.[99]

TRYGAEUS: And not justly?
Did I not climb aboard a beetle for transport
And save the Greeks, so that they now can all fuck and sleep safely in
the country?

---

99. The chorus refers to the sons of Carcinus, who are dancers, as tops.

SERVANT: The girl has had her bath, and all's fine with her rear.
The cake has been baked, the sesame bars are being shaped,
870   And all the other things are ready. All that's needed is the prick.

TRYGAEUS: Come, then, let's make haste
And give Theoria here to the Council.

SERVANT: But who is she?

TRYGAEUS: Why do you ask? This is Theoria.

SERVANT: The one we used to bang on the way to Brauron, when we were a
little tipsy?[100]

TRYGAEUS: You know it! And she was taken with some difficulty.

SERVANT: Master, what a large every-four-years-festival asshole she has!

TRYGAEUS [to the audience]: Well, then, who among you is just? Who in
the world!
Who will take her and keep her safe for the Council?
You there, why are you tracing her perimeter?

SERVANT: Me? Well, it's for the Isthmian[101]
880   Games: I'm taking hold of a spot for my prick to camp in.

TRYGAEUS [to the audience]: You are still not saying who will be the one to
guard her! [To Theoria] You, come here.
I'll take you myself and deposit you right in the middle of them.

SERVANT: That guy is nodding assent.

TRYGAEUS: Who?

SERVANT: Who? It's Ariphrades[102]
Who is imploring you to lead her to him.

TRYGAEUS: But, good fellow,
He will fall upon her, down low, and lap up her soup.
[To Theoria] Come, now, put your gear[103] down on the ground.

---

100. Every four years there was a great festive procession, from Athens east to Brauron, to the
shrine of the goddess Artemis, where maidens ran races and were initiated in a cult.

101. A sexual *double entendre*, as the Greek for "isthmus" can refer to a narrow passage or
place of joining, as of two legs.

102. Apparently renowned for debauchery: *Knights* 1281 ff., *Wasps* 1280–83.

103. It appears the "gear" she puts down is her clothes.

Council! Prytanes![104] Take a look at Opora!
Consider how many good things I've brought to give you!
You can right away lift her legs up in midair and enjoy a feast.   890
And this, you see, is her cooker.

SERVANT: How beautiful!
And it's her cooking that has blackened the area, then.
For before the war she was once the Council's pot-holder.[105]

TRYGAEUS: Now, then, with her in your possession it will be possible
For you to hold a very noble contest tomorrow:
Wrestle with her on the ground,
Stand her on her hands and knees,
Oil up for the pankration[106] and bang and burrow with youthful vigor
With both fist and prick.
On the day after tomorrow, after these events, you will hold horse races,   900
Where one racehorse will ride beside the other,
With chariots turned over on top of each other,
Panting and breathing hard, they will move against each other;
And other chariot drivers will lie with foreskins drawn back,
Having fallen at the turning-twisting points.[107]
But, Prytanes, receive Theoria!
See how eagerly this Prytane took her over!
But you would not have been so eager, if this had been business you had
        to undertake without a
Bribe; in that case, I would have found you holding out your hand.[108]

CHORUS: Good for everyone   910
As man and citizen
Is such a one as he!

---

104. The Prytanes presided over the Council.
105. These had legs and were dark at the top, where the legs met, from smoke.
106. The pankration was an all-out fighting event that combined wrestling and boxing; only biting and eye-gouging were forbidden.
107. It appears that horses, riders, and the chariots themselves are all having sex; "racehorse" is also a sexual position. The word for a turning post in a chariot race can also refer to the vigorous twisting together of an active couple.
108. In order to make a proposal to the Council, one had to go through the Prytanes, whom Aristophanes is accusing of expecting a payoff.

TRYGAEUS: When you gather in your vintage,[109] you'll know even better what sort I am.

CHORUS: Even now it's clear,
For you've become a savior for all human beings.

TRYGAEUS: You'll say this when you drink a cup of new wine!

CHORUS: Except for the gods, we'll always hold that you are first.

TRYGAEUS: I, Trygaeus of Athmonon,
Am indeed deserving of many things from you,
920 Since I have set free the common throng of the people from
terrible hardships
And the country folk from terrible labors, and put a stop to Hyperbolos.

SERVANT: Come then, what must we do next?

TRYGAEUS: What else than to install her with dedicatory pots?[110]

CHORUS: With pots? As if she were a contemptible little Herm?[111]

TRYGAEUS: Well what do you think? Do you wish to use a fatted ox?

SERVANT: An ox? Never, lest it then be necessary to give aid in war.[112]

TRYGAEUS: Then a big fat pig?

SERVANT: No! No!

TRYGAEUS: Why not?

SERVANT: So we don't suffer the piggishness of Theogenes.[113]

TRYGAEUS: Well, which of the remaining choices do you favor?

SERVANT: An "alas-sheep."

TRYGAEUS: An "alas-sheep"?![114]

SERVANT: Yes, by Zeus!

---

109. The verb is from *trugaō*, so the speaker puns on his own name.

110. Pots contained bloodless offerings, beans or porridge, which Trygaeus proposes as appropriate for Peace, but which are less impressive than the great and bloody sacrifices of animals.

111. Herms were phallic statues of Hermes and were common throughout Athens. The word translated as "contemptible" might be more literally rendered as "blaming" or "grumbling."

112. There is a pun here on the words for "ox" and "to give aid in war."

113. A common name, so it is not known with precision who this particular Theogenes was. See also *Birds* 822 and *Wasps* 1183–84.

114. In the dative case, the word for sheep is *oi*, which also means "alas." The translation, "an alas-sheep" is an attempt to convey the pun that Aristophanes' audience would have heard.

TRYGAEUS: But this is an Ionian pronunciation.

SERVANT: As intended, since when someone
　Says in the Assembly that we need to go to war, those seated there may
　　say in fear, in the Ionian
　Fashion, "Alas!"—

TRYGAEUS: Well said!

SERVANT: —and may be mild also in other respects as well.
　Thus, in our manners, we will be lambs to
　Each other and much more gentle toward our allies.

TRYGAEUS: Come now, get the sheep as quickly as possible.
　I'll provide the altar on which we will perform the sacrifice.

CHORUS: How all things—all those that god wills and fortune sets aright—
　Go as intended, and one thing follows another,
　At just the right moment!

TRYGAEUS: How clear this is! For look, the altar is right here at the door!

CHORUS: Hurry now, while a lusty breeze prevails,
　Divinely sent and shifting away from war.
　For now a divinity manifestly shifts its direction toward good things.

TRYGAEUS: Here's the ritual basket with barley corns, a garland, and a
　　butcher knife,
　And here's the fire,
　So nothing is holding you back but the sheep.

CHORUS: Won't you two race against each other?
　For if Chaeris[115] sees you,
　He'll come even uninvited to play his flute,
　And then—I know this well—
　You will of course give him something
　For all his hard blowing.

TRYGAEUS: Come, you, take the ritual basket and the lustral water
　And quickly circle the altar, moving toward the right.

SERVANT: Done. What else? I've gone around it.

---

115. See *Birds* 857 and note, and compare such other freeloading characters as Hierocles at
1052–1126 and the unnamed poet in the *Birds* (904–55).

TRYGAEUS: Come, take this torch and dunk it in the water.[116]

960   [To the lamb] Now shake, you, and be quick about it. [To the Servant] And you,

Hand over some of the barley, and wash your hands and hand me the bowl of lustral water,

And throw some of the barley nuts to the spectators.

SERVANT: Done.

TRYGAEUS: You've thrown them already?

SERVANT: Yes, by Hermes:

Of all these who are here watching,

There is no one who does not have nuts.[117]

TRYGAEUS: The women did not get any.

SERVANT: But tonight the men will give it to them.

TRYGAEUS: But let us pray. Who is here?[118] Wherever are "the many and good"?

SERVANT: Come, let me give some to these,[119] for they are many and good.

970 **TRYGAEUS:** You believe them to be good?

SERVANT: Yes, aren't they, those who have come

And are standing their ground in this very same place,

Even though we are pouring all this water on them?

TRYGAEUS: But let us pray as quickly as possible.

SERVANT: Yes, let us pray.

TRYGAEUS: Most august and queenly goddess,

Revered lady Peace, mistress of choruses, mistress of marriages,

Accept our sacrifice.

---

116. The ritual apparently required the celebrant to use a doused firebrand to shake holy water onto the victim. The consequent shaking of the victim would signal assent to its impending sacrifice.

117. The Greek word for "barley corns" is also slang for penis.

118. Religious ritual included this question, the response being, "Many and good [people]." Trygaeus thus calls the merits of the audience into question. The text then plays, at line 972, on a secondary meaning of good as "courageous."

119. He probably sprinkles the chorus and not the audience in general; the chorus has taken risks to recover Peace.

SERVANT: Do accept it, most honored one, by Zeus,
    And don't do what
    Adulterous women do.   980
    For in fact they open the door a bit
    And stoop to peep out,
    And if anyone pays them any mind,
    They retreat,
    And then if he goes away, they stoop and peep again.
    Don't do any of this to us anymore!

TRYGAEUS: No, by Zeus, but freely reveal all of yourself
    To us your lovers,
    Who have been pining with desire for you
    For thirteen years now,[120]   990
    And wash away battles and tumults
    In order that we might call you Lysimache.[121]
    Bring an end
    To our all-too-clever suspicions
    Which we babble against each other,
    And mix us Greeks together again, making a new beginning,
    With the juicy extract of friendship;
    And blend our mind with a gentler sympathy.
    Grant that our marketplace be filled up with good things,
    With large cloves of garlic from Megara, young cucumbers,   1000
    Apples, pomegranates,
    Little woolen garments for our slaves;
    And grant that we see people coming from Boeotia bearing
    Geese, ducks, pigeons, wrens,
    And that baskets of eels arrive from Lake Copais,
    And that we all in a throng join a jostling mob
    Over these dainties, buying them up

---

120. The war began ten years before the performance of the *Peace*. Perhaps Trygaeus mentions thirteen years either because the number is an estimate that also suggests a bad omen or because he wishes to call attention to important events that preceded the war (such as the conflict between Corinth and Corcyra and Athens' treaty with the latter).

121. Lysimache was a priestess of Athena. Her name means "releaser from battle" and is related to the name of the title character of the Lysistrata ("releaser from armies").

Along with Morychus, Teleas, Glaucetes, and many other gluttons.
1010 And grant further that Melanthius come to the market too late,
After the eels have been sold, leaving him to a tragic lament,
And then to sing a song from his *Medea*,
"Woe, woe, I've lost her; I've been widowed of her
While she was lying among the beets."[122]
And grant that human beings rejoice at this.
Grant these things, most honored one, to us who pray.
[To the Servant] Take the knife. See to it that you slaughter the sheep
Like a top chef.

SERVANT: But it is not permitted.

TRYGAEUS: Why not?

SERVANT: Peace certainly does not take pleasure in slaughters,
1020 Nor in an altar stained with blood.

TRYGAEUS: Okay, take it inside and sacrifice it,
Then after you have removed the thigh bones, bring them back out
And thus the sheep will be kept safe for the choregos.[123]

[Exit Servant.]

CHORUS: Then you must stay outside
And quickly put the split wood here
And everything else required for all of this.

TRYGAEUS: Don't you think I'm arranging the firewood as a first-rate
seer would?

CHORUS: How not? For as regards everything pertaining to a wise man,
What has escaped you?
Don't you think everything that must be thought of by one who's
1030 Esteemed as having a wise mind and resourceful daring?

---

122. This lament is probably drawn in part from a lost *Medea*. Melanthius was either the author or played the role of Jason.

123. The *choregos* was the wealthy citizen assigned to pay the considerable costs associated with the performance of this play; Trygaeus is comically assuring him that he will receive the best meat.

TRYGAEUS: In any event, the wood has been lit, and it's afflicting
   Stilbides.[124]

   I'll bring the table, so a boy servant will not be needed.

[Exit Trygaeus.]

CHORUS: Who would not praise such a man,
   Who saved our sacred city by risking everything?[125]
   [Trygaeus returns with the table, the Servant with the thighs.]
   Thus you will never cease being envied by all!

SERVANT: That's done. Take the thigh bones and put them on [the altar fire].
   I'll go for the innards and sacrificial cakes. [He exits.]   1040

TRYGAEUS: I'll take care of this. [Calling to the Servant] You should have
   been back already!

[The Servant returns with innards and sacrificial cakes.]

SERVANT: Look: I'm here. Do I seem to be holding back?

TRYGAEUS: Roast them in fine fashion now, because someone is coming
   with a laurel crown.[126]

SERVANT: Whoever is he?

TRYGAEUS: He looks like a boaster.

SERVANT: Is he a seer?

TRYGAEUS: No, by Zeus, but it's apparently Hierocles,[127]
   The oracle-collector from Oreus.

SERVANT: What will he have to say?

TRYGAEUS: It's clear he'll somehow oppose the treaty.

SERVANT: No, he's come because of the savory smoke.   1050

---

124. Stilbides was a seer who later went to Sicily with Nicias. Trygaeus implies that his own broad competence enables him to dispense with help from a seer (as Peisetairos eventually rid himself of the priest in the *Birds*).

125. Strauss detects here a reference to Odysseus, though he destroyed a holy city whereas Trygaeus saved one (*Socrates and Aristophanes* 155).

126. The crown or garland suggests he is a professional priest and may expect deference.

127. Hierocles was a prominent Athenian interpreter of oracles.

TRYGAEUS: Let's seem not to see him.

SERVANT: Well said.

HIEROCLES: Whatever is this sacrifice, and to which of the gods?

TRYGAEUS [to the Servant]: Roast in silence, and keep away from the rump.

HIEROCLES: Will you not say to whom you are sacrificing?

TRYGAEUS [to the Servant]: The tail is doing fine.

SERVANT: Fine indeed. Dear Revered Lady Peace.

HIEROCLES: Come now, offer the first fruits, and then hand over the dedicated innards.

TRYGAEUS: It's better to roast them first.

HIEROCLES: But these here are already roasted!

TRYGAEUS: You are meddling, whoever you are! [To the Servant] Cut up the meat.

HIEROCLES[128]: Where's the table?

TRYGAEUS [to the Servant]: Bring the libation.

1060 **HIEROCLES**: The tongue is to be cut out and kept separate.

TRYGAEUS: We remember. But do you know what you need to do?

HIEROCLES: I will if you tell me.

TRYGAEUS: Don't converse with us at all; for we are making holy sacrifice to Peace.

HIEROCLES: "O mortals pointless and childish,—"[129]

TRYGAEUS: Look who's talking!

HIEROCLES: "—you men who in your folly do not comprehend the mind of the gods, you have
Made compacts with glaring-eyed monkeys—"

TRYGAEUS: Oh, my, my!

---

128. Some assign these lines to the servant, others to Trygaeus. There is considerable disagreement over who says what in this section of the play.

129. The grandiose style of Hierocles' speeches here are standard for oracles delivered in verse.

HIEROCLES: Why are you laughing?

TRYGAEUS: I'm pleasantly amused by
  "Glaring-eyed monkeys."

HIEROCLES: "—and trembling gulls put
  Their trust in fox cubs, whose souls are deceitful, and deceitful as well are
    their wits."

TRYGAEUS: Would that you, boaster, had lungs as hot as these I'm cooking!

HIEROCLES: "For if the goddess nymphs did not deceive Bacis,[130]   1070
  Nor Bacis the mortals, nor the nymphs Bacis himself,—"

TRYGAEUS: May you perish, utterly destroyed, if you do not stop Bacizing.

HIEROCLES: "—it was not yet ordained divinely to loosen the fetters of
  Peace, but first—"

TRYGAEUS: —we must sprinkle on some salt.

HIEROCLES: "For this is not yet dear to the blessed gods, to cease from the
  din of battle,
  Until a wolf weds a sheep."

TRYGAEUS: And how, cursed one, could a wolf ever wed a sheep?

HIEROCLES: "So long as the Beetle lays most evil farts while fleeing, and in
  her eagerness for the pangs of birth Akalanthis
  Brings forth blind ones, so long must peace not be concluded."

TRYGAEUS: But what ought we to have done? Never stop making war?   1080
  Or cast lots to determine which side would cry louder,
  Even when it is possible to make a treaty and rule together over Greece?

HIEROCLES: "You will never make the crab walk upright."

TRYGAEUS: You will never in the future have another dinner in
  the Prytaneum,[131]
  Nor will you compose oracles afterwards about something that's already
  been done.

---

130. A famous Boeotian prophet. See also *Birds* 962 (and note); *Knights* 123–24, 1003–04.

131. The Athenians offered meals at public expense in the Prytaneum for officials, dignitaries, and others deemed worthy of honor.

HIEROCLES: "Nor would you ever make smooth the hedgehog's
  rough spines."

TRYGAEUS: Will you, then, ever stop your hoodwinking of the Athenians?

HIEROCLES: In keeping with what oracle was it that you burned thighs for
  the gods?

TRYGAEUS: The most noble one Homer composed, of course:[132]
1090 "Thus thrusting back the hateful cloud of war,
  They chose Peace and established her with a sacrificial victim.
  But when the thighs were burned and they partook of the innards,
  They poured a libation with their cups, and I was leading the way . . ."
  But no one gave a gleaming cup to the oracle-collector!

HIEROCLES: This has nothing to do with me: Sybil did not say it.

TRYGAEUS: But the wise Homer, by Zeus, did make this clever statement:
  "Clanless, lawless, and heartless is he
  Who loves horrid war among his people."[133]

HIEROCLES: "Beware lest a kite somehow seize your wits,
1100 Using some bait to deceive you . . ."

TRYGAEUS [to the Servant]: Yes, do guard against this,
  For this oracle is threatening to seize the innards.
  Pour the libation, and bring here some of the innards.

HIEROCLES: But if this has been settled, I'll be my own bath attendant.[134]

TRYGAEUS: Libation! libation!

HIEROCLES: Pour some for me too, and hand me a share of the innards.

TRYGAEUS: But this is not yet dear to the blessed gods.
  The following must first occur: we pour libations, you go away.
  Revered lady Peace, stay beside us throughout our lives.

HIEROCLES: Serve me the tongue.

TRYGAEUS: Get yours out of here. Libation!

---

132. Trygaeus is faking; his lines may echo Homer, but there is no exact reference.

133. These two lines replicate *Iliad* 9.63–64. Nestor here seeks to persuade Achilles to cease
quarreling with Agamemnon so he can rejoin the fighting against the Trojans.

134. That is, I'll help myself to the innards.

SERVANT: And take these with the libation, quickly. 1110

HIEROCLES: Will no one give me some of the innards?

TRYGAEUS: No, for it is impossible for us to give you any until a wolf weds
a sheep.

HIEROCLES: Please! I'm at your knees.

TRYGAEUS: Your supplication is in vain, fellow.
For you will not make smooth the hedgehog's rough spines.
Come here, spectators, and share in the innards with us.

HIEROCLES: And as for me?

TRYGAEUS: Feed on your Sybil.

HIEROCLES: No, by Earth, don't you two alone eat this!
I'll take them from you; they're up for grabs.

TRYGAEUS: Beat this Bacis, beat him!

HIEROCLES: I call for witnesses!

TRYGAEUS: And I do too, because you're a glutton and a boaster of a man! 1120
Keep striking him with that stick, the boaster!

SERVANT: You do it. I'll peel those sheepskins off him,
Which he acquires by fraud.
Won't you throw off those sheepskins, Mr. Sacrificer?

TRYGAEUS: Did you hear? [Hierocles runs away.] What a crow[135] is he who
came from
Oreus. Won't he fly off that much more quickly to Elumnios![136]

CHORUS[137]: I'm pleased. I'm pleased,
Having been set free from my helmet,
Cheese, and onions.
For I'm not fond of battles, 1130
But of drinking by the fire
With men who are companions and friends—

---

135. Crows were wont to steal food from altars.

136. A place near Oreus, whence Hierocles had come. There was also a sanctuary there, making it an appropriate spot for an oracle-collector.

137. The second parabasis begins here and ends at 1190.

Kindling the sticks that were cut
And dried during the summer,
And roasting some of my chickpeas,
And grilling some acorns,
And at the same time, kissing the Thracian [servant] girl
While my wife is bathing.

1140 **CHORUS LEADER**: Nothing is more pleasant than having the fields sown,
With the god sprinkling rain on them, and some neighbor who says,
"Tell me, what shall we do to pass the time, Comarchides?"[138]
"Drinking our fill would be pleasing to me, at least, since the god is
acting in fine fashion.
So toast three quarts of beans, wife,
And mix in some wheat with them, and take out some figs,
And have Syra call Manes in from the fields.[139]
For it's not at all possible to prune the vines or work the soil today,
Since the ground is sopping wet.
And let someone bring from my house a thrush and the pair of finches.
1150 There is also some cream there and four hares,
Unless a weasel took one of them off during the night.
(There was one inside making I know not what sort of racket and
battle-din!)
Bring three of the hares to us, boy, and give one to my father.
Ask for myrtle branches[140] with berries at Aeschinades' house.
And while on the course of this errand, let someone shout for Carinades,
So he might drink his fill with us
Since the god is doing good
And benefiting our ploughlands."

CHORUS: And when the cicada
1160 Sings his sweet melody,
I take pleasure

---

138. This name could mean either "leader of the village" or "leader of the revels" or both. In the lines that follow (1142–58), the Chorus fantasizes an answer to the imaginary question (1141) of "some neighbor."

139. Syra and Manes were common names for slaves.

140. These were woven into wreaths that were worn or held up at banquets during drinking songs.

In examining my Lemnian vines,
To see if they have already ripened their fruit,
(For this plant is early by nature),
And the wild fig, which I see swelling.
And when it is ripe,
I eat, and I keep at it,
And at the same time I say, "Dear Seasons!"
And I crush and mix thyme to drink,
And then I become fat   1170
At that time of the summer—

CHORUS LEADER: —more than I do looking at a commander, hateful to
    the gods,
With his triple crests and bright crimson uniform,
Which he says is dyed work from Sardis.[141]
But if ever he must do battle in that crimson uniform,
He then dyes it all by himself with a brown dye.[142]
Then he is the first to run away, shaking his crests, like a quick-darting
    cock-horse,[143]
While I stand my ground and guard the nets.[144]
And when they are at home, what they do is unbearable.
For they enroll[145] some of us two or three times,   1180
And strike others out, all haphazardly. The expedition is tomorrow,
But someone has purchased no provisions, for he did not know he
    was going;
Then standing by the statue of Pandion,[146] he sees himself; and at a loss
    because of this nasty
Surprise, he runs off with a sour look on his face.

---

141. Once the capital of Lydia and known for its wealth and luxury.

142. Literally, "a dye from Cyzicus," a city whose well-known coins were brown.

143. Such a mythical creature appeared in Aeschylus. See also *Birds* 800.

144. A comparison to those hunters who stay by the nets toward which wild game is driven.

145. Commanders levied soldiers for particular expeditions by posting their names, but it appears some served more frequently than others. See also *Knights* 1369–71.

146. Citizens of Athens were divided into ten tribes, each named for an ancestral hero. Aristophanes was himself of the tribe of Pandion. On the base of the statue of each eponymous hero were placed notices of draftees from that tribe.

This is what they do to us rustics, but less so to those from the city—
These who throw their shields away before both gods and men.[147]
For all of this these commanders will yet make a public reckoning to me,
    if god is willing.
For they've been unjust to me in many things,
Being lions at home
1190   But foxes in battle![148]

TRYGAEUS: Wow! Wow!
    What a great throng has come to dinner for the wedding feast!
    Here, clean off the tables with this,[149]
    Because there's no further need for it at all.
    Then heap up the cakes and thrushes,
    And a good deal of the hare, and the wheat rolls.

[Enter Sickle-Maker and Potter with sickles and crocks.]

SICKLE-MAKER: Where, where is Trygaeus?

TRYGAEUS: I'm stewing thrushes.

SICKLE-MAKER: Dearest Trygaeus:
    How many good things you've done for us by making peace!
1200   For before, no one would ever buy a sickle, not even at the price of
        a penny,
    But now I'm selling them for fifty drachmas;
    And this potter here is selling his rustic crocks for three drachmas.
    So, Trygaeus, take for free any of these sickles and crocks
    You want. Accept these things as well.
    For from what we have sold and the profits we've gained,
    We bring you these gifts for your wedding.

TRYGAEUS: Come now, put them down beside me
    And come in to dinner as quickly as possible,
    For here's an arms-merchant approaching in anger.

---

147. To throw one's shield away was to abandon the fight and run away.

148. Foxes hide in holes.

149. It is not clear what Trygaeus hands over to be used in the cleaning of the tables, although the next line suggests it is some decoration or garment associated with the military life which he now rejects and mocks.

[Enter an Arms-Merchant accompanied by makers of helmet-crests, breastplates, trumpets, helmets, and spears, each carrying his wares.]

ARMS-MERCHANT: Oh, Trygaeus! How you've destroyed me, root 1210
and branch!

TRYGAEUS: What is it, wretch? Are you sick with crestiness?

ARMS-MERCHANT: You have destroyed my art and livelihood—
And his, and that spear-maker's too!

TRYGAEUS: In that case, what might I pay you for this pair of crests?

ARMS-MERCHANT: What would you pay?

TRYGAEUS: What would I pay? I'm ashamed.
Nevertheless, a lot of work went into the attachment of the hairs,
So I'd pay three quarts of dried figs for the pair of crests,
So I could clean up the table with this one.[150]

ARMS-MERCHANT: Go in and get the dried figs, then. [Trygaeus leaves to
get the figs.]
[To the maker of crests] It's better to get something than nothing, 1220
good fellow.

[Trygaeus returns.]

TRYGAEUS: Take them away! Take them away! To the crows with them!
Away from the house!
They're shedding their hairs! This pair is worthless!
I wouldn't pay even one fig for them!

ARMS-MERCHANT: For what, then, will I—wretched I—use
This breastplate, most beautifully fitted and worth ten minas?[151]

TRYGAEUS: Let this not prove a loss to you!
Take this, of equal value, from me.
For what you have is quite suitable for crapping into—

---

150. Beginning here, and continuing for approximately forty-five lines, Trygaeus' jokes involve the comic transformation of heroic implements of war to mundane and even scatological peacetime purposes.

151. The arms-merchant underscores his woe by using tragic vocabulary: more literally, "this hollow of a breastplate." Ten minas, or 1000 drachmas, was a huge, perhaps an unbelievable sum, for a breastplate.

ARMS-MERCHANT: Stop insulting my wares!

1230 **TRYGAEUS**: —if one steadies it with three stones.[152] Clever, no?

ARMS-MERCHANT: No, for how will you ever wipe yourself, ignoramus?

TRYGAEUS: Like this, slipping my hand through the oar-port, and thus too
   with my other one.[153]

ARMS-MERCHANT: So you'd use both ports?

TRYGAEUS: I would, by Zeus, so I wouldn't get caught stealing an oar-port
   from the ship.[154]

ARMS-MERCHANT: So you're going to sit and shit on a ten-mina corselet?

TRYGAEUS: I will, by Zeus, you accursed rogue:
   Do you think that I would sell my asshole for a thousand drachmas?[155]

ARMS-MERCHANT: Come, then. Get the money.

TRYGAEUS: But, good fellow, it's too tight around my bottom. Take it away; I
   won't buy it.

1240 **ARMS-MERCHANT**: And for what will I use this trumpet,
   Which I once bought for sixty drachmas?

TRYGAEUS: Pour lead into its bell, and then
   On the topside insert a longish rod,
   And you will have a target for the game of flinging wine dregs.

ARMS-MERCHANT: Alas, you're mocking me.

TRYGAEUS: Then I'll recommend something else.
   Pour in lead, just as I said.
   Then attach the pan of a balance, hanging it by little cords,
   And even this will make it possible for you to weigh figs in the field for
   your servants.

---

152. Or "puts three stones next to it [to use for wiping]." Cf. *Wealth* 817.

153. He likens the arm holes of the breastplate to the oar-ports of a ship.

154. Athenians who outfitted warships sometimes drew wages for rowers they never hired,
thus leaving some oar-ports unused and stealing the wages of the absent rowers.

155. A thousand drachmas was the equivalent of ten mina. Trygaeus wishes to indicate that his
posterior is worth a vast amount. See note 151.

ARMS-MERCHANT: You divinity so hard to propitiate![156] How you have
    destroyed me,
Since I once paid a mina also for these.[157]
And now what will I do? For who will buy them?

TRYGAEUS: Go and sell them to the Egyptians,
    For they're suitable for measuring laxatives.[158]

ARMS-MERCHANT: Alas, helmet-maker, how wretchedly we have fared.

TRYGAEUS: He has not fared badly at all.

ARMS-MERCHANT: But what will anyone still use these helmets for?

TRYGAEUS: If he learns how to make handles like these,[159]
    He'll sell them at a much better price than now.

ARMS-MERCHANT: Let's go, spear-maker.

TRYGAEUS: No way, don't leave, since I'll buy these spears of his.

ARMS-MERCHANT: Sure; but at what price?

TRYGAEUS: If they were sawn in two, I'd take them for vine stakes at one
    hundred per drachma.

ARMS-MERCHANT: We're being insulted! Let's get out of here, good fellow!

TRYGAEUS: Yes, by Zeus, because the children of the invited guests are
    already coming out
Here to piss, so—as it seems to me—
They can rehearse what they will sing later.
Whatever you have in mind to sing, boy,
Stand here beside me and rehearse it first.

BOY A: "Now let us begin with those more able to bear arms . . ."[160]

---

156. For calling a human being a harsh or difficult divinity, see also *Clouds* 1264.

157. It is not clear what the Arms-Merchant now shows to Trygaeus.

158. At least as reported by Herodotus (2.77), the Egyptians used laxatives on a routine basis.

159. Trygaeus presumably gestures to the handles on large jars, which suggests a peacetime use for helmets as wine vessels.

160. The children begin to sing portions of war epics; at line 1280 Trygaeus imitates the meter of their songs but radically changes the content.

TRYGAEUS: Stop singing about bearing arms! Especially since Peace
is present,
You with the triply-sick spirit;
You are ignorant and accursed!

BOY A: "And when in their advance they were at close quarters,
They thrust their bucklers and shields, fortified at the center, against
each other."

TRYGAEUS: Shields! Won't you stop reminding us of shields?

BOY A: "Then at the same time were there groans and shouts of triumph
from the men."

TRYGAEUS: Groans of men? You'll shed tears for it, by Dionysius,
If you sing of groans, and of ones fortified at the center at that!

BOY A: But of what then shall I sing? Tell me what things you delight in.

1280 **TRYGAEUS**: "Thus did they feast on the meat of cattle," and things like this:
"They arranged their breakfast and whatever was most pleasant to eat."

BOY A: "Thus did they feast on the meat of cattle, and they set free from
Their harnesses the sweating necks of their horses, when they were sated
with war."

TRYGAEUS: Okay. They were sated with war, and then they started to eat.
Sing this, how after they were sated they kept on eating.

BOY A: "Then when they stopped, they armed themselves—"

TRYGAEUS: —with gladness, I think.

BOY A: "—and went forth from their fortifications, and an unquenchable
shout arose."

TRYGAEUS: May you perish in the worst way, boy, you and your battles!
For you sing of nothing but wars. Whose son are you, anyway?

BOY A: Me?

TRYGAEUS: Yes, you, by Zeus.

1290 **BOY A**: I am the son of Lamachus.[161]

---

161. For Lamachus, whom Aristophanes treats as a war-mongering general, see line 304
and note.

TRYGAEUS: Yuck! I was wondering, as I listened, if you weren't the son of
  some man who
  Wished for battle and then later cried over battle.
  Get out of here and go sing to the spear-carriers.
  Where is Cleonymus's[162] boy?
  [Another youth comes forward.] Sing something before you go in,
  For I know well that you will not sing of troubles.
  For you are the boy of a moderate father.

BOY B: "Some Saean exults over my shield, a faultless weapon,
  Which I unwillingly left behind beside a bush,—"[163]

TRYGAEUS: Tell me, you little pecker, are you singing about your   1300
  own father?

BOY B: "—but I saved my life!"

TRYGAEUS: But shamed your parents!
  But let's go in. I know very well that there's no way you will ever forget
  What you were just now singing about the shield,
  Since you are born of that father.
  The work that remains for all of you who remain out here is now
  To crush and chew all this food, and not to work your jaws in vain.[164]
  But go at it bravely
  And grind with both jaws.
  For your white teeth do no work, rascals,
  If they are not chewing.   1310

CHORUS LEADER: We'll attend to this, at least; but you for your part do well
  to tell us to do so.
  You who used to be hungry, tuck into the hares!

---

162. For Cleonymus, who was famous for dropping his shield on the battlefield and running away, see line 446 and note. The very mention of his name prepares the audience for a shield-dropping joke, which comes a few lines later at line 1300. First, though, Aristophanes presents the boy as reciting the famous shield epigram of the poet Archilochus, thus lending authority to the anti-heroic point of view.

163. These two lines begin Archilochus' anti-heroic epigram, which concludes, "But at least I saved my life. What's that shield to me?/Let it go. Some other time I'll get another not any worse," a sentiment that Trygaeus might applaud (but does not). A "Saean" is a Thracian.

164. More literally, not to pull useless oars.

For it is not every day that it is possible
To chance upon cakes wandering about all unprotected.
So go ahead and start shoveling it in, or I say you'll regret it soon.

TRYGAEUS: Keep an auspicious silence, and let someone bring the bride
out here,
And bring the torches, and let all the people rejoice and cheer us on.
And now take the implements back again to the fields, while
Dancing, pouring libations, and driving Hyperbolus away,
1320 And praying to the gods
That they give wealth to the Greeks,
And that we produce lots of barley
And similarly much wine
And figs to nibble;
And that our wives bear for us,
And that we gather together again all good things,
As many as we lost, in a new beginning,
And put a stop to gleaming iron.
Come here, wife, to the field,
1330 And, my beauty, lie down with me, beautifully.
Hymen, Hymeneus O![165]

CHORUS LEADER: Thrice-blessed,
How justly you now have good things!

CHORUS: Hymen, Hymeneus O!
Hymen, Hymeneus O!

HALF-CHORUS A: What shall we do with her?

HALF-CHORUS B: What shall we do with her?

HALF-CHORUS A: We'll gather her fruit![166]

HALF-CHORUS B: We'll gather her fruit!

HALF-CHORUS A: But let those of us up front
1340 Raise up the groom, men,
And carry him.

---

165. Two names of the god of marriage.
166. The verb is a pun on the hero's name—"We will Trygaeus her." See also 913.

CHORUS: Hymen, Hymeneus O!
    Hymen, Hymeneus O!

TRYGAEUS: You will live beautifully,
    And have no problems,
    Gathering your figs.[167]

CHORUS: Hymen, Hymeneus O!
    Hymen, Hymeneus O!

HALF-CHORUS A: His fig is big and thick;

HALF-CHORUS B: Hers is sweet!   1350

TRYGAEUS: You will say so, at least, when you are eating,
    And drinking much wine.

CHORUS: Hymen, Hymeneus O!
    Hymen, Hymeneus O!

TRYGAEUS: Farewell, farewell, men!
    And if you follow me,
    You will eat cake!

---

167. The word for fig is a double-entendre for the female and the male genitals.

WEALTH

DRAMATIS PERSONAE[1]

CARIO [slave of Chremylos]
CHREMYLOS[2]
WEALTH [the god Plutus][3]
CHORUS OF FARMERS [with **LEADER**]
BLEPSIDEMOS [friend of Chremylos]
POVERTY [the goddess Penia]
WIFE of Chremylos
A JUST MAN
A "SYCOPHANT" [a false accuser, who has harassed the rich with lawsuits in order to get money by settlements]
OLD WOMAN
YOUNG MAN [former lover of Old Woman]
HERMES [the god]
A PRIEST OF ZEUS

[Mute Characters:
CHILD OF JUST MAN
WITNESS OF SYCOPHANT]

---

1. Bracketed material lacks manuscript authority; it is intended only to facilitate a first reading of the play. Line numbers are borrowed from the Greek texts of the plays; they will not always be sequential in English.

2. In the words of the fifth "*hypothesis*," or summary of the play, found in the manuscripts (and dating from Hellenistic commentators), "Chremylos is constructed from *chreos* [debt] and *haimulos* [wily] as 'deceptive': so, 'the one who deceives his debtors—on account of poverty'; and Cario is clearly Greek for 'slave,' . . . and Blepsidemus is a word signifying a beggar, who's looking always to the *demos* [populace]."

3. In *Theogony* (967–74) Hesiod commences his account of "Those goddesses who, having slept with mortal men / Being immortal, gave birth to children like unto gods" with "Demeter, Who, a goddess among goddesses, gave birth to Plutus [Wealth] / Having mingled in erotic affection with the hero Iasion / On a thrice-ploughed fallow field in the fertile land of Crete: / He, noble one, goes across the earth and the wide back of the sea, / Everywhere; and for whomever He encounters, and into whose hands He comes, / He establishes abundance, and to him He annexes great riches." See also the end of the Homeric *Hymn to Demeter* 488–89.

CARIO: How grievous a business it is—Oh Zeus and gods!—
To become the slave of a master who has lost his *wits*!
For if the servant should happen to say what is best,
But the opinion of the owner is against doing these things,
The servant must necessarily share in the evils.
For the divinity doesn't allow the one who is sovereign
To rule over the body, but rather the purchaser.
So be it. . . . But Loxias,[4]
"Who sings oracles from a tripod of beaten gold,"[5]
I blame, with this just blame: that   10
Being a healer and a wise prophet, as they assert,
He sent my master away in a melancholy-mad state,
Who's following along behind a blind fellow,[6]
Doing the contrary of what it befits him to do!
For we who see are the guides of the blind,
But he follows, and also constrains me to do so,
And in regard to these things responds with not even a grunt![7]
. . . [To Chremylos] Now there's no way that I'll remain silent,
If you will not explain why in the world we are following this fellow,
Master, but I will keep bothering you.   20
For you won't beat me while I'm wearing this wreath at least.[8]

CHREMYLOS: By Zeus, I'll take off the wreath, if you cause me any grief,
So that you will suffer worse!

CARIO: Nonsense! I will *not* stop,
Until you explain to me *who* in the world *this* is;
For I ask this out of great goodwill towards you.

---

4. "The Oblique One"—an epithet of Apollo, on account of the obliquity or ambiguity of his oracles.

5. A line in tragic style, perhaps from a tragedy which we no longer have. Aristophanes regularly thus parodies or spoofs the solemn lines from awesome tragedy.

6. Literally, "blind human" (*anthrōpos*)—the divinity of Plutus is not recognizable to Cario.

7. This is Bentley's emendation of the obviously faulty reading of two of the three main manuscripts; the third manuscript has a reading that makes it Plutus whose silence is being referred to by Cario.

8. Worn for the ritual of consulting the oracle at Delphi, from which they are returning.

CHREMYLOS: But I won't hide it from you; because, among my household
    Slaves, I consider you the most trustworthy and thieving.
    I, being a god-revering and just man, have
    Fared poorly and been impoverished.

CARIO: That I know.

30 **CHREMYLOS:** But others are wealthy: temple-robbers, orators,
    And sycophants, and rascals!

CARIO: I am persuaded of it.

CHREMYLOS: So, I went to inquire of the god—
    As regards my own miserable life,
    Believing that the arrows had pretty much been shot;
    But as regards my son, who happens to be my only one—
    Inquiring if *he* ought to change *his* ways,
    So as to be all around wicked, unjust, wholesome in not a single respect:
    On the belief that this would be of advantage in life.

CARIO: What then did Phoebus pronounce, from the sacred wreaths?[9]

40 **CHREMYLOS:** You will learn. For the god plainly said to me the following.
    Whomever I might encounter when I first went out,[10]
    He bade me not to leave off from this person anymore,
    But to persuade him to follow me home.

CARIO: And who was the first you encountered?

CHREMYLOS: This fellow.

CARIO: But didn't you understand the thought of the god,
    Which was expressed—you most benighted one!—most plainly:
    That your son was to practice the *local custom*?!

CHREMYLOS: On what do you base this judgment?

CARIO: It is so obvious that
    Even a blind man is of the opinion that he knows that it is highly
50   Advantageous to practice nothing wholesome nowadays![11]

---

9. Another line in high tragic style, spoofing tragedy. Phoebus is a name of Apollo.

10. A spoofing echo of Euripides' tragedy *Ion* 534ff.

11. Another spoofing echo of a fragment of Euripides: *Tennes*, frag. 695, "there is nothing just nowadays."

CHREMYLOS: It is not possible that *that's* the drift of the oracle!
  It must incline toward something else GREATER. But now if to us
  This fellow would explain whoever in the world he is, and why and
  For what need he has come here, with us two,
  We would learn what the oracle has in mind for us.

CARIO [to the blind Wealth]: Hey, you! Explain yourself, who you might be,
  Or do I do THIS!? You need to talk fast!

WEALTH: I say to you: go holler!

CARIO: Did you hear who he said he is?

CHREMYLOS: He said this to *you*, not to *me*—obviously,
  Because *you* inquired of him in a gauche and harsh fashion.   60
  But [speaking to Wealth] if you are pleased by the ways of an
  Oath-Keeping man, give the explanation to me.

WEALTH: I for my part say to you: go weep!

CARIO: Accept the man and the omen of the god.

CHREMYLOS: By Demeter, you won't stay satisfied!

CARIO: Because if you don't tell me, I will destroy you, evil one, in an
    evil fashion!

WEALTH: Fellow, get away from me, both of you!

CHREMYLOS: Oh yeah!?

CARIO: Now what I say is best, Master:
  I shall exterminate this human, in the worst way!
  For, having placed him on some cliff, I'll leave him
  And go away, from whence he'll fall, breaking his neck!   70

CHREMYLOS: So take him quickly!

WEALTH: No way!

CHREMYLOS: Will you not answer?

WEALTH: But if you two should learn of me who I am, I know well that
  You two will do me some harm, and will not let me go!

CHREMYLOS: But by the gods, we will, if you wish it!

WEALTH: First let go of me.

CHREMYLOS: There, we let go of you.

WEALTH: Now listen. For it seems that it is necessary for me
    To utter what I was prepared to keep secret. . . .
    For, I am *Wealth*!

CHREMYLOS: You most abominable
    Of all men! You, being Wealth, kept silent about it?

80 **CARIO**: YOU are Wealth, in this miserable condition!?

CHREMYLOS: Oh Phoebus Apollo, and gods and lesser divinities!—
    And Zeus! What *are* you saying? YOU, in this state, are really *him*?

WEALTH: Yes.

CHREMYLOS: That One Himself?

WEALTH: The very one.

CHREMYLOS: From where, then, do you say
    You are walking, in this squalid condition?

WEALTH: I am coming from Patrocles'[12] place,
    Who has never bathed since he was born.

CHREMYLOS: How did you come to suffer so badly? Tell me.

WEALTH: Zeus did these things to me, out of envy for humans.
    For when I was a lad, I vowed that
    To the just and wise and orderly
90   Only would I go; and he made me blind,
    So that I would not be able to distinguish any of these.
    Just so, That One envies the worthy.

CHREMYLOS: And yet it is on account of[13] the worthy alone, and the just,
    That he is honored!

WEALTH: I agree with you.

---

12. The name belongs to Socrates' younger half-brother (Plato, *Euthydemus* 297e), who appears to have been a wealthy and prominent office holder during the struggles surrounding the tyranny of The Thirty (Isocrates 18.5–8; Debra Nails, *People of Plato* [Indianapolis: Hackett, 2002], 218–19)—and Socrates is repeatedly satirized as failing to bathe by Aristophanes: *Clouds* 836, *Birds* 1282.

13. "On account of" translates the word *dia*, which can mean either "by means of," "through," or "on account of," "for the sake of"—and this ambiguity is repeatedly present in the lines that follow.

CHREMYLOS: Look here,
    If you could see again, as before,
    Would you avoid the wicked?

WEALTH: I do declare so.

CHREMYLOS: And you would frequent the just?

WEALTH: By all means.
    For I have not seen them for a long time.

CHREMYLOS: That's no wonder; neither have I, who can see!

WEALTH: Now let me go. For you know about me.   100

CHREMYLOS: By Zeus, so much the more will we hold you!

WEALTH: Did I not proclaim that you two were going to give me trouble?

CHREMYLOS: And you, I entreat, be persuaded,
    And don't leave me! For you will not find,
    In seeking, another man better in his ways than me.

CARIO: By Zeus, there isn't another, except me!

WEALTH: That's what they all say. But when they
    Truly happen upon me and become wealthy,
    Their wickedness simply has no limits!

CHREMYLOS: That's so—but not all are bad!   110

WEALTH: But by Zeus, yes, every single one!

CARIO: You'll grieve for that!

CHREMYLOS: But to know how many good things will accrue to you, if
    You stay with us, pay heed, so that you'll learn:
    For I think—I think—with the god's help, be it said,[14]
    That I shall rid you of this illness of the eyes,
    And make you see!

WEALTH: That may you never do,
    Because I do not wish to see again!

CHREMYLOS: What are you saying?!

CARIO: This human is miserable by nature!

---

14. A spoofing echo of Euripides' *Medea* 625.

WEALTH: Zeus, knowing about the follies of these people, if he should
120   Learn, would rub me out!

CHREMYLOS: But doesn't he do that *now*,
He who lets you stumble around?

WEALTH: I don't know. I shudder very much at *That* One.

CHREMYLOS: In truth?—you most cowardly of all divinities!
For do you suppose that the tyranny of Zeus,
And His thunderbolts, would be worth two cents,
If you were able to see again for even a short time?

WEALTH: Don't say these things, you rascal!

CHREMYLOS: Remain calm;
For I shall demonstrate that YOU are *much* more powerful
Than Zeus!

WEALTH: You mean *me*?

CHREMYLOS: By Uranus [Heaven], Yes!
130   Look, [to Cario] on account of *what* does Zeus rule over the gods?

CARIO: On account of money; because he has most of it.

CHREMYLOS: Come, who is it that provides it to him?

CARIO: This One! [Pointing to Wealth.]

CHREMYLOS: And on account of whom do they sacrifice to him? Isn't it on
account of This One?

CARIO: And by Zeus, they straightaway pray to become wealthy!

CHREMYLOS: So isn't This One the cause, and couldn't he easily
Make these things cease, if he wished?

WEALTH: What do you mean?

CHREMYLOS: That not a single one among humans would sacrifice
anymore—
Not an ox, not a cake, not a single thing,
If you didn't wish it!

WEALTH: How so?

CHREMYLOS: How so? There's no way
140   How anyone will be able to *buy* from anywhere, if you aren't
Present yourself, to give the money! So that

The power of Zeus, if he should give you any grief, you can by
    yourself dissolve!

WEALTH: What are you saying? On account of *me*, they sacrifice to Zeus?

CHREMYLOS: That's what I'm asserting. And by Zeus, if anything is shining,
    And beautiful, or charming for humans, it comes about on account
    Of you. For all things are subservient to wealth.

CARIO: In my own case, it is on account of a teeny bit of money that
    I have become a slave—on account of not being equally wealthy.[15]

CHREMYLOS: And they say that the Corinthian courtesans,
    When some poor bloke tries to engage them,   150
    Pay him no mind; but if he's wealthy,
    They turn their assholes to him straightway on this account.

CARIO: And they say the boys do this very same thing,
    For the sake, not of their lovers, but of the money.

CHREMYLOS: The worthy ones don't, but the whores; since
    The worthy don't ask for money.

CARIO: For what, then?

CHREMYLOS: One for a good horse; and one for hunting dogs.

CARIO: That's probably because, being ashamed to ask for money,
    They gloss the baseness over with a name.

CHREMYLOS: On account of *you*, all arts and clever crafts   160
    That exist among humans have been discovered:
    For one of us sits making shoes—

CARIO: And there's another who works at bronze, and one as carpenter—

CHREMYLOS: And one smelts gold, taking the gold from *you*—

CARIO: And one's a thief, by Zeus, and one's a burglar—

CHREMYLOS: And one's a fuller—

CARIO: And one washes fleece—

CHREMYLOS: And one tans hides—

---

15. The scholia at this point lead some to substitute for the phrase after the dash a different phrase: "having been a freeman before."

CARIO: And one sells onions—

CHREMYLOS: And on account of *you*, the nabbed adulterer is plucked![16]

WEALTH: Alas, miserable me! This has for a long time escaped my notice!

170 **CARIO:** Isn't it on account of This One that the Great King preens himself?

CHREMYLOS: Isn't it on account of This One that the Assembly meets?

CARIO: What about the triremes? Don't you fill them? Tell me!

CHREMYLOS: Isn't it This One who feeds the foreign legion in Corinth?[17]

CARIO: Won't Pamphilus[18] come to grief on account of This One?

CHREMYLOS: And The Needle-seller along with Pamphilus?

CARIO: Doesn't Agyrrhius fart on account of This One?

CHREMYLOS: Does not Philepsius relate his stories for your sake?[19]

CARIO: Isn't the alliance with the Egyptians on account of you?[20]

CHREMYLOS: Doesn't Lais love Philonides for your sake?[21]

180 **CARIO:** And the tower of Timotheus[22]—

CHREMYLOS: —may it fall on you!
But are not all affairs brought about on account of *you*?
For, that *you*, most singularly, are the cause of all,
Both of bad things and of good, know well.

---

16. An adulterer caught by the husband could be put to death; "plucking" refers to the alternative punishment, his paying a large sum to have his pubic hairs plucked.

17. A force placed in Corinth by the Athenian general Iphicrates after a Spartan attack in 390 B.C.: Xenophon, *Hellenica* 4.5 (the *Wealth* as we have it was first produced in 388 B.C.).

18. An Athenian general who led a force to Aegina in 389 B.C. (Xenophon, *Hellenica* 5.1.2), and who was apparently charged with theft of public funds (see frag. 14 of the comic poet Plato); his associate Aristoxenus was known as the "needle-seller."

19. Demosthenes (24.134–35) refers to Philepsius and Agyrrhius as prominent political figures, and reports that the former was thrown into prison for embezzlement; his "stories" would presumably be the excuses he gave to the court; Agyrrhius is satirized in *Assembly of Women* 102ff.

20. Athens allied with the king of Cyprus and the Pharaoh of Egypt against Persia in 391 B.C. (Xenophon, *Hellenica* 4.8.24 and 5.1.10).

21. Lais was a legendary courtesan residing in Corinth (see also below, 303–6); Philonides of Melite was an ugly rich man ridiculed in several comic fragments.

22. A very wealthy son of the great general Conon; he would later become a major political and military figure. He apparently built in Athens a tower dedicated to Fortuna.

Cario: For certainly the ones who get the best of their enemies in war, on
each occasion,
Are those who have This One alone sitting on their side!

Wealth: Do I, single-handed, have the power to do so many things?

Chremylos: Yes, by Zeus, and many *more* than these!
So that no one has ever become full of you!
For of all the other things there is surfeit:
Of erotic love— 190

Cario: of bread—

Chremylos: of music—

Cario: of sweets—

Chremylos: Of honor—

Cario: of cakes—

Chremylos: of manliness—

Cario: of dried figs—

Chremylos: Of love of honor—

Cario: of barley-bread—

Chremylos: of generalship—

Cario: of pea soup—

Chremylos: But of *you*, no one has ever become full!
No, if someone might get thirteen talents,
He desires all the more to get sixteen;
And if he accomplishes this, he wants forty,
Or claims that life is not worth living for him.

Wealth: Well, to me at least you two seem to speak well;
Except there is one thing only that I fear.

Chremylos: Explain, concerning what?

Wealth: How I would become master 200
Of this power that you claim I have.

Chremylos: By Zeus! But they all do say
That Wealth is most cowardly![23]

---

23. See Euripides' *Phoenician Women* 597: "Plutus/Wealth is a coward."

WEALTH: No! Least! But I
Am slandered by some burglar! For once when he had broken
And entered, he had nothing to take in the house,
Finding everything locked up;
And so he called my foresight cowardice.

CHREMYLOS: Do not now worry about anything; if you become
A spirited, real man in the affair,
210   I will show you to be sharper in your sight than Lynceus.[24]

WEALTH: How will you, being a mortal, have the power to do this?

CHREMYLOS: I am very hopeful on account of the things
Said to me by "Phoebus Himself, shaking the Pythian wreath."[25]

WEALTH: And *He* also knows about these matters?

CHREMYLOS: So I assert.

WEALTH: Watch out!

CHREMYLOS: Don't give it any thought, Good Fellow!
For—know it well—even if I have to die,
I myself shall do these things!

CARIO: And, if you wish, me too!

CHREMYLOS: And many will be the allies on either side of us—
As many as are just and without a pearl of barley.

220   **WEALTH:** Alas! You speak of rascally allies for us!

CHREMYLOS: Not if they become wealthy again as at the beginning!
But you [to Cario], run swiftly, go—

CARIO: What shall I do? Tell me!

CHREMYLOS: Summon the fellow farmers, whom you will probably find
In the fields, miserably toiling,
So that each, being present here, equally
Would have a share with us in this Wealth.

---

24. One of the Argonauts, who had eyes that could see into the earth. See Apollonius of Rhodes' *Argonauts* 1.153–55.

25. Another spoof on a line from an unknown tragedy.

CARIO: I am on my way; this little piece of meat[26] here
Let someone from within take and bring in.

CHREMYLOS: I'll take care of *that*; you run and get it done.
But you, Wealth, most mighty of all divinities,   230
Come inside here with me; for this house
It is, that today you must
Make full of money, through just and unjust means!

WEALTH: But I am on each occasion pained—by the gods!—to enter
Someone else's house;
For I never reap any good from it.
For if I happen to go into a thrifty man's,
Immediately he buries me in the earth;
And then if some worthy human who is a friend comes along
Asking for a little bit of money to take,   240
He denies that he ever saw me.
But if I happen to go into a mad human's,
I am cast among whores and dice,
And thrown naked out the door in no time.

CHREMYLOS: For you have never happened upon a man of measure.
This is in a sense always my way;
For I have no man who's my rival in enjoying being thrifty—
But also, in turn, at spending, when this is needed.
But let's go in, as I want you to see
Both my wife and my only son,   250
Whom I love very much, after you.

WEALTH: I believe it.

CHREMYLOS: For why would anyone not speak to you what is true?

[Exit Chremylos and Wealth; enter Cario, with Chorus.]

CARIO: Oh you who've often eaten thyme[27] with my master,
Men who are friends and neighbors and lovers of toiling,

---

26. The left-over from the sacrifice to Apollo that Chremylos made before the action of the play began.

27. A diet relying on herbs is a sign of poverty.

Hasten energetically, for the occasion does not admit delay,
But this is the peak moment, when it is necessary to show up and
defend him!

CHORUS LEADER: Don't you see that we have been for some time hurrying,
Eager in spirit, befitting men now feeble with age?
But you probably would demand that I run, before you have explained
to me,
260   Why your master has called me hither!

CARIO: But have I not told you long ago?! But you do not listen!
For the master declares that all of you will in pleasure
Live, leaving behind a cold and harsh life!

CHORUS LEADER: But what, and from what, is this business he declares?

CARIO: You rascals, he's coming here with a certain old man in tow,
Who is filthy, stooped, miserable, shriveled, bald, toothless;
And I think, by Uranus, that he's even circumcised![28]

CHORUS LEADER: Oh messenger bearing golden words, what do you mean?
Explain to me again.
You are making it clear that he is coming with a sack of money!?

270 **CARIO**: I am saying that he has a sack of elderly evils!

CHORUS LEADER: So then: you, for your trickery, wouldn't deserve to
get away
Without punishment, when I have this stick?!

CARIO: Now do you regard me as a human who is by nature such,
In every respect, and would you believe me capable of saying what is in
no way sound?!

CHORUS LEADER: Look how solemn this smooth fellow is! Your shins cry
"Ouch, ouch!" and your feet are longing for the shackles!

CARIO: You've drawn the lot, for jury duty, in your *coffin*,
So why don't you go?! Charon will give you your meal ticket![29]

---

28. A mark of barbarism.

29. A citizen would draw a letter-lot designating which court he would serve in for the day
as juryman, and he would get a ticket at the end of the day that entitled him to receive his pay.
Charon is the ferryman who conveys the souls of the dead across the river Styx to their permanent abode in the underworld.

CHORUS LEADER: Split yourself! You're a Helot[30] brat and by nature
    impudent!
  A trickster, who doesn't have the stomach to explain to us—   280
  Who, wearied with much toil, and not having leisure, have come
  Here eager in spirit, having passed by many thyme plants!

CARIO: But I will no longer hide it from you. For, men, it is *Wealth*
  Whom my master, who's going to make you wealthy, comes bringing!

CHORUS LEADER: Is it really possible for all of us to be wealthy?!

CARIO: By the gods, very Midases (if you'll take the ears of an ass[31]).

CHORUS LEADER: How pleased I am, and delighted!—and I want to dance
  For pleasure, if indeed you are really saying true things!

[The Chorus and Cario begin dancing and continue through line 315.]

CARIO: And I for my part will want—"threttanelo!"—to   290
  Mimic the Cyclops, and, with my two feet thus stamping in rhythm,
  Lead you![32] But come, children, shout repeatedly,
  Bleating the songs of sheep
  And of stinking goats:
  Follow with uncovered, erect pricks; and you goats will have
      your breakfast![33]

CHORUS: And we for our part—"threttanelo!"—will seek you, Cyclops;
  And when we, bleating, find you—hungering,
  With your leather wallet and watery wild herbs, hung over,
  Leading your sheep, and
  Happening to fall asleep somewhere—   300
  We'll take a great burning stake, and put out your eye!

---

30. Helots were the serf-slave people under Spartan domination.

31. Midas, famously given by Dionysus a touch that turned everything to gold, was also cursed with ass's ears by Apollo, as punishment for having dared to judge the latter god the just loser in the great contest with the satyr Marsyas (over who had greater musical wisdom).

32. The scholia explain that the references are parodying a dithyramb of Philoxenus of Cythera, entitled *Loves of Galatea and Cyclops*, in which the word "threttanelo" is used to imitate the sound of the harp, and the Cyclops, dancing the so-called "Cyclops dance," was depicted with a wallet and herbs (see line 298 below).

33. Literally, "drink wine neat": as the scholia explain, this was a word for breakfasting, because that meal often or usually included bread dipped in wine.

CARIO: And for my part, that Circe who mixed the poisons,
　　　Who once in Corinth persuaded the companions of Philonides[34]
　　　That they were swine,
　　　And that they ate kneaded shit, which she kneaded for them,
　　　I shall imitate in all ways![35]
　　　And do you, grunting with love of pleasure,
　　　Follow mother, piggies!

CHORUS: And then you, the Circe who mixed the poisons,
310　　And bewitched and corrupted the companions,
　　　We will catch by love of pleasure;
　　　Mimicing the Son of Laertes,[36] we shall hang you up by the balls,
　　　And befoul your nose with dung like a goat!
　　　A very gaping Aristyllus,[37] you will say:
　　　"Follow mother, piggies!"

CARIO: But enough now: leave off the jesting,
　　　And turn to another style;
　　　I, going now in secret
　　　Want to take from the master
320　　Some bread and meat—
　　　Which having chewed, it's back to the toil.

[Cario goes inside.]
[A Short Dance and Song by the Chorus]
[Chremylos comes out.]

CHREMYLOS: To bid you "cheerful welcome," men who are neighbors,
　　　Is now old-fashioned and musty;
　　　But I salute you, because you have come, eager in spirit,
　　　And keyed up, and in no slothful fashion!
　　　See that you stand by me in the rest,
　　　And become really the saviors of the god!

---

34. For Philonides, see above on line 179.

35. This mingles the legend of Odysseus with that of Philonides.

36. In the *Odyssey* (22.178), Melanthius is hung up, with his hands and feet tied to a board, by Odysseus.

37. The scholia indicate that the "gaping" of Aristyllus refers to his notoriety in oral sex, apparently as a coprophiliac—referred to also in *Assemblywomen* 647, and frag. 551.

CHORUS LEADER: Be bold: for you will seem to see in me Ares!
    For terrible would it be, if for the sake of three obols in money
    We used to jostle one another in the Assembly each time,   330
    But I would let someone take Wealth himself!

CHREMYLOS: And now I see Blepsidemos here
    Approaching also. It's obvious that
    He has heard something of the affair, by his pace and speed.

BLEPSIDEMOS: What's afoot then? From whence and in what way
    Has Chremylos suddenly become wealthy? I don't believe it!
    But—by Heracles!—there was much talk among those sitting in the
      barbers' shops,
    To the effect that the man has suddenly become wealthy!
    But this is to me the wonder: that   340
    Having fared worthily, he should call in his friends!
    This is not what's done, according to local custom anyway!

CHREMYLOS: But I will speak hiding nothing:[38] by the gods,
    Oh Blepsidemos, we are faring better than yesterday,
    So that it's possible to share! For you are one of the friends.

BLEPSIDEMOS: But have you truly become, as they say, wealthy?!

CHREMYLOS: I will be, very shortly, if the god is willing—
    For there is, . . . there is, . . . a certain risk in the business.

BLEPSIDEMOS: What's that?

CHREMYLOS: What?

BLEPSIDEMOS: Speak and finish whatever you were just saying!

CHREMYLOS: If we get things right, it's prosperity forever!   350
    But if we slip, totally rubbed out!

BLEPSIDEMOS: The business appears evil,
    And does not please me; because immediately
    To become thus over-wealthy, and at the same time to be fearful,
    Is not at all healthy for a working man.

CHREMYLOS: How not at all healthy?

---

38. Another spoofing echo of Euripides, *Phoenician Women* 503.

BLEPSIDEMOS: If you come having stolen—by Zeus!—
    Some silver or gold from
    The god there, and then perhaps you have remorse . . .

CHREMYLOS: Apollo shield me from such! By Zeus, I have not!

360 **BLEPSIDEMOS:** Stop chattering, good fellow; for I know clearly!

CHREMYLOS: Do not suspect any such thing of me!

BLEPSIDEMOS: Alas! There is nothing simply sound about anyone,
    But all are overcome by gain!

CHREMYLOS: By Demeter, *you* don't seem healthy to me!

BLEPSIDEMOS: How greatly he has changed from his former ways!

CHREMYLOS: By Uranus, fellow, you're mad with melancholy!

BLEPSIDEMOS: His look is shifty;
    It is obvious that some completely wicked thing has been done.

CHREMYLOS: I know what you're croaking about!—Supposing me to have
370   Stolen something, you're seeking a share!

BLEPSIDEMOS: Seeking to share?—In what?

CHREMYLOS: Well that's not it, but something else is afoot.

BLEPSIDEMOS: So it's not theft—but violent robbery?!

CHREMYLOS: You're possessed by an evil divine spirit!

BLEPSIDEMOS: So you haven't committed any fraud at all?

CHREMYLOS: Not me!

BLEPSIDEMOS: Heracles! Come, where should one turn?
    For you're not willing to explain the truth!

CHREMYLOS: You're accusing before knowing from me what the affair is!

BLEPSIDEMOS: Look, man, for only a little trifle,
    I am willing to take care of this—before the city learns:
    I'll seal the mouths of the orators with some coins!

380 **CHREMYLOS:** And—by the gods!—you seem to me to be ready
    To spend three hundred drachma and reckon it twelve hundred!

BLEPSIDEMOS: I envisage one who is sitting on the rostrum,
    Holding the bough of supplication, with his children

And his wife—no different from
The Heraclidae of Pamphilus![39]

CHREMYLOS: No, you who are beset by an evil divine spirit! But it is
Only the worthy and the just[40] and the moderate-thinking,
Whom I am going to make wealthy henceforth!

BLEPSIDEMOS: What are you saying?
You've stolen that much?!

CHREMYLOS: Ai yi yi! With these evils
You are destroying me!

BLEPSIDEMOS: You are destroying yourself, it seems to me!

CHREMYLOS: No indeed, since it is Wealth, you villain, that I have!

BLEPSIDEMOS: YOU have wealth? Of what sort?

CHREMYLOS: The god Himself!

BLEPSIDEMOS: And where is he?

CHREMYLOS: Inside.

BLEPSIDEMOS: Where?

CHREMYLOS: My place.

BLEPSIDEMOS: YOUR place!?

CHREMYLOS: Certainly.

BLEPSIDEMOS: Won't you go to the crows!? Wealth, at your place!!

CHREMYLOS: By the gods!

BLEPSIDEMOS: Are you speaking the truth?

CHREMYLOS: I declare it.

BLEPSIDEMOS: In the name of Hestia?

CHREMYLOS: By Poseidon.

BLEPSIDEMOS: You mean the sea god?

CHREMYLOS: If there is another Poseidon, then by that other!

---

39. Apparently the famous painter Pamphilus portrayed, in a scene from mythic tradition, the children of the dead Heracles with their grandmother supplicating the king of Athens for protection from the persecution of Eurystheus, a powerful Mycenean king.

40. Some major manuscripts have "dextrous" instead of "just."

BLEPSIDEMOS: But you aren't sending him [Wealth] around to us,
  your friends?!

CHREMYLOS: This is not yet what's to be done at this time.

BLEPSIDEMOS: What do you mean? Not time for sharing?

400 **CHREMYLOS**: No, by Zeus!—because what's necessary first . . .

BLEPSIDEMOS: Is what?

CHREMYLOS: Is for us two to make him see.

BLEPSIDEMOS: Who see? Explain!

CHREMYLOS: Wealth—even as before, somehow.

BLEPSIDEMOS: Because he really is blind?

CHREMYLOS: Yes, by Uranus!

BLEPSIDEMOS: So it's not without reason then that he never comes to me!

CHREMYLOS: But if the gods are willing, he'll arrive now!

BLEPSIDEMOS: So isn't it necessary to bring in some doctor?

CHREMYLOS: What doctor is there in the city now?
  For there's no pay, and so no practice of the art.

BLEPSIDEMOS: Let's look. [He looks around the audience.]

CHREMYLOS: But there isn't any!

BLEPSIDEMOS: Nor does there seem to me to be.

410 **CHREMYLOS**: But by Zeus, what has been planned for a while
  By me—to have him lie down in the temple of Ascelpius—
  Is what is most effective.

BLEPSIDEMOS: Yes, by far, by the gods!
  Don't spend time now, but accomplish it!

CHREMYLOS: Indeed, I'm on my way!

BLEPSIDEMOS: Hurry!

CHREMYLOS: I shall! [Starts to hurry off.]

[Enter Poverty.]

POVERTY: Oh, it is a brazen deed, and impious, and against the law,
  That you two little humans, beset with an evil divine spirit, dare to do!
  Where, oh where, are you fleeing? Why aren't you staying?

BLEPSIDEMOS: Heracles!

POVERTY: I shall destroy you evil ones, in an evil fashion!
 For you two have dared a piece of daring that is intolerable,
 Such as no one else ever has done,   420
 Neither god nor human. As a consequence, you two shall die!

CHREMYLOS: But WHO are *you*!? For you seem to me to be ghastly pale!

BLEPSIDEMOS: Perhaps she's a Fury from tragedy;[41]
 She stares in a mad and tragic way, at any rate.

CHREMYLOS: But she doesn't have torches.

BLEPSIDEMOS: Well then, she'll weep!

POVERTY: Who do you *suppose* Me to be?

CHREMYLOS: A tavern hostess,
 Or a pudding-seller. Otherwise you wouldn't be
 Yelling so much at us when you've been done no injustice!

POVERTY: In truth?! So you two haven't committed the most terrible of
 Things, in seeking to throw me out of the entire land?!   430

CHREMYLOS: Well, wouldn't the pit for criminals' corpses be left for you?
 But you better tell who you are, very quickly!

POVERTY: I am SHE who will today make you two pay the judicial penalty,
 For seeking to make *me* vanish from here!

BLEPSIDEMOS: So then is she that neighborhood barmaid,
 Who's always cheating me with the cup-measures?

POVERTY: I'm *POVERTY*—who've been living with you two all these
  many years!

BLEPSIDEMOS: Leader Apollo and gods! Where might one flee?

CHREMYLOS: Here, what are you doing? Oh you most cowardly of beasts!
 Will you not stay?!   440

BLEPSIDEMOS: Least of all!

---

41. Perhaps a reference to the *Eumenides* of Aeschylus. When it is pointed out to Blepsidemos that she does not have the torches that Furies were believed to carry, he ceases to fear her.

CHREMYLOS: You're not staying?!—
But we, two real men, are going to flee one woman?!

BLEPSIDEMOS: Yes, for she's *Poverty*, you rascal!—Than whom no
Animal more destructive has ever existed by nature!

CHREMYLOS: Stand! I beseech you, stand!

BLEPSIDEMOS: By Zeus, not me!

CHREMYLOS: Now I say that it will be the most terrible deed by far,
Of all deeds, that we will be doing, if
Leaving the god deserted, we will flee,
Fearing this woman, and won't fight!

BLEPSIDEMOS: Trusting in what sort of weapons or power?
450   For what breastplate, what shield,
Has this most abominable one not made to be pawned?

CHREMYLOS: Be bold! For I know that this god by himself
Will set up a victory trophy over her ways!

POVERTY: You two, you rubbish, dare to mutter,
Having been caught in the act of doing terrible things?

CHREMYLOS: And you, worst of lost ones, why do you revile
Us, coming forward when you have been done nothing unjust?

POVERTY: Nothing! Oh before the gods! Do you believe
You do me no injustice in trying to make Wealth
460   See again?

CHREMYLOS: Why in this are we doing you an injustice,
If we provide good for all humans?

POVERTY: What good would you two devise?

CHREMYLOS: What?—First, throwing *you* out of Greece!

POVERTY: Throwing Me out! And what would you two believe
Would be a greater evil you could do to humans?

CHREMYLOS: What?—Well, if we were going to *forget* to do this very thing!

POVERTY: And now about this, I am willing to enter into a debate with
        you two,
First off; and I would demonstrate that I alone

Am the cause of all good things for you,
And that through me you live! And if not,   470
You two do now whatever this is that seems best to you.

CHREMYLOS: You dare to say this, you most abominable one?!

POVERTY: And *you* learn it! For I think that I'll rather easily
Demonstrate that you are completely in error,
If you claim that you will make the just wealthy.

CHREMYLOS: Oh clubs and stocks, won't you come help?

POVERTY: You shouldn't rage and shout before you've learned.

CHREMYLOS: And who could refrain from shouting
When he hears such things?

POVERTY: He who thinks well.

CHREMYLOS: What judicial penalty shall I write up for you,   480
If you're defeated?

POVERTY: Whatever suits your opinion.

CHREMYLOS: Nobly spoken.

POVERTY: For it is the same that you two ought to suffer, if you two lose.

CHREMYLOS: Do you believe twenty deaths sufficient?

BLEPSIDEMOS: For her, yes; but for us two, only two will suffice.

POVERTY: It won't be long before you undergo this, for what
Just thing would anyone still have to say on the other side?

CHORUS LEADER: But now you must say something wise by which you can
win against her,
By speaking opposing arguments, and showing no softness!

CHREMYLOS: For my part I think that this is known plainly to all alike:
That it is just for the worthy among humans to prosper;   490
And for the wicked and the atheists, surely the contrary.
Now it is this that we desire, and have with toil figured out, so
That there has come into being a plan that is noble, and well-born, and
useful for every work.
For, if Wealth now should see, and not wander about being blind,
He will go to the good among humans and will not leave them,

While He will flee the wicked and the atheists; and then he will make
Everyone worthy and wealthy, surely, and reverencing the divine.
And who would ever devise something better for humans than this?

BLEPSIDEMOS: No one! I am a witness of this on your behalf. Don't ask
her this!

500 **CHREMYLOS**: For, as life *now* is disposed for us humans, who would not
Consider it to be mad and, moreover, beset with an evil divine spirit?
For many humans are wealthy, being rogues,
Having acquired unjustly; and many who are very worthy
Fare badly, starve, and spend most of the time with You.
I assert that this would not be, if Wealth were once to see, and stop her!—
Taking a path by which he would provide great good to humans.

POVERTY: Oh you two—of all humans the most easily persuaded, to
become unsound!
Two old men, partners in driveling and missing the point!
If what you two long for were to come to pass, I assert that it would not be
to your profit.

510 For if Wealth were to see again, and to divide himself equally,
No one among humans would care for art or wisdom;
And if both of these disappear for you, then who will be willing
To work in bronze, or to build ships, or to sew, or to make wheels,
Or to make shoes, or to work in stone, or to launder, or to tan hides,
Or, having broken the surface of the earth with ploughs, to harvest the
fruit of Demeter—if it were
Possible for you to live in idleness, without care for all these?

CHREMYLOS: You are driveling drivel! For all these things you have gone
through now
The servants will toil at for us!

POVERTY: From where will you have servants?

CHREMYLOS: We'll buy them with the money, of course!

POVERTY: But in the first place, who'll be the seller,
520 When he too has money?

CHREMYLOS: Some merchant wishing to gain,
Who arrives from Thessaly, where there are the most slaves.

POVERTY: But in the first place, no one at all will be a slave trader,
  According to the argument you're uttering. For who of the rich will be
    willing to
  Do this, risking his own life [literally, "soul"]?
  So you yourself will be constrained to plow and to dig and to toil at the
    other things,
  Wearing out a life much more painful than the one now!

CHREMYLOS: Let this curse be on your head!

POVERTY: In addition, you won't be able to sleep in a bed, because there
    won't be any;
  Nor even in covers; because who'll be willing to weave when there's gold?
  Nor will you two be able to perfume with drops of scent your bride when
    you lead her home,
  Nor to adorn her with the expenses of variegated dyed robes.   530
  And indeed what more is there to wealth if you lack these things?
  But through me, all these things that you two need are readily provided;
  For I sit like a mistress constraining the craftsman
  Through need and poverty to seek a livelihood.

CHREMYLOS: What good are *you* able to provide?—except burns from
    the bath,[42]
  And the uproar from starving little kids and old hags?
  And I can't count for you the number of the lice and the mosquitoes and
    the fleas
  Who torment, humming around the head,
  Waking one up and saying, "you will starve, so get up!"
  Besides these things, instead of a cloak, one has a rag; instead of a bed,   540
  Straw full of bugs who wake up the sleepers;
  And you have a rotten rush mat instead of a rug; instead of a pillow,
  A big stone for your head; instead of bread, you'll eat
  Mallow shoots; and instead of cakes, withered radish leaves;
  Instead of a bench, the top of a shattered jug; instead of a
    kneading trough,

---

42. The poor had to crowd one another around the stove in the public baths.

The rib of a wine cask—and that broken! So then don't I
Show you to be the cause of many goods for all humans!

POVERTY: You haven't been speaking of *my* life, but knocking that
of beggars!

CHREMYLOS: Don't we declare that Poverty is sister to Beggary?

550 **POVERTY**: You're the ones who say that Dionysius is the same as
Thrasybulus![43]
But my life doesn't suffer these things—by Zeus!—nor will it!
For the life of a beggar, about which you speak, is to live having nothing;
But the life of the poor man is to live frugally and with labors,
And there is no surplus for him, but neither does he lack.

CHREMYLOS: How blessed—by Demeter!—is his life as you go through it,
If, having been frugal, and toiled, he leaves not enough for a tomb!

POVERTY: Try to joke and make a comedy, careless of being serious—
Not knowing that I produce better real men than does Wealth,
Both in judgment and in form. For through *him* they have gouty feet,
560 And they're pot-bellied, and fat in the calves, and licentious fatsos;
While with *me* they're lean, wasp-waisted, and baleful for enemies!

CHREMYLOS: For it is probably from starvation that you provide them the
wasp-waists!

POVERTY: I now conclude, concerning moderation; and I teach you two,
That orderliness dwells with me—but with Wealth is *hubris.*

CHREMYLOS: It's certainly very orderly to steal and to break through
house walls!

BLEPSIDEMOS: By Zeus, how is it not orderly, if one has to escape notice?

POVERTY: And now consider the orators in the cities, how when
They are poor, they are just, as regards the populace and the city,
But when they get rich from the common funds, they immediately
become unjust:
570 Plotting against the majority, and making war on the populace.

---

43. Dionysius was a famous tyrant. Thrasybulus led the liberation of Athens from The Thirty
tyrants.

CHREMYLOS: But as regards none of these things, at least, do you lie, even if
you are a malicious slanderer.
Still, don't preen yourself on this account; you shall weep,
Because you seek to persuade us of this—that Poverty is better
than Wealth.

POVERTY: And you at any rate have in no way been able to refute me in
this matter,
But you chatter and flap about!

CHREMYLOS: And why does everyone *flee* you?

POVERTY: Because I make them better! The evidence is seen especially in
Children: for they flee their fathers when the latter are prudently
thinking about what is best for them.
Thus it is a difficult task to discern the just.

CHREMYLOS: So then You will assert that Zeus does not correctly discern
what is superior;
For That One also has Wealth! 580

BLEPSIDEMOS: —And HER, he sends to us!

POVERTY: You are both blind in your thinking, with the blindness
of Kronos![44]
Zeus is surely poor—and *this* I shall now plainly teach you.
For if he were rich, how is it that when he himself made the
Olympic contest,
So that all the Greeks would gather every five years,
He announced that he would crown the winners among the contestants
With an *olive wreath*? Surely, he would have required gold, if he'd
been rich!

CHREMYLOS: It's exactly in this way that That One clearly honors Wealth!
Being thrifty and wishing not to spend any of him,
He lavishes nonsense on the victors and keeps Wealth for himself!

POVERTY: You seek to tar him with a shame greater than that of Poverty, 590
If he, being wealthy, is so illiberal and so fond of gain!

---

44. Implying antiquated thinking, belonging to the eon (the reign of Kronos) before the reign
of Zeus.

CHREMYLOS: May Zeus destroy you, after crowning you with an
olive wreath!

POVERTY: You have the gall to deny that all good things come to you
Through Poverty!

CHREMYLOS: It's possible to learn this from Hecate—that is,
Whether being wealthy or being poor is better: for she tells
Those who have, and are wealthy, to send her a monthly meal,
While the poor among humans steal it before it's set down![45]—
But perish, and cease to mumble
Anymore about anything;

600   For you will not persuade, not even if you were to persuade!

POVERTY: Oh city of Argos, listen to what sort of things he is saying![46]

CHREMYLOS: She's calling Pauson[47] to be her messmate!

POVERTY: The suffering I am enduring!

CHREMYLOS: Go from us to the crows, quickly!

POVERTY: Where on earth shall I go?

CHREMYLOS: Go to the pillory! But you shouldn't delay—
Get it over with!

POVERTY: Yet you two shall send for me,
To come back here again!

[Poverty exits.]

610 **CHREMYLOS**: Come home at that time; but now be hanged!
It is better for me to be wealthy,
And to let you bewail at length, beating your own head!

BLEPSIDEMOS: By Zeus, I for my part am willing, being wealthy,
To feast with my children
And wife; and, having bathed,

---

45. On the thirtieth day of every month, the rich were supposed to have a meal put at one of the shrines to Hecate (a goddess of magic—cf. *Wasps* 804) situated where three roads met; and these meals (actually scraps, according to Demosthenes—54.39) became a dole for paupers.

46. A spoofing echo of Euripides' *Telephus*—of which we possess only fragments. Cf. *Knights* 813.

47. A painter, who is also teased for his poverty at *Acharnians* 854 and *Thesmophoriazusae* 949.

To proceed glistening from the baths—
And to the craftsmen,
And to Poverty—blow a fart!

CHREMYLOS: This worn out hag has left us.
But let's me and you as quickly as possible   620
Lay the god down in the temple of Asclepius!

BLEPSIDEMOS: And let's certainly not take any time, lest someone else
Should come, preventing the doing of some of the work at hand.

CHREMYLOS: Boy! Cario! You need to carry out the blankets,
And bring the god Himself, with customary observances,
And whatever else is well arranged within.

[A Short Dance and Song by the Chorus]
[The following morning . . .]

CARIO: Oh you old men who have sopped up the most soup
With the smallest barley cakes at the feasts of Theseus![48]
How good your fortune is! How blessedly you fare!—
As do others, who partake of worthy character!   630

CHORUS LEADER: What is it, you best among your friends?
For you evidently come as a messenger of something worthy!

CARIO: The master has fared in most lucky fashion,
Or rather Wealth Himself has: for "instead of being blind,
The pupils of his eyes are opened and made bright,
Through chancing upon a propitious healing song of Asclepius!"[49]

CHORUS LEADER: What you say brings me joy, what you say makes
me cheer!

CARIO: Joy it is, whether you wish it or you don't!

CHORUS LEADER: I will cheer for Asclepius, favored in his offspring,[50]
And a great beacon for mortals!   640

---

48. The feasts of Theseus included meager public meals for the poor, consisting of soup and barley cakes, hollowed as scoops.

49. The scholia say that this contains a quotation from Sophocles' lost play *Phineus*.

50. A reference to families of doctors spread over Greece, who were reputed to be descendants of Asclepius.

WIFE [of Chremylos]: What ever is the shouting about? Is there a
Report of something worthy? For it is this I have been longing for,
During the time I've been sitting within, waiting for him.

CARIO: Quickly, quickly bring wine, Mistress, so that
You too can drink! For you very much like to do that!
And I bring you all good things together!

WIFE: And where is he?

CARIO: In what's to be said you will soon know.

WIFE: Well then, finish whatever you have to say!

CARIO: Just listen, as I relate to you
650   The entire affair, from the feet to the head.

WIFE: Not on my head![51]

CARIO: Not even the good things
Which have now come to pass?

WIFE: Not any trouble, now!

CARIO: Well:[52] as quickly as possible we arrived at the god,
Bringing this man who was in miserable condition then,
But now is blessed and happy if anyone is—
First, indeed, we took him to the sea,
And then washed him.

WIFE: By Zeus, he was then
Happy!?—an old man, being washed in the cold sea!?

CARIO: And then we went to the sanctuary of the god;
660   And when on the altar a cake and preparatory sacrifices
Had been consecrated—"fuel for the Hephaestean flame,"[53]
We laid Wealth down, as was suitable.
And each of us put together a bed of straw.

WIFE: And were there others beseeching the god?

---

51. "On your head" was a common phrase used to curse.

52. The long speech of Cario's that follows is a comic equivalent of speeches by messengers that are common in tragedy.

53. A spoofing quotation from an unknown tragedy.

CARIO: There was one, Neoclides,[54] who's blind,
    But in stealing overshoots those who see;
    And many others, who had all sorts of illnesses.
    And as he put out the lamps,
    The servant of the god enjoined us to sleep,
    Saying that if anyone perceived a noise   670
    He should keep silent. We all lay down in orderly fashion.
    But I wasn't able to sleep; I was distracted
    By a pot of porridge that lay
    A little above the head of an old hag—
    And to which I had a preternatural desire to creep.
    Then, opening my eyes, I saw the priest
    Stealing the muffins and the figs
    From the sacred table! After this,
    He circled around to all the altars
    Upon which were left cakes—   680
    Then he "consecrated" these in a certain sack.
    So I, believing that there was much piety in the deed,
    Went after the pot of porridge.

WIFE: You greatest wretch among men! Didn't you fear the god?

CARIO: By the gods, I did—lest
    He should get to the pot ahead of me, with his chaplets;
    Because this priest had previously instructed me!
    But the old hag, when she perceived my noise,
    Stretched out her hand; and I, hissing,
    Took it with my teeth as if I were a brown snake;[55]   690
    She drew back her hand at once,
    And lay wrapping herself up quietly,
    Farting from fear with a stench worse than a weasel!
    At that point I gulped much of the porridge,
    And, when I was full, ceased.

---

54. An orator and "sycophant." See *Assemblywomen* 254, 398–407.

55. These snakes were ritually kept in sacred precincts, and twin snakes were closely associated with Asclepius, whose famous doctor's symbol is the staff around which two snakes are entwined.

WIFE: The god didn't approach you?

CARIO:　　　　　　　　　　　　　　Not yet.
　　After this I did do something ridiculous.
　　For as he approached, I
　　Farted a great fart (because my stomach was inflated).

700　**WIFE:** Well, surely on account of that he was revolted by you!

CARIO: Nope; but Iaso,[56] who was following, blushed a bit,
　　And Panacea turned away,
　　Holding her nose: because I don't fart frankincense!

WIFE: But He Himself?

CARIO:　　　　　　　　Oh, by Zeus, he didn't mind!

WIFE: Well then, you're saying the god is a rude fellow!

CARIO: By Zeus, I am not! After all, he IS a shit-eater.[57]

WIFE:　　　　　　　　　　　　　　　　You wretch!

CARIO: After these things, I at once hid myself,
　　In fear; and That One went around
　　Examining all the illnesses in a very orderly fashion.
710　Then a boy placed before him a stone pestle,
　　And mortar, and a little box.

WIFE: Stone?

CARIO:　　By Zeus, not the box!

WIFE: But how did you see, you worst of lost ones,
　　When you claim you had hidden yourself?!

CARIO:　　　　　　　　　　　　　Through my cloak:
　　For by Zeus, it has not a few holes!
　　He first of all went about
　　Grinding a medicinal ointment for Neoclides, into which he put
　　Three heads of Tenian garlic; then he pounded
　　And mixed, in the mortar, fig-tree sap
720　And bitter mastich; then, moistening it with Sphettian vinegar,

---

56. Iaso and Panacea were daughters of Asclepius.
57. The scholia explain that this refers to the fact that doctors examine excretion.

He turned up his eyelids and applied it to him—
So that the pain would be greater; and he screamed
And shouted, sprang up, and ran away. The god said laughing:
"Now sit there plastered,
So that I stop you from swearing oaths[58] in the assemblies!"

WIFE: What a lover of the city is the Divinity, and wise!

CARIO: After this, he sat down next to Wealthikins,
    And first he touched his head,
    And then, taking a clean cloth,
    He wiped around the eyes; and Panacea   730
    Spread a red cloth over his head
    And his whole face; then the god whistled,
    And there darted out of the sanctuary two serpents,
    Of a size more than natural!

WIFE: Oh dear gods!

CARIO: These two, quietly plunging under the cloth,
    Licked his eyelids, as it seemed to me;
    And before it would be possible for you to drink ten goblets of wine,
    Oh Mistress, Wealth stood up seeing!
    And I clapped my hands with pleasure,
    And woke the Master. But the god immediately   740
    Made himself disappear, along with the serpents, into the sanctuary.
    And how do you suppose the ones lying with him
    Embraced Wealth, and stayed up the whole night,
    Until the day broke!
    And I praised the god very much,
    Because he quickly made Wealth see,
    But made Neoclides more blind.

WIFE: What power You have, Master and Leader!
    But tell me, where is Wealth?

CARIO: He's coming.
    But there was a crowd around him of more than natural size.   750

---

58. The meaning of the Greek term is uncertain; it seems to signify some sort of obstructive affidavit procedure in the Assembly.

For the just, who before had a scanty life,
Greeted him and
All took his hand out of delight;
But as many as were wealthy and had much,
Having acquired their livelihood by unjust means,
Knitting their brows, looked angry.
The others, however, followed along—wreathed,
Laughing, and speaking phrases of good omen; and
The shoes of the old men beat a rhythmic step.—

760   But come! [To chorus] All together with one voice,
Dance and jump and make a choral procession!
For no one will come in bringing to you the message,
That there is no barley in the bag!

WIFE: By Hecate, and I want to crown
You—with a chain of barley cakes[59]—as a reward for good tidings,
For having brought such reports!

CARIO: Don't delay anymore,
As the men are near the doors already!

WIFE: Come, I'm going in to fetch welcoming sweets,
As if for newly-purchased—eyes![60]

[Exit Wife.]

770   **CARIO**: And I want to go to meet them!

[Exit Cario.]
[A Short Song and Dance by the Chorus]
[Enter Wealth.]

WEALTH: And I make obeisance first to the Sun,
Then to the famous plain of Pallas Athena,
And the entire land of Cecrops,[61] that welcomes me.
And I am ashamed of my misfortunes,

---

59. Bringers of good tidings were customarily crowned; the barley cakes are peculiarly suited to Cario, with his focus on food.

60. It was a custom to welcome newly purchased slaves by showering them with sweets as they entered the house for the first time.

61. The first legendary king of Attica.

Of the sort of humans with whom I consorted without realizing it—
While those who were deserving of my company,
I avoided, knowing nothing! Alas for me,
That neither the former nor the latter did I do correctly!
But now, reversing all these things,
I will show henceforth to all humans that   780
I gave myself to the wicked involuntarily.

[Enter Chremylos.]

CHREMYLOS: Go to the crows! —How difficult are the friends
Who show up immediately when one is prospering!
For they prod and they crush my calves,
Each making a show of some goodwill.
Who has not greeted me?! What elderly mob
Has not encircled me in the agora?!

WIFE: Oh dearest of men—welcome to you—and to you!
Come now, it is the lawful custom:
Taking hold of you, I pour the sweets over you, thus![62]   790

WEALTH: No! For when I am entering a house
For the first time with sight, it is
Fitting that nothing be carried out, but only carried in.

WIFE: Then You won't accept the sweets?!

WEALTH: Inside, next to the hearth, as is the lawful custom!
And then we would avoid the vulgarity.
For it is not fitting for The Teacher[63]
To throw little figs and sweets to the spectators,
And with these to force a laugh from them.

WIFE: You speak very well; for Dexinikos[64] there   800
Was getting up from his seat to rob the figs!

[They go in.]

---

62. Both "you's" in this line refer to Wealth.

63. The producer, who was Aristophanes himself. The producer was designated "The Teacher" because his main concern was instructing the chorus and actors.

64. Some otherwise unknown member of the original audience.

[A Short Dance and Song by the Chorus]
[Enter Cario.]

CARIO: How sweet it is, men, to fare happily,
    And without any outlay from home!
    For a heap of good things has burst into our homes
    Without us doing anything unjust!
    To be wealthy thus is indeed a sweet affair!
    The flour bin is full of white barley,
    And the amphora of dark, flower-scented wine.
    And with silver and gold are all our wallets full, in wondrous fashion.
810   And the cistern is full of olive oil; and the little cups
    Teem with myrrh, and the attic with dried figs.
    Every cruet and platter and pot
    Has become bronze; the rancid trenchers
    For fish are seen to be silver.
    The privy has suddenly become ivory for us.
    And we servants gamble with golden coins.
    We wipe our bottoms no longer with stones,
    But with garlic stalks, out of luxury, each time.
    And now the master, wreathed, is inside slaying for sacrifice
820   A pig and a billy-goat and a ram.
    The smoke has driven me out. I could no longer
    Remain within, for it pained my eyes.

[Enter Just Man followed by boy carrying an old cloak and shoes.]

JUST MAN: Follow along with me, boy, so that to the god
    We may come.

CARIO: Well, who's this coming here?

JUST MAN: A man who before was miserable, but is now fortunate!

CARIO: Obviously you are one of the worthy, as you appear.

JUST MAN: Very much so.

CARIO: So what do you need?

JUST MAN: To the god
    I'm coming; for he is the cause for me of great goods!
    For I, inheriting from my father sufficient property,

Came to the aid of friends in need, 830
Believing it to be useful in life.

CARIO: And presumably the money quickly left you!

JUST MAN: Exactly!

CARIO: So after this, you were miserable.

JUST MAN: Exactly! And I thought that those whom for so long
I benefited, when they were needy, I would have as friends
Who were really firm, if I should ever be in need;
But they turned away and seemed not to see me anymore.

CARIO: And did it laughing!—I know!

JUST MAN: Exactly!
For the drought in my coin jars was destroying me.

CARIO: But not now! 840

JUST MAN: Which is why I am coming to the god—
To give a just prayer of thanks.

CARIO: But what, in the name of the gods, is the old cloak for,
Which this little boy who's with you is carrying? Explain.

JUST MAN: This too I am going to dedicate to the god.

CARIO: So presumably you were initiated into the greater mysteries while
wearing it?[65]

JUST MAN: No, but I shivered in it for thirteen years!

CARIO: And the shoes?

JUST MAN: And these have spent winters with me.

CARIO: So you're bearing these also to dedicate?

JUST MAN: Yes, by Zeus!

CARIO: Refined gifts that you've come bearing for the god!

[Enter Sycophant, accompanied by Witness.]

---

65. The mystery rite of initiation, celebrated at Eleusis, where it was the custom to wear and
dedicate old clothes. See *Frogs* 404–7.

850 **SYCOPHANT**: Alas! Beset by an evil divine spirit, how wretchedly I've
      been destroyed!
    And triply beset by an evil divine spirit, and fourfold, and fivefold,
    And twelvefold, and a thousandfold! Ai yi yi!
    With so prolific a divine spirit am I bound up!

CARIO: Apollo and the dear gods avert it!
    Whatever evil is it that the fellow has suffered?

SYCOPHANT: Have I not now suffered harsh evils,
    With everything in my home utterly taken,
    On account of this god—Who will be blind
    Once again, if acts of court justice be not lacking!

860 **JUST MAN**: In my opinion I am pretty sure I know what's the matter.
    For a certain man arrives who's faring badly;
    And he's likely to be minted wickedness.

CARIO: Well by Zeus, his destruction is nobly done!

SYCOPHANT: Where, where is he who promised that through himself alone
    He would make us all wealthy immediately,
    If again as at the beginning he had sight? But he
    Has instead destroyed some people!

CARIO: And to whom has he done this?

SYCOPHANT: ME! Here!

CARIO: But you were one of the wicked and the housebreakers?

870 **SYCOPHANT**: By Zeus, there's no soundness in any of you,
    And there's no way that you don't have my goods!

CARIO: How arrogantly—Oh Demeter!—has the sycophant
    Entered! He's plainly suffering from the hunger of an ox.

SYCOPHANT: You shall not delay in proceeding at once to the agora,
    For there you must be racked on the wheel to
    Make you say what crimes you have committed!

CARIO: You'll howl for that!

JUST MAN: By Zeus the Savior! Deserving of much
    From all the Greeks is the god who
    Wretchedly destroys the wretched sycophants!

SYCOPHANT: Alas, alas! *You*, too, are partaking in the mockery?!— 880
  For from where did you take this cloak?!
  Yesterday I saw you wearing a rag!

JUST MAN: I don't hold you in awe, for I bought
  This ring-amulet from Eudamus for a drachma.[66]

CARIO: But there's nothing in it against the bite of a sycophant!

SYCOPHANT: But is this not great hubris?! You two jeer,
  But what the two of you are up to here you have not said:
  For you're not up to any good here!

JUST MAN: By Zeus, not for you, you can be sure!

SYCOPHANT: For you two are about to feast from my goods, by Zeus! 890

CARIO: May you truly, along with your witness,
  Burst yourselves from emptiness!

SYCOPHANT: Do you deny it? There is within, you most cursed one,
  Much salted fish and roasted meat!
  Sniff-sniff, sniff-sniff, sniff-sniff, sniff-sniff, sniff-sniff.

CARIO: What are you—beset by an evil divine spirit—smelling?

JUST MAN: Maybe it's the cold—
  Since he's wearing such a rag!

SYCOPHANT: Are these things to be tolerated, Oh Zeus and gods?!—
  That these people are insolent to ME?! Alas, how I am pained,
  That being a worthy man and a friend to the city I suffer evilly! 900

JUST MAN: YOU a friend to the city and worthy?!

SYCOPHANT: Like no other man!

JUST MAN: So answer my questions—

SYCOPHANT: About what?

JUST MAN: Are you a farmer?

SYCOPHANT: Do you suppose me so melancholy-mad?

JUST MAN: Then a merchant?

---

66. According to Theophrastus (*Enquiry into Plants* 9.17.2), "Eudamus the seller of medicines had a great reputation in the art." A drachma is not a cheap price.

SYCOPHANT: Ye-e-s, or at least, that's my excuse, when chance requires.[67]

JUST MAN: What then?—have you learned some craft?

SYCOPHANT: By Zeus, no!

JUST MAN: So how do you support yourself, or from what source, since you
   do nothing?

SYCOPHANT: I am one who cares for the affairs of the city,
   And of all the private persons!

JUST MAN: You! Having learned *what*?

SYCOPHANT: "I will!"[68]

JUST MAN: How then would you be worthy, you housebreaker,
910   If you make yourself hated, through what is not at all your business?

SYCOPHANT: Because is it not fitting that my own city be
   Done good deeds by me, as much as is in my strength, featherbrain?

JUST MAN: So being a busybody is doing good deeds?!

SYCOPHANT: Indeed: coming to the aid of the established laws,
   And not leaving it to another if someone does wrong.

JUST MAN: Are there not jurors for that purpose whom the city
   Appoints to rule?

SYCOPHANT: But who prosecutes?

JUST MAN: "The one who wills."

SYCOPHANT: So then I am that one!
   Therefore the affairs of the city fall on me.

920 **JUST MAN:** By Zeus, then it has a wicked leader!
   But would you not "will" *this*: keeping quiet
   To live in idleness?

SYCOPHANT: But you are speaking of the life of a sheep,
   If no occupation is evident in life!

JUST MAN: You would not learn new ways?

---

67. To be a merchant could exempt one from military service. Cf. *Assemblywomen* 1027.

68. This is a legal expression referring to the right of any citizen ("he who wills") to initiate a legal action in certain cases—which enabled the sycophants to bring their lawsuits against the rich.

SYCOPHANT: Not if you would give me
   Wealth Himself and the fennel of Battus![69]

JUST MAN: Quickly lay down your cloak! . . .

CARIO: It's YOU he's speaking to!

JUST MAN: Then undo your sandals! . . .

CARIO: All these things are said to YOU!

SYCOPHANT: Let him among you come against me here
   "Who wills!"

CARIO: Then I am he!!

SYCOPHANT: Alas, alas! I'm being stripped in daylight!   930

CARIO: For you would deserve it, eating by meddling in others' business!

SYCOPHANT [to Witness]: Do you see the things he's doing? I call you to
    witness these things!

JUST MAN: But he's leaving in flight—the one you brought to be a witness!

SYCOPHANT: Alas I'm alone and surrounded!

CARIO: Now do you shout?

SYCOPHANT: Alas, alas again!

CARIO [to Boy]:   You, give me the rag,
   So that I can clothe this sycophant.

JUST MAN: No indeed! For it's been sacred to Wealth for some time.

CARIO: But where will it be offered up more nobly,
   Than draped around a wicked man and a housebreaker?
   But Wealth it is fitting to adorn with august robes.   940

JUST MAN: What's to be done with this footwear? Tell me.

CARIO: These I shall nail on his forehead immediately,
   As on an olive tree.[70]

SYCOPHANT: I am leaving. For I know that I am much weaker than
   You. But if I get some partner,

---

69. Silphium or giant fennel was the source of the wealth of the city of Cyrene, whose founder
was Battus.

70. Offerings were often nailed to olive trees in sanctuaries.

Even if he's fig-wood,[71] this strong god
I shall make pay a judicial penalty today,
Because he, being one alone, is plainly dissolving
The democracy, having persuaded neither the Council
950   Of the citizens nor the Assembly!

JUST MAN: And now, since it's with my panoply
That you are going, run to the bath;
And then stand there as the chorus leader of warmth.
For I held that station once.

CARIO: But the keeper of the bath will grab him by the balls
And throw him out the door; for on seeing him he'll recognize
The minting of wickedness!
But now let's go in, so that you may pray to the god.

[Exit Cario, Just Man, and the boy.]
[A Short Dance and Song by the Chorus]
[Enter Old Woman with an attendant carrying a tray of sweets.]

OLD WOMAN: Have we then, you dear old men,
960   Really arrived at the house of this new god,
Or have we completely missed the way?

CHORUS LEADER: But know, that you have arrived at the very doors—
Young lady: for you inquire as one in bloom.

OLD WOMAN: Well, I'll call now for someone of those within.

[Chremylos comes out.]

CHREMYLOS: No need—for I myself have come out.
But you ought to say why exactly you have come.

OLD WOMAN: Dearest one, I have suffered terrible things, illegal things!
For from the time when this god began to see,
He has made life unlivable for me!

970 CHREMYLOS: What's the matter? —Or is it not, presumably, that you too
Were a "sycophant,"[72] among the women?

---

71. A play on the word "fig-wood" (*sykinos*)—used metaphorically for something cheap and worthless—and the word "sycophant."

72. Here there is a double-entendre: the verbal form of "sycophant" was slang for sexual congress.

OLD WOMAN: By Zeus, I was not!

CHREMYLOS: But you were drinking, when you hadn't drawn an
  inscribed lot?[73]

OLD WOMAN: You're mocking. But I am itchy in a pitiable fashion!

CHREMYLOS: Won't you then speak and finish the account of the
  tearing apart?

OLD WOMAN: Listen now: I had a dear youth,
  Poor, but otherwise handsome and noble and
  Worthy; for if I was in need of something,
  He did it all for me in a lovely and beautiful way;
  And I served him, in all these ways.

CHREMYLOS: What was it in particular that he needed each time from you?   980

OLD WOMAN: Not many things. For he was uncustomarily bashful in
  regard to me.
  But he would ask for twenty silver drachmas,
  For a cloak; and eight, for shoes;[74]
  And for his sisters he would ask to buy a little garment;
  And for his mother a little cloak.
  And he would need four bushels of wheat.

CHREMYLOS: By Apollo, these are not many things that
  You've mentioned, but it is clear that he *was* bashful in regard to you!

OLD WOMAN: And these things he asked me for, not out of greed,
  He said, but out of affection,   990
  So that by wearing my cloak he would be reminded of me!

CHREMYLOS: You describe a fellow most uncustomarily passionate in love!

OLD WOMAN: But now, the brute is no longer of the same mind,
  But very altered entirely!
  For when I sent to him this flat cake,[75]

---

73. A jesting reference to the lots by which citizens were assigned to juries, the pay for which
supported many of the poor: a woman would not of course participate.

74. These are moderate prices: in the *Assemblywomen* 413 it is said that the cheapest cloak
cost sixteen drachmas.

75. There is a double entendre, to which the old woman is oblivious, in the words for "flat
cake," "sweets," and "milk cake," which are all slang for the female genitalia.

And the other sweets on the board,
Promising that I would be
Coming in the evening, —

CHREMYLOS: What'd he do to you? Tell me!

OLD WOMAN: He sent back to us this milk cake,
1000   On the condition, that I never again go there,
And in addition to these things, he said, on sending them back, that
"It was long ago that the Milesians once were brave."[76]

CHREMYLOS: It's obvious that he's not wicked in his ways,
But now that he's wealthy, he's no longer pleased by lentils!
Before, on account of poverty, he'd eat anything!

OLD WOMAN: And yet, before, every day—by the twin goddesses![77]—
He always came to my door!

CHREMYLOS: To see if you were being carried out to your funeral?

OLD WOMAN: By Zeus, only out of passionate love to hear my voice!

CHREMYLOS: (So as to get a gift.)

1010 **OLD WOMAN:** And by Zeus, if he perceived me out of sorts,
He would call me the pet-names "duckling" and "little dove!"

CHREMYLOS: (And then probably ask you about shoes.)

OLD WOMAN: And at the Great Mysteries, when I was riding
In my cart,[78] if someone looked at me,
I would be beaten on[79] the whole day on account of this—
So jealous the youth was!

CHREMYLOS: (Because he liked to feed alone, probably!)

OLD WOMAN: And he said I had altogether beautiful hands.

CHREMYLOS: (When they stretched forth twenty drachmas.)

1020 **OLD WOMAN:** And he said of my skin that it was sweet to smell.

---

76. A proverb—originally a line of the poet Anacreon.
77. Demeter and her daughter Persephone.
78. That is, in the ritual procession; only the rich could afford carts.
79. There is a double entendre, unintended by the old woman, in the Greek verb (which is slang for sexual congress).

CHREMYLOS: (If you poured Thasian wine, in all likelihood, by Zeus!)

OLD WOMAN: And how I had a look that was soft and beautiful!

CHREMYLOS: (The fellow wasn't a fool, but knew
That the old lady was a rutting sow, and he fed himself off the estate.)

OLD WOMAN: So, my dear man, in doing these things the god acts
    incorrectly,
While claiming always to help those who are done injustice.

CHREMYLOS: Well, what *shall* he do? Say, and its done!

OLD WOMAN: It's just, by Zeus, to compel
The one done well by me to do well to me in return,
Or else it is not just that he have any good.   1030

CHREMYLOS: Didn't he pay you every night?

OLD WOMAN: But he declared that he would never leave me so long as
    I lived!

CHREMYLOS: (Rightly indeed; but now he thinks that you no longer live.)

OLD WOMAN: Oh my dear! I have melted away with grief!

CHREMYLOS: (It's rather that you've rotted away, it seems to me!)

OLD WOMAN: You could draw me through a ring!

CHREMYLOS: (If the ring happened to be a barrel hoop!)

OLD WOMAN: And now here comes the youth,
The one I happen to have been accusing for so long!
Likely going to a revel.

CHREMYLOS: So he appears.   1040
He proceeds wreathed, and holding a torch.

YOUNG MAN: I greet you!

OLD WOMAN: What's he say?

YOUNG MAN: Dear ancient one,
You have swiftly become grey, by Uranus!

OLD WOMAN: I am made wretched by suffering such hubris!

CHREMYLOS: It's probably been a long time since he's seen you.

OLD WOMAN: What time, you wretch!—He was with me yesterday!

CHREMYLOS: Then he has undergone the opposite of what happens to
　　the many;
　　For being drunk, as is likely, he sees more sharply.

OLD WOMAN: No, but he is always unrestrained in his ways!

1050　**YOUNG MAN:** Oh Poseidon of the sea and elderly gods!
　　How many wrinkles she has in her face!

OLD WOMAN: Ai yi yi!
　　Don't bring the torch close to me!

CHREMYLOS:　　　　　　　　　(Well spoken indeed!
　　For if only one spark seizes her,
　　She'll burn like an ancient harvest-wreath!)

YOUNG MAN [to Old Woman]: Do you want to fool around with me
　　for a while?

OLD WOMAN:　How?—You rascal!

YOUNG MAN [taking some nuts from the tray]: Right here, taking hold
　　of the nuts.

OLD WOMAN:　What game?

YOUNG MAN: How many teeth you have![80]

CHREMYLOS:　　　　　　　　　　　But even I know that:
　　For she has maybe three or four!

YOUNG MAN: Pay up! For she has only one molar!

1060　**OLD WOMAN:** You wretch among men! In my opinion, you're not sane,
　　To give me a washing before so many men!

YOUNG MAN: You would profit from it, if someone were to wash you!

CHREMYLOS: No indeed; since now she's dolled up for sale;
　　But if this white makeup were washed off,
　　The tatter of her face would be plain!

OLD WOMAN: For an old man, you don't seem to me to be sane!

YOUNG MAN: He's maybe trying you out, and feeling your tits,
　　Thinking he's escaping my notice.

---

80. A common child's game was betting on guessing the number of nuts someone held.

OLD WOMAN: By Aphrodite, not mine, you crude fellow!

CHREMYLOS: By Hecate, no! For I'd be crazy!   1070
But young man, I won't let
You hate this girl.

YOUNG MAN: But I am excessively fond of her!

CHREMYLOS: Yet she accuses you.

YOUNG MAN: What's the accusation?

CHREMYLOS: She asserts that you're hubristic, and that you say,
"It was long ago that the Milesians once were brave."

YOUNG MAN: I won't fight with you over her.

CHREMYLOS: What do you mean?

YOUNG MAN: I'm abashed by your age, since
I would never allow another to do this;
But now, go away, take the girl and enjoy yourself!

CHREMYLOS: I know, I know what's in your mind! You probably don't think   1080
It's worthwhile to be with her anymore.

OLD WOMAN: Who's the one "allowing"?

YOUNG MAN: I won't get into a discussion with a woman who's been
thoroughly screwed
By thirteen thousand years/comrades![81]

CHREMYLOS: All the same, since you considered it worth it to drink
the wine,
You have to drink the dregs also.

YOUNG MAN: But she is completely ancient and rotten dregs!

CHREMYLOS: Then a straining cloth will remedy everything!

YOUNG MAN: I'm going inside; for I want to go to the god
To dedicate these wreaths that I have.

OLD WOMAN: And I for my part also wish to say something to Him!   1090

YOUNG MAN: But then I am not going in!

---

81. The word has this twofold meaning.

CHREMYLOS: Pluck up, don't be afraid!
For she won't commit rape!

YOUNG MAN: You speak very nobly!
For I spent enough time before, plastering her down below!

OLD WOMAN: Go ahead; I'll go in behind you.

[Exit Young Man, Old Woman, and her attendant.]

CHREMYLOS: How intently—Oh Zeus the King!—does the old woman,
Like a barnacle, stick to the youth!

[Exit Chremylos.]
[A Short Dance and Song by the Chorus]
[Enter Hermes.]

CARIO [coming out of the house]: Who's knocking at the door? . . . What
    is this? . . .
Looks like no one! But indeed the door
Will wail with sorrow for having made an untoward noise!

HERMES: You! I say:
1100   Cario! Stay!

CARIO: Tell me, you:
Were you the one knocking so hard on the door?

HERMES: NO, by Zeus, but I was about to; you anticipated me by opening!
But run fast and summon the master,
And then the wife and the children,
And then the servants, and then the dog,
And then yourself, and then the pig!

CARIO: Tell me,
What's up?

HERMES: Zeus, you rascal, wishes
To grind you up together in the same bowl,
All at once, and throw you into the pit!

1110   **CARIO:** Let the tongue be cut of the herald of these things!
For what reason does he plan to do these things to us?

HERMES: Because you have carried out the most terrible of actions!
For from the beginning of the time when Wealth has started to have

Sight, no one has offered incense, or laurel,
Or barley-cake, or consecrated animal, or any other single thing,
As sacrifice to us gods anymore!

CARIO: No, by Zeus, nor
Will offer sacrifice! For before, you exercised bad providential care of us!

HERMES: The other gods are of less concern to me,
But me! —I'm finished, I'm worn out!

CARIO: You're prudently moderate.

HERMES: For before, I had from the barmaids 1120
All good things, starting from dawn: wine cake, honey,
Figs—as many things as it was likely that Hermes would eat.
But now, I'm starving and cooling my heels.

CARIO: Isn't that just, for you who sometimes used to punish
When you had such goods?

HERMES: Alas, alas!
Alas—for the flat cake that is cooked on the fourth![82]

CARIO: "You long for what is not present, and you call in vain."[83]

HERMES: Alas for the ham that I used to eat!

CARIO: Hop on the inflated bladders, here in the open air![84]

HERMES: And for the hot innards that I used to eat! 1130

CARIO: There's probably some pain churning in *your* innards!

HERMES: And alas for the cup with equal parts water and wine!

CARIO: If you take a sip from this, and then run off, you won't be going
too soon!

HERMES: Wouldn't you help your friend a little?

CARIO: If he needs something, and I'm able to be of assistance.

---

82. The fourth day of each month was traditionally celebrated as the birthday of Hermes, when these cakes were dedicated to him.

83. Another mocking echo of solemn tragedy. According to the scholia, this is a line from a (lost) tragedy, referring to Heracles seeking his beloved, Hylas.

84. A play on words: at a Dionysian festival day named "Askolia"—a word that sounds as if it could mean "ham-less"—a game was played of hopping on inflated bladders.

HERMES: If you could just provide me with some well-baked bread,
 And if you could give me some fresh meat to devour,
 From what you're sacrificing within.

CARIO: But it's not for export!

HERMES: And when you had lifted some little pot of the master's,
1140   I always made you escape notice!

CARIO: On condition that you got a share, you housebreaker![85]
 For a firm, well-baked cake always came to you!

HERMES: And then you yourself would eat this!

CARIO: For you did not share equally with me in the whippings,
 When I was caught being a thorough rascal!

HERMES: Don't be a bearer of grudges, if you've captured Phyle;[86]
 But in the name of the gods, receive me into the household!

CARIO: Then will you leave the gods and remain here?

HERMES: Yes. For it is much better with you.

1150   **CARIO**: What? Does deserting seem to you to be civic?

HERMES: For every fatherland is wherever one prospers![87]

CARIO: What benefit would you be to us by being here?

HERMES: You will install me as the Hinge-god by the door.

CARIO: The Hinge-god? But there's no work for the "shifty."[88]

HERMES: But as the Commerce-god.

CARIO: But we're wealthy; why
 Do we need to provide for Hermes the Retailer?

HERMES: But as the Deceiver.

---

85. Hermes was the god of thieves and thievery.

86. The taking of Phyle was the first big stage in the overthrow of the Thirty tyrants by the democrats, after which there was declared a general amnesty (Xenophon, *Hellenica* 2.4).

87. Another line spoofing tragedy.

88. "The Hinge-god" designates a traditional role of Hermes, whose statues were placed next to the hinges of the outer door of homes, to ward off other thieves; the words for "hinge" and "shifty" are related, and there is a pun here. In what follows, Hermes tries to find employment by mentioning a series of his traditional roles.

CARIO: Deceiver?! Least of all!
For now there's no work of deception, but straightforward mores.

HERMES: But as the Guide.

CARIO: But the god now sees,
With the result that we don't need a guide anymore. 1160

HERMES: Well, I'll be the Contest-god. Now what will you say?
For this is most congenial to Wealth,
To provide musical and gymnastic contests![89]

CARIO: How good it is to have many epithets!
For this one has discovered how to make a living for himself!
Not without reason do all the jurors frequently
Hasten to get themselves enrolled in many drawings!

HERMES: So I can come in on these terms?

CARIO: And also you wash
The tripe yourself, after you've gone to the well—
So that you'll immediately seem to be The Server.[90] 1170

[Exit Cario and Hermes.]
[A Short Dance and Song by the Chorus]
[Enter Priest.]

PRIEST: Who can tell me clearly where Chremylos is?

[Enter Chremylos.]

CHREMYLOS: What is it, best one?

PRIEST: What else but bad news?
For from the time when this Wealth began to see,
I've been destroyed by hunger! For I have nothing to eat,
And I'm suffering these things while being a priest of Zeus the Savior!

CHREMYLOS: And what's the reason, in the name of the gods?

PRIEST: No one thinks it worthwhile to sacrifice!

CHREMYLOS: Why is that?

---

89. The wealthiest citizens paid for the public contests.
90. Hermes had a traditional role as personal servant to Zeus: Aeschylus, *Prometheus* 966.

PRIEST: Because all are rich! And indeed before,
When they had nothing, the merchant would come
1180   To sacrifice something because he was preserved; and another
Because he had been acquitted in a case of justice; and one who had
Fine auspices from his sacrifice would invite me, the priest to dine;
      but now,
Not a single one sacrifices anything at all, nor comes in—
Except that more than a myriad use it to relieve themselves in!

CHREMYLOS: Well, don't you receive the lawful share from these?

PRIEST: So I myself have decided to bid good-bye to Zeus the Savior,
And to settle down right here!

CHREMYLOS: Pluck up! For you'll do so in noble fashion, if the god
      is willing,
For Zeus the Savior is himself here,
1190   Having come of his own accord.

PRIEST: What you say is all good!

CHREMYLOS: Now we're this moment about to perform—stay around—the
Installation of Wealth, where formerly He was installed—
Always guarding the back chamber of the goddess.[91]
But let someone give out here lit torches,
So that you can lead the god's procession with one!

PRIEST: Certainly
These are the things that ought to be done!

CHREMYLOS: Someone call Wealth outside!

OLD WOMAN: And me, what shall I do?

CHREMYLOS: Take the pots that we'll use in the
Installation of the god and carry them on your head
Solemnly. —And you've come with your festive dress!

1200 **OLD WOMAN**: But what about the *reason* I came?

CHREMYLOS: All will be taken care of for you.
For the youth will come to you in the evening.

---

91. Athena, in the back room of whose temple on the acropolis the city's treasure was stored
in the days of the Athenian empire—whose wealth is now to be more than restored.

OLD WOMAN: But if indeed—by Zeus!—you pledge to me that
He is coming to me, I *will* carry the pots!

CHREMYLOS: And now these pots are doing the opposite of what other
Pots do: for in other pots the "old woman"[92] is on the top,
But now the pots are on top of this old woman!

CHORUS LEADER: We also shouldn't tarry, but take up
The rear; for we need to follow behind these, singing.

[Actors and Chorus dance and sing in procession out.]

---

92. The word for "old woman" is also a word for the scum that forms on the top of heated or cooked liquids in pots.